EDUCATION, POLITICS, AND PUBLIC LIFE

Series Editors:
Henry A. Giroux, McMaster University
Susan Searls Giroux, McMaster University

Within the last three decades, education as a political, moral, and ideological practice has become central to rethinking not only the role of public and higher education, but also the emergence of pedagogical sites outside of the schools—which include but are not limited to the Internet, television, film, magazines, and the media of print culture. Education as both a form of schooling and public pedagogy reaches into every aspect of political, economic, and social life. What is particularly important in this highly interdisciplinary and politically nuanced view of education are a number of issues that now connect learning to social change, the operations of democratic public life, and the formation of critically engaged individual and social agents. At the center of this series will be questions regarding what young people, adults, academics, artists, and cultural workers need to know to be able to live in an inclusive and just democracy and what it would mean to develop institutional capacities to reintroduce politics and public commitment into everyday life. Books in this series aim to play a vital role in rethinking the entire project of the related themes of politics, democratic struggles, and critical education within the global public sphere.

SERIES EDITORS

HENRY A. GIROUX holds the Global TV Network Chair in English and Cultural Studies at McMaster University in Canada. He is on the editorial and advisory boards of numerous national and international scholarly journals. Professor Giroux was selected as a Kappa Delta Pi Laureate in 1998 and was the recipient of a Getty Research Institute Visiting Scholar Award in 1999. He was the recipient of the Hooker Distinguished Professor Award for 2001. He received an Honorary Doctorate of Letters from Memorial University of Newfoundland in 2005. His most recent books include *Take Back Higher Education* (co-authored with Susan Searls Giroux, 2006); *America on the Edge* (2006); *Beyond the Spectacle of Terrorism* (2006), *Stormy Weather: Katrina and the Politics of Disposability* (2006), *The University in Chains: Confronting the Military-Industrial-Academic Complex* (2007), and *Against the Terror of Neoliberalism: Politics Beyond the Age of Greed* (2008).

SUSAN SEARLS GIROUX is Associate Professor of English and Cultural Studies at McMaster University. Her most recent books include *The Theory Toolbox* (co-authored with Jeff Nealon, 2004) and *Take Back Higher Education* (co-authored with Henry A. Giroux, 2006). Professor Giroux is also the Managing Editor of *The Review of Education, Pedagogy, and Cultural Studies.*

Critical Pedagogy in Uncertain Times: Hope and Possibilities
Edited by Sheila L. Macrine

The Gift of Education: Public Education and Venture Philanthropy
Kenneth J. Saltman

Feminist Theory in Pursuit of the Public: Women and the "Re-Privatization" of Labor
Robin Truth Goodman

Hollywood's Exploited: Public Pedagogy, Corporate Movies, and Cultural Crisis
Edited by Benjamin Frymer, Tony Kashani, Anthony J. Nocella, II, and Richard Van Heertum; with a Foreword by Lawrence Grossberg

Education out of Bounds: Reimagining Cultural Studies for a Posthuman Age
Tyson E. Lewis and Richard Kahn

Academic Freedom in the Post-9/11 Era
Edited by Edward J. Carvalho and David B. Downing

Rituals and Student Identity in Education: Ritual Critique for a New Pedagogy
Richard A. Quantz with Terry O'Connor and Peter Magolda (forthcoming)

Educating Youth for a World beyond Violence
H. Svi Shapiro (forthcoming)

America According to Colbert: Satire as Public Pedagogy post-9/11
Sophia A. McClennen (forthcoming)

Citizen Youth: Culture, Activism, and Agency in a Neoliberal Era
Jacqueline Joan Kennelly (forthcoming)

EDUCATION OUT OF BOUNDS

REIMAGINING CULTURAL STUDIES FOR A POSTHUMAN AGE

Tyson E. Lewis
and
Richard Kahn

EDUCATION OUT OF BOUNDS
Copyright © Tyson E. Lewis and Richard Kahn, 2010.

All rights reserved.

First published in 2010 by
PALGRAVE MACMILLAN®
in the United States—a division of St. Martin's Press LLC,
175 Fifth Avenue, New York, NY 10010.

Where this book is distributed in the UK, Europe and the rest of the world,
this is by Palgrave Macmillan, a division of Macmillan Publishers Limited,
registered in England, company number 785998, of Houndmills,
Basingstoke, Hampshire RG21 6XS.

Palgrave Macmillan is the global academic imprint of the above companies
and has companies and representatives throughout the world.

Palgrave® and Macmillan® are registered trademarks in the United States,
the United Kingdom, Europe and other countries.

ISBN: 978-0-230-62254-8

Library of Congress Cataloging-in-Publication Data

Lewis, Tyson E.
    Education Out of bounds : reimagining cultural studies for a
    posthuman age / Tyson Lewis and Richard Kahn.
        p. cm.—(Education, politics and public life series)
    Includes bibliographical references.
    ISBN 978-0-230-62254-8 (alk paper)
    1. Critical pedagogy. 2. Monsters—Symbolic aspects. 3. Political
    science—Philosophy. 4. Social sciences—Philosophy. I. Kahn, Richard V.,
    1969– II. Title.

LC196.L49 2010
370.11'5—dc22   2010018768

catalogue record of the book is available from the British Library.

Design by Newgen Imaging Systems (P) Ltd., Chennai, India.

First edition: December 2010

10 9 8 7 6 5 4 3 2 1

Printed in the United States of America.

Boarman

This guy's no tame pig.
No even-toed ungulate or woodsy
grubber, he's the spear-skinned

hound, the boar-dog root and thistle
who kills the young and carries
mourning, hung cross a stick.

He looks at you and his Neptune
eye is a bent spoon of absinthe,
a gilled shadow that sees—then,

whorls ear and pupil into one. His
fossil jaw is the mollusk-dyed shade
of Tyrian emperor, ornate bruise pig-

ment, violet and feathered grackle.
The swine's got snout. He's all
beetle root and bone, horned with

the forest beard, a spiral of moth bristle,
victim of the crimson hog typhoid.
When he sleeps, tonight, in his bed

or sty, listen for the human moan
of dream, a purred sorrow, wet air
loosed from fang lock.

                  —*Anne Keefe*

CONTENTS

PREFACE

Rousseau famously begins his book *Emile or On Education* (1762) with the following passage:

> Everything is good as it leaves the hands of the Author of things; everything degenerates in the hands of man. He forces one soil to nourish the products of another, one tree to bear the fruit of another. He mixes and confuses the climates, the elements, the seasons. He mutilates his dog, his horse, his slave. He turns everything upside down; he disfigures everything; he loves deformity, monsters.

Rousseau's educational practice is an attempt to purify humanity by returning to "the Author's" intended path. The monstrous appears as an educational obstacle that must be overcome through strict isolation from all forms of societal "degradation," "mixing," "mutilation," "disfigurement," and "deformity." Thus Rousseau posits a purified ontology of the human that education must preserve against contaminating influences. On the level of affect, Rousseau insists on weaning the child of his or her desire for monstrous disfigurations and mutilations of the perfect symmetry, simplicity, and unity of a natural state. Rather than desire these perversions, Rousseau's education will induce a sense of horror and moral repulsion at the sight of all monsters. In other words, the community that Rousseau hopes to rebuild through natural education is one that must exclude monsters.

In this book we are questioning the ontological claims of Rousseau as an efficacious starting point for theorizing democratic education. Instead of purity, we are positing the ontological priority of the monstrous, of the contamination and indetermination that emerges when we suspend the distinctions of nature versus culture that Rousseau presupposes. Thus instead of purity as an ethical mandate, we will advocate for a critical theory of disfiguration that lies at the very heart of our collective social, political, and economic worlds. Beyond the immunization of the self against the threat of degeneration, we will examine the possibilities for an education that exists in the indeterminate zones where tried and true boundaries between self and other, friend and enemy, and nature and culture seem to give way to the meeting between strangers and foreigners that, for Rousseau, bear the threat of turning everything upside down.

When Rousseau turns his back on the monstrous, he turns his back on politics. For us, democracy at its most radical is disfiguring, dislocating, and thus monstrous beyond measure. Rather than purity of the self or of community, democracy opens up to a perpetual rupture through contaminating interference with the common sense of a community. The monstrous is in other words the imaginative disorganization of categories and subject roles through which new democratic insurgencies stake a claim and through which a novel imagination dreams of impossible new forms of liberation, new forms of unrepresentable common life.

Although Marx once denounced Thomas Badington Macaulay for being a bourgeois ideologue (at best a parliamentary reformer and at worst a colonial apologist), for our purposes Macaulay's description of liberty is an important one that cannot be reduced to simply ideological mystification or abstract poetic musing. For instance, in his essay on Milton (1825), Macaulay weaves a startling allegory that reconnects politics to the monstrous and thus to the very forms of contamination and creaturely excesses that Rousseau held in contempt:

> Aristotle tells a pretty story of a fairy, who, by some mysterious law of her nature, was condemned to appear at certain seasons in the form of a foul and poisonous snake. Those who injured her during the period of her disguise were forever excluded from participation in the blessings which she bestowed. But to those who, in spite of her loathsome aspect, pitied and protected her, she afterwards revealed herself in the beautiful and celestial form which was natural to her, accompanied their steps, granted all their wishes, filled their houses with wealth, made them happy in love and victorious in war. Such a spirit is Liberty. At times she takes the form of a hateful reptile. She grovels, she hisses, she stings. But woe to those who in disgust shall venture to crush her! And happy are those who, having dared to receive her in her degraded and frightful shape, shall at length be rewarded by her in the time of her beauty and glory!

Liberty is a shape-shifter (a fairy with great powers of transformation), a creature of appearances and disguises whose nature resides precisely in unnatural deformations. Rather than Liberty as a classically inspired woman of virtue [as in Delacroix's famous painting

La Liberté guidant le peuple (1830)], for Macaulay, the figuration of Liberty finds roots in folktales and pantheistic myth that induce the shock of a monstrous stranger disorganizing the boundaries of the community with its "hisses" and its "stings." Rather than a classically imbued form of virtue, nobility, and reason that culminates in the promise of modernity as a triumph over aristocracy, Liberty in Macaulay's description inaugurates a kind of altermodernity with a different genealogical lineage that breaks with the classical tradition in order to fully embrace the complex and monstrous dimensions of Liberty as a *resource* rather than as a danger. Rather than bar the monstrous from the community (as with Rousseau) we see in Macaulay a counter-ethic: the invitation of the monster *as the founding gesture of a coming community*.

What is an education of and in liberty? This book traces the outlines of a monstrous education that does not retreat from the "hateful reptile" of Liberty but rather finds in its stings the beauty of a coming community—a community that emerges from within a "frightful shape" of a multitude of strange sensations and even stranger imaginative narratives. While venom to some, the fangs of Liberty are far from poisonous. It is in the stings that education out of bounds finds its dislocating location—with beasts—with strangers.

ACKNOWLEDGMENTS

We would like to especially acknowledge Henry and Susan Searls Giroux for graciously affording us the opportunity to publish this book in their excellent series, for the show of support for radical pedagogical theory that goes beyond the "bounds" of what many publishers and/or scholars might have thought acceptable, and for their long-standing leadership as critical researchers and public intellectuals. Also, to Douglas Kellner, our mutual mentor and friend, who has himself provided invaluable resources and lots of guidance over the years—our most sincere love and thanks. And our gratitude to Michael Hardt for his enthusiasm for the project and willingness to support it. Additionally, we should note that our work together first blossomed years ago in a graduate education class conducted by Peter McLaren, and it was Peter who germinated the idea of doing something on David Icke and reptoids—a topic that we then knew little to nothing about. Gracias, Peter! Finally, thanks are extended to Marta Pires, Tyson's graduate assistant, who has spent hours tracking down obscure references to all things monstrous and meticulously formatting chapters. She was invaluable to the project.

Tyson would individually like to acknowledge his parents, Steven and Allyson Lewis, for encouraging his savage imagination at a young age as well as his nonhuman animal companions (past and present)—Bitsy, Natalie, Sweetpea, and Maybell (the littlest one of all). Last but not least, he could not have completed this project without the help of his wife, Anne Keefe, whose passion, creativity, and critical insights proved time and time again invaluable resources for unlocking the wonder of the bestiary.

Richard would like to generously thank Tyson for his ongoing friendship, extremely hard work on this project, and highly peculiar surplus of genius that is both an inspiration and a bellwether of sorts. Second, great kudos go to Steve Best, who will undoubtedly disdain aspects of this book as fetishistically posthumanist and not liberationist enough for his liking. Somebody has to hold the line on animal liberation praxis and Steve does so unfailingly. Even here, Richard is with him. In this vein, again, blessings and a cosmic cry of solidarity to all the activists of every stripe and every species whose labor helps to realize a planet free from domination. Richard stands with you and attempt to speak from within a state of zoë, as described by Hildegard of Bingen in the twelfth century: "I am the supreme and the fiery force who kindles every living spark. And I breathe forth no deadly thing, yet I permit them to be. And I am the fiery life of the essence of God: I flame above the beauty of the fields; I shine in the waters; I burn in the sun, the moon, and the stars. And, with the airy wind, I quicken all things vitally by an unseen, all-sustaining life. For the air is alive in the flowers; the waters flow as if they lived; the sun lives in its light; and when the moon wanes, it is rekindled by the light of the sun as if it lived anew." All people who refuse to imagine a world perpetuated by a force such as this should consider themselves Richard's enemy.

Introduction

THESE MONSTROUS TIMES:
FROM BESTIARY TO POSTHUMANIST
PEDAGOGY

> Even he who does not resemble his parents is already in a certain sense
> a monstrosity.
>
> —Aristotle, *Generation of Animals*

Monsters come in all shapes and sizes.[1] There are zoological monsters (biological anomalies violating "natural laws") that defy taxonomical classification by blurring distinctions between genuses and species. Opposite of natural monsters there are technological monsters such as terminators, cyborgs, and robocops—all of which undermine dichotomies between the artificial and the organic, the prosthetic and the natural. There are also supernatural/paranormal monsters that escape scientific explanation or material verification, turning our heads toward heaven or hell. Then there are psychological or pathological monsters who challenge definitions of sanity, normality, and good old-fashioned common sense. Last but not least there are political/social/ideological monsters that violate social laws by transgressing sacred and profane boundaries of the community. Here, "monster" is used as a politically derogatory term indicating the threat of the "social outcast" to the solidarity of the community. On the flip side, the excluded, oppressed, and marginalized often lobby the same charges in reverse, describing the consensus of the political or economic community as a "monstrous" abuse of natural rights. What do these valences of the monstrous have in common? What unifies such disparate phenomena under the sign "monster"? In other words, how do we organize this disparate field in order to *understand* and *learn from* the monster? This book revolves around these central questions and can be seen largely as an attempt to theorize the interwoven dimensions of imagination, ontology, and politics of monsters to define a new approach to an education *out of bounds.* When tried and true categories are under threat or have been suspended—categories of us versus them, inside versus outside, human versus animal, inclusion versus exclusion, destruction versus production—the monster appears as an important conceptual category. Neither a miracle nor simply a natural phenomenon, a monster is a profane "twilight creature" (Daston and Park 2001, 192) betwixt and between this world and the next. As "boundary-creatures" (Graham 2002, 11), monsters embody a "simultaneous demonstration and destabilization of the demarcations by which cultures have separated nature from artifice, human from non-human, normal from pathological" (12). In other words, monsters indicate (a) the breakdown of boundaries (their suspension) but also (b) powerful taboos against breaking such boundaries (Cohen 1996). Because monsters lie within a paradoxical space (boundary-creatures), they serve a variety of political, social, psychological, and economic functions (both symbolic and material).

How are we to navigate this ambiguous field of the monstrous? It is our contention that we must remain on the level of the imaginary and chart its various permutations in order to organize and evaluate the possible political narratives that map these monstrous times. Drawing on Brian Massumi's work (2002a), we argue that the imagination is an act of "thinking feeling" (134). In this sense, the imagination is not a set of fixed images of self and other but rather an active diagram between the contingencies of pre-subjective affect and the common notions of a rational, cognitive subject. Poised between visceral reflex and rational reflection, the imagination is a *resonance* between sensations and sense, cognition and affect, critical distance and sensorial immanence. In short, the imagination is the sensation of thought's becoming. Massumi summarizes imagination as follows: "The mutual envelopment of thought and sensation, as they arrive together, pre-what they will have become, just beginning to unfold from the unfelt and unthinkable outside: of process, transformation in itself" (ibid.). Stated differently, the imagination is the topological modeling of transformations beyond quantification and beyond a definitive end—an incubator of monsters. Like the monster, the imagination itself is the outside of thought's inside (betwixt and between dichotomous relations) and therefore is the central terrain of struggle over (and potentially against) boundaries.

Yet the imagination as a composite diagram interacts not only with pre-subjective/pre-conscious affects but also with the larger social field. It is, in other words, both embodied in impersonal individuations and embedded in social, political, economic, educational, and ecological relations (Protevi 2009). Emerging from the complex relays below, above, and between subjects, the imagination produces multiple forms of the monster, each of which has its own political, social, and economic valences. Because we conceptualize the imagination as neither a faculty/sub-faculty of mind nor a reified image nor a virtue (see, for instance, Higgins 2009) but rather as a relay of resonances between forces, we will refer to the imagination as a diagram of oscillating vectors, each with its own internal velocity, direction, and capacity for rendering new constructions of self and other in excess of predefined subject positions within the common sense of a community. For our purposes here, we have chosen to focus on two intersecting relations of force defining the imaginative diagram: the political/social and the biomorphic vectors.

First, the political/social vector of the imagination is organized in relation to savage and superstitious affective cathexes to power. Utilizing Antonio Negri's work (1991), we would argue that the superstitious vector of the political imagination is sustained through fear and linked with servitude to Power as a territorializing force. Superstition is a form of immunizing imagination, retreating from the shock of affective stimulation and collective becoming into the safety of the ontological purity of the community safeguarded by a transcendental Power of the sovereign, of law, and so on. It is, in short, a fascistic imagination for a ruler to bring order to the polis by imposing rule from above. On the opposite imaginative polarity, Negri finds in Spinoza's work an emphasis on a productive and revolutionary imagination that does not retreat from the event of sensational rupture but rather finds in the diagram of thought feeling a new form of constituting, insurgent power. This savage imagination moves against existing forms of Power, opening up the possibility of new possibilities via the intensification of new embodied and embedded relations. In direct contradistinction to superstitious imaginings, the savage imagination offers a critique of all transcendence or centralized/structured authority (all forms of Power). The savage imagination, for Negri, is important precisely because it "begins to make the constitutive scheme concrete" (149). Even if this savage form of imagination which is dynamic and contagious results in a "vacillation" of the individual mind (confused results), the vacillation is "the first element of the constitutive rhythm" (ibid.) composed of a real and significant power to reappropriate collective social and economic life. In this sense, imagination is not simply "illusion" but rather a "real material force" that is "always excessive, going beyond the bounds of existing knowledge and thought, presenting the possibility for transformation and liberation" (Hardt and Negri 2009, 99). The monstrously savage imagination is a zone of becoming-insurgent against Power.

The savage imagination has radical implications, but it can potentially result in collapsing the multiplicity of powers of becoming into an imaginative diagram of anthropocentric valorization that validates human interests and therefore puts nonhuman animals in a position of sacrifice. In other words, Negri's theory of imagination might be savage, but it has not yet maximized its liberatory dimensions. The determining factor in this production lies with the particular form of intersection between the social/political and biomorphic vectors of the imagination. As with the social/political register, the biomorphic imagination contains within itself two radical polarities: at one extreme we find anthropocentric intensities while at the other zoocentric sensitivities. As a corrective to anthropocentric dominance and hierarchization, a zoocentric imagination (a) problematizes taken-for-granted divisions between human and nonhuman animals and (b) returns the human to its internally exiled animality. According to Margot Norris (1985), the zoocentric imagination offers a critique of anthropocentrism through art, theory, and practice that "allow[s] the animal, the unconscious, the instincts, the body, to speak again" (5). A zoocentric imagination understands that any critique of transcendence must be located within the immanence of a form-of-life that is monstrously beyond measure. Similarly, Alan Bleakley (2000) has argued that the imagination must be returned to the animal commonwealth—which includes both literal and figurative animal relations—in order to generate new forms of ecological activism and awareness. While acknowledging Norris's invaluable contribution to undermining the "anthro" in anthropocentrism, we would also like to point out her uncritical retention of "centrism" as a dominant framework. Here we would advocate a more decisive shift from "zoocentrism" to "zoömorphism," where the former maintains a center/margin imaginary while the latter implies an ontological dimension of relationships prior to and beyond an imperialist cartography.

And yet, without a savage critique of Power, zoömorphic thought feelings all too easily fetishize animal becomings without a critical capacity to understand how animality itself can be recuperated by Power in order for further exploitation and domination (Shukin 2010).[2] Only when savage and zoömorphic vectors are combined can the imagination enable us to critically narrativize our relations to the monster where tried and true constructions of self and other have been radically shaken and destabilized. A zoömorphic and savage imagination remains on the terrain of the monstrous in order to amplify collectively creative resources in the struggle against the hierarchical and exploitative deployment of Power.

Perhaps it would be possible to organize the human-animal monsters that emerge from the intensification of the political and biomorphic vectors of the imagination. While this diagram of imaginative becomings is in a sense reductive and misses the complexity of how these vectors shift and how the monsters that are produced contain multiple, contextually specific meanings, we can use it as a useful heuristic model, even if this model must ultimately be rejected.

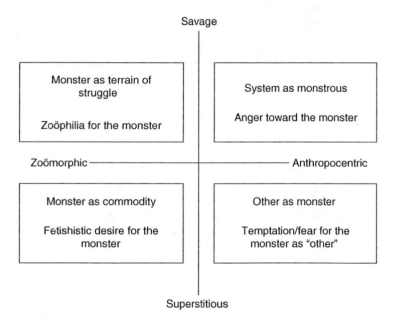

Briefly, the savage and anthropocentric quadrant produces monstrous imaginings that demonize economic, cultural, or social systems that are discriminatory or exploitative. As we will demonstrate in our Intermezzo, much of critical theory is located in this quadrant. In opposition to these monsters, the alienated, human community is privileged as a "hero" capable of "taming" or "killing" the irrational beast using the tools of reason (as in liberal humanist versions of the narrative) or creative labor (as in the Marxist humanist version). While important within many civil rights and proletarian struggles, here the monster is reduced to nothing more than an allegory of *human* system building gone terribly wrong. In other words, the political struggle is organized around the killing of the monster in order to overcome alienation. If full humanization remains the goal, then anthropocentric assumptions concerning the superiority of the human over and against creaturely others remains a highly problematic dimension of these imaginings and their concurrent narratives of struggle, liberation, and communist equality.

The anthropocentric and superstitious quadrant is perhaps the most typical imaginative matrix to emerge from the state of exception. When all boundaries are being challenged, there is a desire to retreat into the "safety" and "familiarity" of the anthropocentric community under threat of invasion by monstrous outsiders, foreigners, or strangers. In this case, the monster, as a sublime excess, must be dominated or tamed through colonial force or pedagogical intervention. Here the creaturely is once again appropriated in order to negatively code the other as "subhuman" producing a monster that demeans human and nonhuman animals as criminal, pathological, abnormal, or perverse. At stake in policing the dialectic of fear and desire for the monstrous is the (re)production of the "ontological hygiene" (Graham 2002, 60) of the community. This ontological purity is maintained through a "sacrificial strategy" (Kearney 2003, 26) in which the monster is ritualistically produced/discovered only to be expelled from the heart of the community as stranger. While acting to rejuvenate the law of the community, such rituals remind participants that the monster as scapegoat is never external enough—in fact it is always hauntingly too close for comfort, exposing the insidious fact that at the core of the law (purity) resides the very limit of the law (the monstrous)! In a brilliant analysis of cynocephalus—a monster that is part human and part canine—and the chivalric subject of medieval romantic literature, Jeffery Cohen (1999) argues that a little bit of the "species-mingling flesh" of this creature "is always found staining the 'domain of the subject'" because "the proximity of the monster is a formal necessity to keep in motion the identity-giving process of its continued exclusion" (134). In other words, monster and hero are locked within a shared space between the natural world and the social world, a zone of (aggressive) contact outside yet founding the law— what Cohen refers to as a "zone of uninhabitability" (ibid.).

A quintessential examination of the monster as boundary defining/deconstructing is seen in Adorno and Horkheimer's analysis of the Odysseus myth. For Adorno and Horkheimer, Odysseus is the proto-bourgeois individual attempting to return to the security, fixed property, and recognizability of the community. In this epic myth, monsters form the obstacles to Odysseus's journey home—obstacles that are not so much external as they are necessary supports for the development of bourgeois subjectivity. In other words, civilized community is only recognizable as such through a return, mediated by the struggle to overcome the barbarism of the monstrous. Quoting Adorno and Horkheimer (2002),

> All the adventures Odysseus survives are dangerous temptations deflecting the self from the path of its logic. Again and again he gives way to them, experimenting like a novice incapable of learning—sometimes, indeed, out of foolish curiosity, like a mime insatiably trying out roles. "But where dander threatens/That which saves from it also grows": the knowledge which makes up his identity and enables him to survive has its substance in the experience of diversity, distraction, disintegration; the knowing survivor is also the man who exposes himself most daringly to the threat of death, thus gaining the hardness and strength to live. (38)

In other words, exposure to the monstrous is a learning experience for Odysseus who is capable of developing his characteristic cunning and Enlightenment reason through this subterfuge of monstrous combatants. Thus the monster (embodied in the temptations of Scylla and Charybdis or the stupidity of Polyphemus) is both the allure of the different that tempts Odysseus and his crew away from community and the support for the reaffirmation of a rational, human community—they are necessary externalities to the construction of the community, its disavowed supplement—a temptation that must be sacrificed in order to constitute the homeland. To give into the monstrous is nothing less than a betrayal of the community and yet, existence without the monster would be tantamount to a disintegration of the boundaries that define community in the first place. Thus when Circe utilizes her magic powers to transform Odysseus into a pig (a creature whose hairless condition is reminiscent of the human animal minus the supplement of Enlightenment reason), the pact of renunciation and sacrifice that binds Odysseus to community is threatened. And yet, by overcoming these obstacles, Odysseus and his crew rejuvenate and ultimately strengthen the law of human reason to dominate nature and affect. In other words there could not be a homeland without a monstrous stranger, barbarian, or savage that provides the backdrop for heroic returns, for sacrificial purification.

A zoömorphic and yet superstitious imagination gives birth to monsters of another sort—monsters of extreme desire, monsters that are commodified and sold on a market that itself is never up for critique. On the cultural front, R. L. Rutsky (2007) highlights the surge of interest in heroic mutants such as The Amazing Spiderman, the X-Men, and other cyborg creations, all of which save humanity from a host of enemies precisely because of their monstrous natures. In these cases, a zoömorphic imagination takes flight and embraces all shapes and sizes of surrealist fancy without distinctions or savage suspicions. The monsters in these scenarios are not threatening to consensus politics as such but rather have been absorbed into the system of exchange, and animal-becomings are seen as fashionable statements within the circulation of hybrid identities and alternative lifestyles [everything from New Age Shamanism (chapters two and three) to bestiality porn (the conclusion to this book)]. Border-crossing is no longer "subversive" but rather part and parcel of the postmodern capitalist expropriation of life in all its mutant forms.

In other words, the twilight zone of monstrous uninhabitability has expanded, erasing the differential that separated the ontological purity of the community from the sacrifice of "species-mingling flesh." This construction of the monster represents what Giorgio Agamben might refer to as a "state of emergency" (Agamben 1999a) where the state of nature and the nature of state collapse in on one another creating a perpetual no-man's-land between inclusion and exclusion, friend and enemy, life and death, human and animal. In other words, the state of emergency is where the exception becomes the rule and law and language no longer can act to safeguard a community from the "transformation of all social life into a spectacular phantasmagoria" (Agamben 1993b, 79) of desirable monsters. If the community and the monster are conjoined twins, then, in the state of spectacular emergency, the disavowed, externalized supplement of the law has become coterminous with the law—fear and temptation become immanent to the life of the community, which is always itself in a state of ontological and political crisis. If the monster can no longer be excluded from the gates of the community as in the Odyseus myth, then myth no longer functions as a narrative safeguard against invasions. Invasion itself becomes the narrative (un)grounding of the state of exception.

Finally, the last quadrant represents that maximal intensification of zoömorphic and savage vectors of the imagination. Here the system is coded as monstrously set against life and in turn life itself is considered as a monstrous terrain of struggle of humans and a host of literal and figurative animal-becomings against Power. As a plateau of maximum insurgency, this final quadrant occasionally arises in order to open up a new location for a democratic politics of life. Moving from an anthropocentric logic of immunization, both quadrants on the left of the graph embrace contamination—yet with a key difference. Rather than anger or fear/temptation, these quadrants promote desire (as with commodification of the monster in the state of exception) or outrageous love [as the radical potentials for a new, democratically zoöphilic community (see the conclusion to this book)].[3] If, as Michael Hardt and Antonio Negri (2004) argue, the monster is an "ever present possibility that can destroy the natural order of authority in all domains, from the family to the kingdom" then today the "the monster effect has only multiplied" (195). Rather than simply a supplement to the law (Cohen) or an a-political indetermination of the law and its outside (Agamben), the monster becomes a model of exodus from a relation to the law (Hardt and Negri)—a figuration of absolute democracy itself as a force that cannot be fully territorialized. In fact, this construction of the monster is defined by two important features: becoming-ontological and formal immeasurability. For Negri (2007), the multiplication of the monstrous is a "becoming-ontological" in the sense of an embrace of the biopolitical production of life without recourse to qualifications of an "essence" or an "authentic identity," and it is immeasurable in the sense of infinite innovations and generations of new modes and forms of living. The monster in its most radical potentiality therefore brings "the hope for and the choice of a life that is not hierarchically ordered or prefigured by forms of measure" (52). This is a monster truly out of bounds.

If Cohen (1996) proposes that we "read cultures from the monsters they engender" (3), then we further suggest that the bestiary is an important technology for organizing and evaluating the various monsters (political, pathological, economic, etc.) emerging from the present moment. Agreeing with Frances Bartkowski (2008), we need a new kinship bestiary that enables us to recognize the zoömorphic and savage possibilities of a monstrous imagination for redefining social, political, economic, and ecological activism.[4] The *bestiarum vocabulum* is a compendium of beasts, some imagined and some real, others a strange hybrid between the two. Made popular in the Middle Ages, the bestiary is more than simple natural history. Rather it is a unique text that transforms nature into culture—where the word of God imbued every creature in heaven and earth with a particular meaning—and culture into nature. They are, as Bartkowski argues, "fables of the human-animal borderlands" (60) where monsters dwell. As the bestiary testifies, the monster does not exist simply on the outside of the boundaries of community, class, or public. It is a complex externality that is outside as much as it is inside, both mythical and natural, both simultaneously close and distant. In a zone of in-between that suspends the law of recognition, identification, and belonging (to a particular class, race, gender, species), monsters are a form of "domestic foreigness" (Braidotti 1996, 141) that are both strange and familiar. As Debra Hassig argues, medieval bestiaries explored the zones of indistinction between the known and the unknown, the human and the animal, the divine and the natural, creating an imaginative space that inevitably transgressed the boundaries which they upheld. For Hassig (1995), bestiaries were a politically contested genera that simultaneously perpetuated anti-Semitism by casting the Jew as the idolatrous hyena and provided an imaginative space for medieval feminist critique (see, for instance, the *Response du bestiarie* written by an anonymous woman as a critique of the misogynous message of Richard of Fournival's *Bestiarie d'amour*) (8). Bestiaries are collections of our narrative constructions of monsters and as such help us navigate the zone of uninhabitability—the bestiary is a zoömorphology.

Uncovering the catalogue of monsters that constitute these monstrous times is an aesthetic, political, and *pedagogical* project. As a technology for organizing the monstrous, the bestiary reveals the difficulty of maintaining the coordinates of a zoömorphic and savage imagination in the face of superstitious beliefs in the legitimacy and universality of Power. If certain valences of the monster can be progressive, helping to enliven imaginative critiques of Power, then others might very well be put in the service of extending the Power of capitalism and the nation-state to control and police. Emerging from within this crisis, the contemporary bestiary is a pedagogical technology that must be struggled over, for the creatively productive and destructive force of the imagination is what is at stake. In this sense, our use of the bestiary is meant to cut across two extreme positions in educational philosophy: the rejection of the imagination as inherently dangerous—leading to an imbalance between powers and desires (Rousseau 1979)—or the imagination as inherently linked to freedom (Greene 2000). Both positions ultimately miss the complexity of the imagination as composed of contradictory vectors of force that can be intensified or depleted through interactions with affects and social determinants. Our bestiary is an attempt to organize various permutations of this imaginative diagram in order to better understand how imagination is both dangerous and liberatory. In particular, the bestiary is a function of a particular kind of pedagogy—a pedagogy that we call "exopedagogy." Here the prefix "exo" designates the beyond, an education out of bounds, whose location resides at the very limits of the recognizable—where we learn to study the zone of uninhabitability that indicates the untimely arrival of a swarm of monsters and strangers. It is, in other words, a pedagogy that concerns the sudden appearance of "strange facts" (Daston and Park 2001) that exist beyond the field of common sense. If monsters have traditionally been banned from philosophy as dangerous obstructions to be sacrificed or as mere illusions (Kearney 2003), then so too has education more often than not been involved in projects that (a) repress the monstrous within or (b) project the monstrous onto the outside world. Drawing on Althusser's theory of the school as an Institutional State Apparatus, Badmington (2004) argues that schools attempt to naturalize the human in order to conceal the historical, "profoundly non-original" (126) origin of the human within the unformed of the monstrous. Either way, the uncanny relation between the self and other, the animal and human, the foreign and familiar is misplaced, and our interior alterity is sacrificed in order to achieve a false presence or identity that substantiates the formation of a community predicated on mutual belonging. Schools betray the monstrous multitude as an unruly beast that must be tamed and gentrified through either sacrifice or separation.

Exopedagogy helps us navigate the various narratives of the monstrous emerging from our state of phantasmagoria—reactionary monsters, commodified monsters, and creative/constituting monsters. At its best, exopedagogy utilizes the bestiary in order to intensify the savage and zoömorphic vectors of a radical imagination beyond the law of the community (the sacrificial strategy), the law of capitalism (the expropriation of surplus-value), and the law of the human (the anthropocentric valorization of human creative power, linguistic production, and cognitive capacity). In this sense, exopedagogy is both savagely critical and creatively posthuman—producing new political narratives emerging from seemingly uninhabitable terrains.

Exopedagogy intensifies the zoömorphic and savage vectors of the imagination through imaginative play between the human and the animal, leading to new political narratives. While posthumanist scholars such as Norris (1985) and Davide Panagia (2009) remain critical of narrative—in the first place as a gentrification of zoocentric thought and in the second as the territorialization of sensation—what we want to argue is that narrative as such is not the enemy, but rather the type of narrative. Certain forms of monstrous narration, animated by zoömorphic and savage vectors of imaginative force, produce uncanny events for the further generation, acceleration, and intensification. Drawing on Deleuze and Guatarri's distinction (1987) between "order" and "organization" (158), we could argue that a narrative organization remains a hierarchical and centralized stratification of imaginative vectors of force whereas a narrative order promotes momentary rest before increasing experimentation and savagely zoömorphic involution (innovation beyond hybridization of two species or evolution of a single species). A critical bestiary is essential in charting the imaginative valences of the monstrous in order to build new narratives that are democratic and creatively open.

In this sense, pedagogy is the re-presentation of the example (the model citizen, the fully humanized subject, the revolutionary proletariat, or the "A" student) whereas exopedagogy is the *re-presentation of the exceptional* (the monster that emerges from the uninhabitable hinterlands of the community and of capitalist production). In fact, our project focuses on the *bestiary as an aesthetic pedagogy organizing the study of the exceptional*—a technology for producing new literacies of the monstrous through the intensification of both the zoömorphic and savage dimensions of the imagination. It is an aesthetic alternation of consciousness that releases the subject from habituated patterns of thought in order to construct an intensive thought feeling out of bounds of common sense. In this sense, the critical bestiary is a "monstrous curriculum" immanent to the development of a posthuman form of intelligence, stimulating zoömorphic and savage imaginative vectors for new political narratives beyond the capture of the communal law or the desires of the capitalist marketplace.[5]

Exopedagogy exists in an unhomely home—an uncanny, imaginary location that is neither inside nor outside, self nor other. For Freud (2003), the uncanny is a misidentification of a difference that turns out to be the self—an estrangement of self and other in a moment of indistinction. The uncanny is not a state of recognition but is rather a dwelling in the suspension of recognition, belonging, and common sense when confronted with the extimate—or as Freud would say "something that should have remained hidden and has come into the open" (148). What is this "something"? It is the surplus common that exists in excess of the political or economic community.[6] Because there is no position outside the monstrous (outside of the real subsumption of society and ecology by capitalism) we cannot find a "safe" location that legislates judgments from the position of authoritative knowledge or inherited/pre-organized values, and in this sense, we must struggle to reclaim the monster from within the monster as a form of uncanny dwelling. We cannot, in other words, simply transcend various permutations of monstrous forms.

The uncanny home of exopedagogy is the zone of indistinction, disfiguration, and deformation that profanes the sacred parameters of community and self precisely by exposing the subject to potentiality to be or not to be this or that—the monster whose flesh is a "pure potential, an unformed life force" that "constantly expands social being, producing in excess of every traditional political-economic measure of value" (Hardt and Negri 2004, 192). Education is no longer as John Dewey (1980) once described an "embryonic society" but is rather—to appropriate the title of Bhanu Kapil's poetic dislocations—an "incubation" machine for "humanimal" monsters.

In this sense, the exopedagogical "classroom" (whether imaginary or material) is a home, but not a "safe" or "comforting" retreat where the human subject can find privacy and repose with other like-minded friends and family against the noise of the rabble outside. The dangers of this concept of the home for educational theory and practice are clearly outlined in Helen Marie Anderson's call (2007) for a radical pedagogy of homeplace. The home as exclusive private property and interiority are always, as Anderson argues, predicated on an exclusion that limits responsibility to those within a finite circle of close acquaintances. Also agreeing with Anderson, this criticism does not mean a complete rejection of the home for absolute nomadism—a claim that undermines the work of the oppressed to form new notions of the home (and homeland) in opposition to oppression, marginalization, and exclusion. What we would call a monstrous home is a locality that always includes an uncanny confrontation with its repressed excess: the monstrous contaminant that undermines notions of public/private dichotomy. The "dirty home" (Lewis and Cho 2006) is an alternative spatial topography that suspends the public and the private by exposing the remnant of the monstrous other within the most private and autonomous places—realizing the political potential of homeplace by revealing the foreign kernel that remains lodged in the most intimate of spheres. Thus the home is no longer static and sanitized but rather is dynamic and contaminated—a location that is always a dislocation and thus an opening to exodus and the coming community. As Roberto Esposito (2010) demonstrates, the original meaning of the common emphasized "dirtiness" or "contamination" over and against immunizing logics of purity and chastity. In this sense we choose to read the home of exopedagogy as a castle or landscape full of intrigue, suspense, and uncanny close encounters of the third and fourth kinds—a location of struggle to reclaim the monster over and against capitalist separation or political scapegoating. If exopedagogy lacks a proper object (the example), then it also lacks a proper location/place/homeland. It is joyously dirty, filthy! In sum, exopedagogy can be summarized in relation to the following dimensions:

1. Location: Out of bounds of community sacrifice or capitalist separation (the uncanny home).
2. Curriculum: The organization of the exceptional (the critical bestiary as a zoömorphology).
3. Operation: The intensification and acceleration of zoömorphic and savage dimensions of the imagination.
4. Goals: New narratives of absolute democracy and new practices of posthumanist politics.

Exopedagogy means that we have to move beyond the prescribed limits of educational cultural studies, which more often than not relegate themselves to the critical analysis of film, television, and Internet (Giroux 1994, 2001; Kellner 2003b). Certainly the media spectacle of capitalism circulates through the monstrous—both in terms of form (the bloated information highways of the Internet, blockbuster spectacles, and supersaturated technophilic cultural productions) and in terms of the content—and it is also clear that young adults are clamoring for monstrous curricula based on best-selling monster novels such as *Twilight* and *The Host* (both by Stephanie Meyer). Authors such as Annalee Newitz (2006) persuasively argue that monsters in the media are a powerful allegory for the violence of capitalism. She writes, "Mutated by backbreaking labor, driven insane by corporate conformity, or gorged on too many products of a money-hungry media industry, capitalism's monsters cannot tell the difference between commodities and people" (2). Her analysis of movie monsters such as zombies and robots as articulating the fears of capitalist crisis and postcolonialist haunting is a powerful reminder that monsters speak to very real social, political, and economic concerns within global capitalism. Henry Giroux (2010) provides a similar argument in his recent analysis of the zombie as a defining monster of capitalism. Broadening the scope of this research we turn to natureculture assemblages whose linguistic, affective, and social productions form the narrative materials for organizing the contemporary bestiary. Through an analysis of these monstrous narratives we hope to find new resources for an exopedagogy that continually moves beyond boundaries set between human and nonhuman animals, beyond the exclusivity of the humanist community, and beyond the historical specificity of class while not abandoning the problematic of labor, exploitation, and commodity fetishism. In other words we are proposing an *exo-public* pedagogy dwelling in the uninhabitable realm of the monsters at the edge of the map of the imagined world.

Looking toward exopublic spheres, we pose the questions: What is the contemporary bestiary that defines the monstrous antagonism of counter-revolution and revolt? What pedagogies, literacies, and imaginative curricula do these natureculture assemblages deploy? Here we argue that figures such as the feral child, the alien, and the faery are important monsters for examining various intensities that arise when the social/political and biomorphic vectors of the imagination cross, collide, and accelerate. These figures rest on three different thresholds that define the contemporary posthuman age:

1. Feral Child: between the human animal and the nonhuman animal, the state of nature and the nature of state. This monster is the result of a humanist paradigm fueled by an anthropocentric and superstitious imagination. As we will demonstrate in chapter one, the feral child is a pathological monster tainted or infested with animal gesticulations and desires that rupture the divisions between human and nonhuman producing equal mixtures of fear and desire that haunt the ontological purity of the community.
2. Alien: between inside and outside, inner-space and outer-space. Our analysis of David Icke's alien reptoid hypothesis as a form of exopedagogy (chapter two) will illustrate the complexity of Icke's monstrous imagination. While exhibiting certain zoömorphic and savage qualities, ultimately his work is ambiguous, sliding into a superstitious fear of the animal other (now located as the ultimate space-traveling alien) while simultaneously singing the praises of posthumanist becomings.
3. Faery: between nature and culture, premodernity and postmodernity. Another example of exopedagogy, faery faith attempts to break free from anthropocentric paradigms by promoting certain zoömorphic and savage critiques of capitalism. Yet at the same time, there are residual imaginative elements that compromise the potential of faery faith to move beyond commercialization.

By looking at media culture, human-nonhuman actor networks, and educational practices emerging from countercultures we will examine multiple dimensions of the feral, the alien, and the faery in order to provide new affective, cognitive, and linguistic tools to intensify the generative, creative, and democratic powers of the monster against communal temptation/fear and capitalist desire. If exopedagogy is monstrous, let us all become monsters and in this way experiment with new forms of democratic imagination.

Intermezzo

MARXISM AND THE BESTIARY

Perhaps one of the most important and yet overlooked bestiaries is Marx's own fantastically monstrous conception of capitalism. For some, it might appear to be rather strange that Marx's "science of history" is peppered with continual references to irrational occult figures that transgress the human and animal boundary. For this camp, the aesthetic of horror and suspense is no more than an ornamental digression that leads the reader astray from the scientific focus of Marx's *Capital*. Others, such as Marshall Berman (1982), argue that we should not forget the *literary* nature of Marx's works, and that his literary gestures cannot be completely separated from his overall dialectical method. What is *Capital* after all if not a gothic tale of horrors where the reader is left in perpetual uncertainty as to his or her fate (is capitalism destined to consume the world or to be vanquished by the proletariat?), where suspense holds the reader in the grip of the unfolding drama of struggle, where linear historical narrative suddenly complexifies into labyrinthian descriptions of political and economic intrigue? Although Robert Tucker (1967) anchors Marx's narrative structure in myth, he nevertheless finds its literary equivalent in Robert Louis Stevenson's gothic description of alienation in *Dr. Jekyll and Mr. Hyde* (1886). Bonnie Honig (2001) further argues that political philosophy as such should be read as a gothic narrative. In defense of the gothic aesthetic against critics such as Richard Rorty and his romanticism, Honig suggests that a gothic approach to the study of social reality sensitizes us to the paradoxes and ambiguities of foreignness (or in our case, the monstrous).[1] For Marx, the gothic enables the savage suspicion of our domesticated visions of the freedoms of the market and the eternal profitability of industry, intensifying the affective expression of alienation and, simultaneously, multiplying the sensation of constituting powers of revolt and revolution. We would like to suggest that the inclusion of imaginative references to a host of gothically inspired demonic forces and animal-hybrid creatures in *Capital* is not simply literary and philosophical but also pedagogical. The choice of gothic imagery enlivens and intensifies the pre-critical, pre-conscious *sensation* of disturbance and distortion, creating new resonances between thought and feeling within the diagram of the imagination.[2] The centrality of gothic imaginings as part of Marx's overall pedagogy is noted by Marx (1990) himself: "There is a definite social relation between men that assumes, in their eyes, the fantastic form of a relation between things. In order, therefore, to find an analogy, we must have recourse to the mist-enveloped regions of the religious world" (165). The mist-enveloped regions of the occult are, in a dialectic turn, the very allegorical channels through which we can demystify the supernatural forces of capitalist production. The use of allegory is not simply literary but also pedagogical, creating a chain of imaginative resonances between thought and feeling that make capitalism more real precisely through the unreality of the analogy.[3] In what follows, we will examine three monsters in Marx's critical bestiary—the vampire, the werewolf, and the Medusa—revealing how each embodies a different dimension of capitalism's own demonic qualities—qualities that have only intensified since Marx's original observations.[4] In other words, our bestiary provides an important resource for mapping imaginative lines of flight.[5]

Yet our analysis of Marxist bestiaries, past and present, will not simply be laudatory. We insist that the bestiary as a way of organizing imaginary relations to the monstrous conditions of economic emergency are complex terrains of thought feeling that include anthropocentric and superstitious dimensions, setting a precedence for the appropriation of the monster as an allegory for vicious and predatory capitalism. Although Negri argues that Marx was the first to discover the proletariat as a revolutionary monster (Casarino and Negri 2008), a close reading of Marx's work reveals that "the monster" is a purely derogatory concept implying a distortion of an authentically human species-being. If the proletariat is monstrous, it is not because of its productive capacities or political insurgencies but rather because the proletariat under the division of labor represents a negative state of alienation. Marx (1990) writes, capitalism "converts the worker into a crippled monstrosity by furthering his particular skill as in a forcing-house, through the suppression of a whole world of productive drives and inclinations, just as in the states of La Plata they butcher a whole beast for the sake of his hide or his tallow" (481). In this quotation, Marx separates the monster from productive and generative capacities of the proletariat, equating the monster both with alienation and slaughter. The world historical occupation of the

proletariat is therefore to overcome this crippled, monstrous state by
becoming fully human. Marx thus misses the connection between
the infinite productivity of human species-being and the figure of the
monster as a positive, zoömorphic force of creation and ontological
destabilization of the categories of human and animal that both bind
and separate species under capitalism. In fact, we would argue that
Marx could not imagine this connection precisely because the historical conditions were not yet fully developed. It is our contention that
Hardt and Negri are able to name the monster as a political project
precisely because of the global reach of bioproduction (the production
of social, economic, and political life). It is in the interaction between
pre-subjective affective vectors and social/political/economic determinants of an extensive and intensive form of bioproduction that a
zoömorphic and savage imagination becomes possible. In what follows we will provide a brief overview of Marx's own bestiary—its zoömorphic limitations and its savage resources—and then move on to
Michael Hardt and Antonio Negri's more contemporary compendium
of beasts in order to see how they inherit the most progressive aspects
of Marx's savage imagination in order to intensify monstrous insurgencies against Power. If Marx famously inverted Hegel's idealism,
then we would argue that Hardt and Negri likewise have inverted
Marx's analysis of the monster, revealing its potentially progressive
valences. In conclusion we will return to the vampire, werewolf, and
Medusa in order to demonstrate how these figures can be reclaimed
for a posthumanist political agenda.

The Vampire and Immunization

Capital's gothic bestiary begins when Marx famously argues that capitalism is a monster that has three dominant forms. First, he describes
capitalism as having a vampire-like desire for profit at the expense of
human life. Quoting Marx (1990) directly, "dead labor which, vampire-like, lives only by sucking living labour, and lives the more, the
more labour it sucks" (342). Living labor (which generates value) is
appropriated by capital, transforming it into dead labor (materialized
in the form of the commodity and invested back into the expansion and
intensification of the forces of production). As Steve Shaviro (2002)
argues, the vampire is a premodern, precapitalist, aristocratic figure
who is a "feudal master, and not a capitalist" (284). Yet despite the
anachronistic imagery, the figure of the vampire is revealing precisely
because "his ravages are captured by, and brought within the scope
of, the capitalist world market" (285). We would agree with Shaviro's

analysis but for different reasons. If Shaviro argues for the transubstantiation of blood into information and the commodity-form, then
we would argue that such a reading misses the force of Marx's provocative metaphor. It is not blood that is replaced by information but
rather blood *as information has become commodified*. In other words,
blood has not become dematerialized as pure information but rather
has become a form of "biomedia" (Thacker 2003) where materiality
acts as a support function for information recodification and control.
Thus the vampire metaphor uniquely reveals the taste for the control
over life that marks modern *biopower* as a power that invests in health,
reproduction, and genetic fitness of total populations. Labor power is,
as Paulo Virno (2004) argues, a unique commodity precisely because
it cannot be separated from the body that contains the physical, mental, linguistic, and affective potential/capacity necessary for the production of surplus value. Thus labor power is the one commodity that
remains tethered to flesh and blood. Given recent genetic science, and
its emphasis on DNA mapping and stem cell research, our most intimate and private spheres have become commodified into biomedia.
In such cases, the very seeds of life have entered into the sphere of
exchange-value and capitalism has become a form of nano-capitalism
or micro-capitalism that produces increasingly intimate spaces for the
extraction of profits. In other words, capitalist expropriation of labor
power is no longer restricted to the molar level of organized, disci-
plined, and efficient human laborers, but has extended to take hold of
life's seemingly immeasurable molecular movements.

   If contemporary biopolitics has ancient genealogical roots in the
premodern figure of the vampire, this also means that the vampire is
equally transformed by contemporary capitalist social relations. To
understand both the continuity and the radical break that constitutes
the modern vampire we have to understand the particular logic of
modern biopolitics. Roberto Esposito (2008) argues that the precise
mechanism or technology of modern biopolitics is immunization.
Immunization here is not simply a historically specific technology/
discourse of biopower. For Esposito, it is the dialectical image that
captures the two aspects of biopolitics in a relation of imminence to
one another: *bios* (life) and *nomos* (law). Immunization enables us to
understand the internal complexity of this relationship as both affir-
mative/productive and equally negative/lethal. Through immunization "the negation doesn't take the form of the violent subordination
that power imposes on life from the outside, but rather is the intrin-
sically antinomic mode by which life preserves itself through power"
(46). Of course, we are all familiar with medical immunization that

allows minimal exposure to a weakened viral source in order to make the body stronger and more resistant to future infection. For Esposito, this is more than simply a medical procedure and instead forms the backbone of an overarching political paradigm. The classical case of political immunization turned autoimmune disease is in fact Nazi Germany where the health and purity of the Aryan race are only secured through the mass murder of the other as bearer of infection and disease. Thus as Esposito argues, "the therapeutic purpose" behind extermination is an attempt to eliminate the "presence in life of death; a life that is already dead because it is marked hereditarily by an original and irremediable deformation; the contagion of the German people by a part of life inhabited and oppressed by death" (137). What is most startling in the case of Nazi Germany is that this immunitary paradigm ultimately turns against the population it is meant to protect, eating it away from the inside as a form of "auto-immune" illness, hence Hitler's final command that all Germans commit suicide rather than surrender to the allies. Esposito finds the same tendency at work today in the global war against terror in which "it is excessive defense that ruinously turns on the same body that continues to activate and strengthen it" (148).

For Esposito, the temptation of the community is always to immunize itself against the monster, the stranger, the foreigner as exceptions produced above and beyond the logic of legal recognition and civic belonging. Immunity for Esposito always collapses into a form of autoimmune disease where the community folds back upon itself in a moment of what Giorgio Agamben (1998) would call "thanatopolitics" as a politics of death. Yet we would argue that the central struggle over immunization is not so much political as it is economic. It is in the struggle over the length of the working day as well as the question of the wage that capitalism embodies at the deepest level the principal model for immunity: both releasing productivity on unprecedented levels while also negating this productivity internally through crisis management. If Esposito sees in the novel *Dracula* the ultimate metaphor of a society attempting to immunize itself against the monstrous contaminant of disease, then it is no coincidence that Marx used the allegory of a vampire to explain the ability of capitalism to extract surplus value out of the labor process, transforming living labor (the life of the surplus common) into dead labor, transforming blood into "liquid" profit. To increase profits, capitalism must "inject" itself with the very viral life form that threatens its collapse: the insurgent powers of collective, living labor. Exposure to the virus of living labor is tempered through internal crisis management that strengthens and expands the vampire of capital. It is only through exposure to the risk of internal revolt of the working class against labor control that capitalism grows to monstrous proportions. Yet, it is precisely the injection of living labor into the system that, according to Marx, will in the end lead to a capitalist autoimmune disease in the form of falling rates of profit and worker revolution. In short, the vampire exposes the dialectical instability of the immunization paradigm of capital that cultivates the seeds of its own destruction.[6]

WEREWOLVES AND THE COMMODITY FORM

While the living dead might be the most potent image of capitalism's monstrous nature to date, Marx (1990) also argues that capitalism's "werewolf hunger for surplus labor" is "a live monster that is fruitful and multiplies" (217). The werewolf is shape-shifter, a changeling that contains within itself a dual nature that cannot be reconciled, or dialectically sublated, into a synthetic whole. Although there are many traditional interpretations of the werewolf, one line of inquiry is critically important for our analysis. For some, the transformation of the human into the wolf is not simply a demonic hoax or superficial alteration of appearances but rather a complete transformation that affects even the soul of the human. Whether this transformation is akin to somnambulism or the work of a demon that possesses not only the body but also the spirit of the human, the moment of becoming-wolf signifies a significant mutation where human understanding is replaced by a voracious appetite for flesh and violence. Montague Summers (2003) summarizes this bizarre phenomenon: "Not without reason did the werewolf in past centuries appear as one of the most terrible and depraved of all bond-slaves of Satan. He was even whilst in human form a creature within whom the beast—and not without prevailing—struggled with the man" (123). This depiction is instructive because it casts the werewolf as a bond-slave and the human as a conflicted creature torn apart at the center. According to I. Goulart's book *Admirable and Memorable Histories* (1607), the wretched state of the werewolf was caused by a "melancholike humor" that led the sick to "imagine themselves to be transformed into wolves" (cited in Otten 1986, 41). Typical of melancholia, the werewolf cannot find satisfaction with this world and its objects nor with itself as a conflicted creature. Returning to Marx's provocative allegory, it would appear that the werewolf provides the imaginary backdrop for his description of the commodity and its own internally split nature. For Marx, the commodity is a useful object that is also produced for exchange. Quoting Marx (1990),

> The usefulness of a thing makes it a use-value. But this usefulness does not dangle in mid-air. It is conditioned by the physical properties of the commodity, and has no existence apart from the latter... Exchange-value appears first of all as the quantitative relation, the proportion, in which use-values of one kind exchange for use-values of another kind. (126)

Thus exchange value is a common feature that can be found in each object but also abstracted from it—an abstraction necessary for recognition in the market as an exchangeable good. Stated differently, use value is a qualitative aspect of the commodities, their uniqueness and singularity, while exchange value is a quantitative aspect. Unusually, while the commodity contains within itself a dual nature, it cannot simultaneously make both visible at once. The two existing (and yet exclusive) natures of the commodity make it impossible to fully enjoy both the use and the exchange value of a commodity simultaneously. Here we return to the werewolf-like *structure* of the commodity form, which is forever split and thus unable to reconcile its own nature. The result is the fetishistic character of the commodity that can never fully equal itself by attaining full presence—every presence is predicated on an absence. Forever shape shifting/oscillating between use value and exchange value, the commodity restlessly multiplies itself throughout society ultimately to be internalized by the subject.[7] The werewolf hunger of capitalism is therefore not simply the lust for profit but also a metaphysical lust for *full presence*.

While Marx examines the fetishistic form of the commodity, he does not provide a complete analysis of the paradoxical effects that the fetish has on the fetishist. Drawing unique connections between medieval melancholia and modern capitalist fetishism, Agamben (1993a) writes,

> Considered from this point of view, the fetishist confronts us with the paradox of an unattainable object that satisfies a human need precisely through its being unattainable. Insofar as it is a presence, the fetish object is in fact something concrete and tangible; but insofar as it is the presence of an absence, it is, at the same time, immaterial and intangible, because it alludes continuously beyond itself to something that can never really be possessed. (33)

This peculiar position of the fetish changes the fetishist, who, like the fetish, must fully alienate him or herself, "constantly tending toward an *other*, a creature essentially nonhuman and antihuman" (50). Thus the human fetishist becomes nonhuman, a creature that has no name (can no longer be identified as Marx's *homo faber*). This modern fetishist is a recasting of the ancient melancholic werewolf who likewise attempted to possess a lost object precisely by its absence—an alienated being whose consciousness is split within itself. If the gothic image of the werewolf supplied Marx's imagination with the raw material for his critique of political economy, then so too the werewolf returns in the form of the fetishist who has been bitten by and subsequently infected with capital's own hunger, leaving the human in a crippled state of alienation.

MEDUSA AND THE STATE

The third seemingly anachronistic monster in Marx's bestiary is Medusa. In the preface to the first edition of Volume One of *Capital*, Marx (1990) writes,

> The social statistics of Germany and the rest of Continental Western Europe are, in comparison with those of England, wretchedly compiled. But they raise the veil just enough to let us catch a glimpse of the Medusa head behind it...Perseus wore a magic cap that the monsters he hunted down might not see him. We draw the magic cap down over eyes and ears as a make-believe that there are no monsters. (91)

Here Marx draws upon the ancient Greek myth of Medusa in order to explicate another dimension of social relations within capitalism: ideological mystification. If Perseus utilized the cap to hide from monsters, we use the cap to veil the monster within: capitalism. Without this cap, the bourgeoisie would not be able to sustain itself as a class. According to Georg Lukacs (1971), the preeminent theorist of class consciousness, the distinctive feature of bourgeois consciousness is that it is unable to grasp social totality without moving beyond itself. The contradictions of capitalism cannot be held together in a mediated totality, reducing society to a number of independent and autonomously functioning institutions each with their own internal laws of motion and regulation. While these local laws might be true in an abstract sense, they are never concretely true with relation to the totality of social relations within capitalism. Thus, under capitalism, "free" political/juridical status of the worker masks his or her "enslavement" to a capitalist system, where the only freedom is the chance to sell themselves into a system that is decisively organized against their material interests. The free, autonomous individual is a veil that conceals the objectification of human labor power as a commodity. In fact, Etienne Balibar (2009) has recently argued capitalism is never satiated and leads to "over-exploitation" (110) that threatens the worker with ever escalating levels of violence despite "humane" laws that "guarantee" worker rights. The dual nature of capitalism as an internally contradictory system of use and value, freedom and violence cannot be fully comprehended by bourgeois consciousness, which is not a psychological or intellectual defect but rather the necessary result of its structural location within the relations of production. As Lukacs (1971) describes,

> But the veil drawn over the nature of bourgeois society is indispensable to the bourgeoisie itself... Either they must consciously ignore insights which become increasingly urgent or else they must suppress their own moral instincts in order to be able to support with a good conscience an economic system that serves only their own interests. (66)

To remove the veil and thus to force this subject to stare into the face of the Medusa of capitalism is literally to collapse the structure that gives consistency to the bourgeoisie—turning them into "stone."

If what fascinates Marx is the use of Perseus's veil to hide from the horrors of the Medusa, we must return to the original myth in order to understand the full power of this analogy missed by Marx's initial reading. Perseus ultimately handed over the decapitated head of Medusa to his patroness, Athena, who utilized the head as a sign of civic strength to ward off foes. Thus what was once terrifying and monstrous becomes the emblem of the state—a protective talisman. From this perspective, states function to gentrify and tame the destabilizing power of the monster in order to maintain certain norms and values that enable the community of citizens to recognize one another—the humanist state of enlightened reason finds its protector in the savage and animalistic monsters it disavows! Medusa becomes a shield against the antagonism that the Medusa symbolized in the first place. As with the vampire, the monster as dangerous contaminant is appropriated through the immunizing logic of the state in order to strengthen/fortify the state against the perceived illness and disease of the monstrous. Marx's analysis of capitalism's Medusa qualities could act as a powerful mytho-poetic genealogical anchoring point for contemporary critiques of Power over and against revolutionary movements, demonstrating the appropriating, immunizing, and reactive nature of the nation-state.[8]

Just as the Medusa acts as an allegory for ideology and ideological critique in Marx's model of historical materialism, we equally cannot ignore that monstrous animality is gendered female, indicating a close connection between patriarchy, anthropocentrism, and superstition. Medusa was once a beautiful young virgin who participated in the cult of Athena. Poseidon, who could not resist her beauty, brutally raped Medusa, which led to her ultimate banishment as a monster. If, as Julia Kristeva (1991) argues, women are the original strangers, then Medusa is the ultimate foreigner, cast out on a lone island, with statues of frozen warriors her only companions. Medusa is a monstrous hybrid: woman and snake, living yet socially dead, desirous yet dangerous—a creature that suspends all the boundaries of the proper and the improper. According to Rosi Braidotti's genealogy (1996) of teratology (the science of monsters), it is often those on the fringes of community that are defined as the monstrous, including the African and Asian *homo monstrosus*—a racialized other that would become the half-man, half-ape "missing link"—as well as the female body whose maternal imagination could give birth to monstrous hybrids that seemed to combine phylogenic traits of the human animal and the nonhuman animal. And, as we learn from Foucault (2003a), biopolitics requires the invention of race as well as the sexual monster (Foucault 1980) to act as convenient scapegoats for the promotion of the life of the population. In all cases, gender and race are the "primary operators" (Braidotti 1996, 150) that mark the terrain of the monstrous against the ontological hygiene of the community. As Horkheimer and Adorno argue, women are included precisely by their exclusion from a patriarchal order. Charting the history that links "primitive" divisions of labor, the Christian witch trials, and finally the bourgeois family structure, Horkheimer and Adorno (2002) argue "Women gained admission to the world of mastery on behalf of the whole of exploited nature, but in a broken form" (207). Women, as representative of dominated nature, are included only through an exclusion. Returning to the Odysseus myth, Penelope is merely the embodiment of a patriarchal lack of patriarchy, and Circe, the hideous temptress of men, symbolizes the allure of pleasure constitutive of the repression that defines the bourgeois, male psyche. In both cases, the patriarchal order depends on the structural function of these exclusions (woman as wife or whore, virgin or monster). As Horkheimer and Adorno write, women as wives or as sorceresses "merely serve the purposes of male self-preservation" (57). Interestingly it is Athena who safeguards the patriarchal law of purity and chastity in the Medusa myth—Athena punishes Medusa (the female victim) rather than Poseidon (the male perpetrator). In other words, the only way for the community to maintain its "purity" (to keep its hands clean) is to legitimate an internal exclusion—Athena as goddess functioning in the name of patriarchal authority—to exclude/scapegoat the illegitimate monster (Medusa). There is a complex set of exclusions at work in this myth that function to maintain the perception of communal ontological hygiene, of collective "virginity" and "chastity." The paradox is clear: at the very heart of the community there lies an exclusion (the divine) whose function it is to exclude (the monster). Like Agamben's description (1998) of *homo sacer*, Medusa is a "double exception" (84) poised between the human and the divine, but unlike Agamben's description, it is the violence of patriarchy and its fear of contamination by the violated female body that is at stake.

Historical materialism is a reflective shield that enables Marx to gaze upon the monstrous in its totality, in all its contradictions without suffering the fate of the bourgeoisie. Yet the shield of historical materialism, while revealing these contradictions, also introduces the distance of science as an objectifying practice above or outside of Medusa, who must be "dissected" from a safe and secure location. Louis Althusser (Althusser and Balibar 1979) is the perfect example of this distancing from Marx's gothically savage imagination. The scientization of Marx's bestiary reduces the power of his monstrous contaminations to mere flights of residual mystification that conceal the emerging scientific core. Equally missed in this scientific reductionism is the importance of using the monster as a potential gateway for thinking beyond mere critique (or negation) into the open space of the monster as a new model of transformation outside of anthropological assumptions concerning the ontological purity of the human. It is to this posthumanist project that we must now turn.

THE CONTEMPORARY BESTIARY: FROM CAPITALIST DEMONS TO MULTITUDINOUS SWARMS

In this section, we will outline the central features of Hardt and Negri's bestiary in order to illustrate a key shift in the construction of the monster. Not only does the monster become a constituting and generative multitude of actors, but also Marx's anthropocentrism begins to show its limits when faced with a new posthumanist emphasis on difference and multiplicity that lacks a firm grounding in human essence our authentic existence. First we will overview their general theory of the multitude as a monstrous form of insurgent political and economic revolution and then, by positioning their analysis in relation to exopedagogy, argue that their theory provides a way of connective education, imagination, and cognition in order to form a coming community of monsters. We have chosen to focus on Hardt and Negri because more than anyone else they have most directly carried the mantle of Marx's savage project into the present historical moment. For Negri (2008), "Monstrous means that all the terms of the labour relation and of society have been caught up in the innovation of the forces of production and therefore present themselves in indeterminate and unqualifiable figurations" (47). With the "real subsumption" (Hardt and Negri 1994, 15) of society under capitalism, the rules of capitalist exploitation have exploded the limits of the factory walls to permeate and define all social relations—causing a series of perpetual emergencies in a variety of sectors of the economy and social life simultaneously. If space itself has been colonized by capitalism, then so too has time (Negri 2003a). Rather than an external/transcendent measurement of labor time in the factory, time has become a material substance that expands beyond the limits of the workday to become indistinguishable from life as such. Thus labor is precisely *wherever* and *whenever* there is social life. Yet the state of emergency, where society and factory coincide in a monstrous state of immeasurability (Hardt and Negri 2009), is not a cause of despair. Immanent to this no-man's-land of indistinction between inside and outside, we find the multitude laboring in vast networks across the globe building the capacities, capabilities, and the habits that form the affective and cognitive dimensions of a new sociality out of bounds. Thus, the monstrous is not simply a designation of capitalism's extended control (as in Marx's bestiary of industrialized capitalism). It is also and equally the location of insurgent power of innovation, cooperation, and collectivization that characterizes the multitude. If, according to Negri, the beginnings of modernity construct the political and economic fields in relation to the monster (Hobbes' leviathan and Marx's vampire) then so too it is on the plane of the monster that we must locate the generative powers of creation and production beyond the limits of this modernity. Therefore, it has been Negri's mission to "reclaim the monster" (Casarino and Negri 2008, 196) and fight against the underlying logic of capitalist exploitation and the nation-state from within the unformed and unruly flesh of the monster. In fact, we could argue that the political clarion call of Hardt and Negri's book *Multitude* (2004) is best summarized in the following: "Today we need new giants and new monsters to put together nature and history, labor and politics, art and invention in order to demonstrate the new power that is being born in the

multitude" (194). As such, Hardt and Negri utilize the *bestiary* as
a contemporary critical methodology for charting the mutations of
becoming that mark the modern and postmodern worlds, finding in
the monstrous imagination the resources for critique of the immunizing knot of biopower, the enchantment of the commodity form, and
the co-opting power of the state.

In the hands of Hardt and Negri, the monstrous is a dynamic,
boundless, and infinitely creative ontological becoming that constantly produces the commonwealth outside all measure. This positive definition of the monster beyond its relation to law hinges
on a key rethinking of Marx's definition of surplus. Capitalism
has always been driven by the production of surplus value, which
is value generated by expropriated labor over and above the value
necessary for its own reproduction. While labor power is capable of
producing a value greater than its individual worth, the constituting
powers of intellectual and immaterial labor (intelligence, experience,
knoweldges, desires, affects) also produce a common surplus that
cannot be fully expropriated by capital. Rather than simply romanti-
cize the capacities to produce new valences of becomings, Hardt and
Negri's work challenges us to make a critical distinction between
the *separation* and *incorporation* of the common. Cesare Casarino
draws on Hardt and Negri's recent work to make this distinction
explicit: "*Surplus value is living surplus as separation (in the form of
value par excellence, namely money). Surplus common is living surplus
as incorporation (in the forms of the common, including and especially
our bodies)*" (Casarino and Negri 2008, 23). The surplus common
is a living incorporation of the commonwealth rather than a privat-
ization that separates the monstrous dimensions of becoming from
the multitude. The surplus common does not reside on the terrain
of the nation-state or in the factory—it is the surplus that exists in
exodus from the common sense of the community, the boundaries of the nation-state, and the efficiency of capitalist production.
The surplus common is in other words *extraneus*—the surplus generated from the creative plentitude of collective labor that cannot
be restrained or fully incorporated into capitalist production (i.e.,
mortified into dead labor through the production of surplus value).
Hardt and Negri (2004) summarize, "We have also focused on the
fact that the production of the common always involves a surplus
that cannot be expropriated by capital or captured in the regimentation of the global political body" (212). The exclusion of the surplus
common is not simply negative; rather it is positive and highly productive. Living-labor, as Hardt and Negri (1994) argue, is "always

subjugated but always liberating itself" (5–6) through a process of self-valorization (i.e., always in the production of the common surplus that is a "dynamic rupture of the system" of capture and control that marks the capitalist process [9]). The surplus common is a line of flight from capitalist appropriation and political territorializations, forming a collective excess that runs ahead of capitalism into the open possibilities of labor out of bounds—a labor that constructs its own values immanent to the life of the multitude. It is therefore the goal of leftist politics to organize this surplus in order to maximize freedom and joy—maximize the Dionysian power of becoming—over and above *both* private property of liberal subjects and the public property of the nation-state. "This monster is common" (Casarino and Negri 2008, 205)—the power of common living within the biopolitical against the biopower of capitalism. In other words, the monster is the surplus common that supersedes all measure—it is always wherever and whenever there is bioproduction within global capitalism. Hardt and Negri's productive and positive reading of the surplus common is the most politically progressive narrative structure for understanding the potential role of the monster. The monster as an ambiguous sight/site is liberated from its iterative relation to law and becomes the imaginative force of exodus itself—a "divine violence" (Benjamin 1978).

As a constituting power that lacks a fixed identity, the monster is a constant, creative, joyful becoming rather than a static being. For Hardt and Negri, the multitude is the form of this becoming, a living-in-common that emerges from and against the extended state of emergency. In Hardt and Negri's genealogy, the multitude has been characterized throughout modernity as "a savage beast" that "must be dominated, tamed, or destroyed, overcome or sublimated" (Negri 1999, 325) by either the public (as its respectable, domesticated, and gentrified formation) or the community (as its immunized other). The multitude is what the community deems the excessiveness of alterity and the public deems irrational noise of the streets and the nation-state deems barbarian. From inside these boundaries, the multitude becomes a threat, its elocution nothing more than senseless babble, its demands nothing more than irrational complaints, and its actions nothing more than assaults against the common sense organization of community or nation-state or capitalist productive processes. Freed from the dialectic of sacrifice that constitutes the community's relation to the monster, the multitude as monstrous no longer is predicated on fear/temptation but rather pure desire to construct new becomings and thus increase the power to act and produce in the world beyond separation (the capitalist expropriation of the commonwealth) and sacrifice (the scapegoating function of the monster in the community).

The multitude is not designated by identity or similitude but rather by internal difference, multiplicity; it is both polymorphous and expansive. The multitude is in other words, the quintessential stranger, the extraneous writ large, which exists both inside and outside the political field. The stranger breaks kinship ties that are based on blood (familial), political affiliation (national), or cultural identity (communitarian). It is a kinship that is unstable, mutant, and thus open to perpetual contamination. As Hardt and Negri (2009) argue, the monster is a "figure of sublime disproportion and terrifying excess, as if the confines of modern rationality were too narrow to contain their extraordinary creative powers" (95). At the same time, Negri (2003a) argues that the multitude (as monstrous) is "something very beautiful" (98). If community is predicated on the aesthetics of the beautiful (symmetry, proportion, and harmonious identity that scapegoat the monstrous as dangerous), then the multitude is (like Medusa) a *beautiful form of the monstrous*—a productive and life-enhancing notion of the sublime that ruptures the boundaries of the community through the insurgent joy of collective labor.[9] Presenting an excess over and above recognition (i.e., the surplus common) that defines who belongs and who is excluded, the multitude *suspends* the distinction between the sublime and the beautiful, rendering such terms obsolete—producing a sublime beauty through a close encounter with the surplus common. It is the strangeness of the multitude that poses problems of contamination to kinship networks based in genetics, traditions, or political alliances but also opens up new horizons beyond the sacrificial logic of the community—a utopian space that is not so much "over there" as it is "right here" in the coming community that is immanent in the movements of the multitude. As Negri (2008) writes, "Utopia [a beautiful sublime par excellence] today means exodus and metamorphosis" (32) in the state of exception.[10]

Rather than articulation of a particular through which all other struggles are temporarily organized and sutured (hegemony), the multitude is polymorphous lacking a head (like Medusa's body) or, alternatively, composed of multiple heads (like a hydra) and thus is a distributed/decentralized form of network intelligence. Using the provocative metaphor of the swarm, Hardt and Negri (2009) write, "When a distributed network attacks, it swarms its enemy: innumerable independent forces seem to strike from all directions at a particular point and then disappear back into the environment" (91). Rather than a mindless set of drones that collapse into uniformity and opposed to simple and pure spontaneous anarchy, the multitude has a certain "swam intelligence" that emphasizes the "collective and distributed techniques of problem solving without centralized control or the provision of a global model" (ibid.). Such intelligence arises through ever more complex and global communications networks that form the fabric of social life without having to posit the essence of a working-class identity or the formal structure of a hegemonic project of articulation. Emphasizing the swarm suggests that intelligence is no longer conceptualized along liberal humanist lines of the autonomous individual and universal (and thus fully abstract) reason. Rather reason is embodied in collective practices composed of internal singularities. By developing its own swarm intelligence and by amplifying its own productive networks of communication, the multitude labors to realize a state of absolute democracy—a democracy for everyone without limits. The goal is the constitution of a new, open-ended notion of the commonwealth that cannot be territorialized into a nation-state or held captive by any form of community, hierarchical organization, or communicative speech act of public discourse. This new body is "pure potential, an unformed life force, an in this sense an element of social being, aimed constantly at the fullness of life" through the constant expansion of the surplus common (192). In other words, if capitalism thrives off of intellectual or cognitive labor (the general intellect), then the multitude's swarm intelligence does not simply reappropriate the property of the state or of capitalism but rather "de-appropriates" (Negri 2003b, 101) the general intellect, releasing its productivity into the circulation of the surplus common.

While new communication networks within the real subsumption of global social relations by capitalism have made this political possibility a reality for Hardt and Negri, there are clear historical antecedents of the present multitudinous uprising (including the infamous WTO protests in Seattle). Peter Linebaugh and Marcus Rediker's magisterial book entitled *The Many-Headed Hydra: Sailors, Slaves, Commoners, and the Hidden History of the Revolutionary Atlantic* (2000) can be read as a textbook analysis of the historical tendency of the multitude to struggle for the common against the rise of capitalist expropriation. From the very beginning of English colonial expansion in the seventeenth century, the battle over the commonwealth was characterized in mythic allegory as a struggle between Hercules and the hydra. Those attempting to order the new global system of labor

variously designated dispossessed commoners, transported felons, indentured servants, religious radicals, pirates, urban laborers, soldiers, sailors, and African slaves as the numerous, ever-changing heads of the monster. But the heads, though originally brought into productive combination by their Herculean rulers, soon developed among themselves new forms of cooperation against those rulers, from mutinies and strikes to riots and insurrections and revolution. (4)

The hydra was a multiplicity, an internally differentiated network of all those striking a blow against authority of church and state, private property, and imperial rule. This "motley crew" explored alternative forms of social organization that did not sacrifice the commonwealth and instead intensified collaboration across race, class, and gender divisions in order to subvert Power and poverty. In fact, the notion of the common itself became a hydra-headed beast expanding its points of reference beyond the English agrarian traditions to include West African village life and Native American long-fallow agriculture— forms of social existence that "encompassed all those parts of the Earth that remained unprivatized, unenclosed, a noncommodity, a support for the manifold human values of mutuality" (26). Thus, the multitude as a monstrous contamination is the lost history of revolution and of becoming-communist. The hydra is part of the political bestiary of the multitude—both a superstitious rendering of the multitude from the perspective of the community under threat and, once de-appropriated, a savagely democratic imaginative diagram of creative production beyond dialectics of fear (which define the common property of the community) and desire (which fuel the commodification of monstrous becomings as surplus value).

Although Hardt and Negri's theory of the multitude can be criticized for residual anthropocentristic assumptions concerning living labor, linguistic creativity, and cognitive development (Lewis, in press), nevertheless, they help intensify the savage and zoömorphic dimensions of the Marxist imagination more than any other contemporary theorists working within this lineage. Drawing heavily from a host of posthumanist theories, Hardt and Negri (2000) argue that the multitude is composed of "barbarians" who see nothing as permanent, who are out of the boundaries of community. More than anything, the barbarians signal what Hardt and Negri argue is an "*anthropological exodus*" (215) from the human opening up a new, creative, and highly experimental zone of becoming. Stated differently, Negri (2007) argues for a process of "anthropological metamorphosis" (54) of self and other beyond preconstituted subjectivities circulating within capitalism or defined by the law of the community. The first condition of this metamorphosis is "the recognition that human nature is in no way separate from nature as a whole, that there are no fixed and necessary boundaries between the human and the animal, the human and the machine, the male and the female, and so forth" (ibid.). In fact, Hardt and Negri (2005) write, "The new world of monsters is where humanity has to grasp its future" (196). The monstrous future of the human transforms the human beyond recognition by the state or by the community. This post-human teleology renders the scapegoating function of the monster obsolete precisely because it calls into question the anthropocentric assurances of human superiority, rationality, certainty, autonomy, and self-awareness that found the ontological purity of the community (even Marx's own communist utopia). In other words, posthumanist skepticism undermines the fundamental "dignity" and "centrality" of the human against which all other life is measured, opening up a newly expanded and intensified field for zoömorphic imaginative becomings.

For Hardt and Negri, the savage and zoömorphic imagination plays a crucial role in this overarching project of the multitude and in the formation and structure of swarm intelligence. While it is not uncommon to argue that one's enemies are "insects" (allegorized in science fiction films such as *Starship Troopers* [1997]), Hardt and Negri turn to Rimbaud (2004) who positively described the Commundards defending revolutionary Paris against government forces as "ants" and the barricades as "anthills" (92) thus inverting the negative symbolism of insect life. It is not that insect colonies are the same as human societies, but rather that there are differences of degree rather than differences of kind within the manifestation of collectively embodied swarm intelligences. Drawing certain theoretical and political implications out of ant behavior, the "savage beast" that is the multitude becomes a savagely posthuman assemblage forged through the zoömorphic imaginative impulse to become-animal, become-creaturely, become-multitude. The unruly flesh of the multitude folds within itself the nonhuman logic of animal swarms, thus opening up a threshold between nature and culture, *zoë* and *bios*.

Quoting Donna Haraway (1992), "Nature is not a physical place to which one can go, nor a treasure to fence in or bank, nor an essence to be saved or violated ... It is not the 'other' who offers origin, replenishment, and service ... " (296). Rather nature for Haraway is "artifactual," a topos of "common places—locations that are widely shared, inescapably local, worldly, enspirited; i.e. topical" (ibid.). In other words, nature as a "commonplace" is part of the artifactual surplus common of the multitude—a multitude that defines itself in exodus from anthropological divisions that separate *bios* (as active and infinite) and *zoë* (as passive and finite).[11] Haraway argues that nature is a "co-construction among humans and non-humans" (ibid., 297) and in this way is both a constituted and constituting force. Indeed, nature cannot be cast as merely a finite set of resources and threatened ecologies existing outside the political common but rather is an active force that structures sensation and in turn impacts the development of imaginative worlds both directly and indirectly.[12] What is needed here is a return to Deleuze and Guattari's theory (1987) of "transversal communications" (11), which situates the commonwealth in a radically open system/field that traverses fidelities to anthropocentric fantasies of human exceptionalism. When Hardt and Negri turn to ant colonies to theorize the swarm intelligence of the multitude, they are envisioning a surplus common (the common of commons, or a *transversal* commonwealth) populated with imaginative resonances between humans and nonhumans, social and environmental ecologies—a reconstruction of an embodied, unruly, and fleshy intelligence capable of anthropological exodus through imaginative translations and filiations without bounds.

If, as Cary Wolfe (2010) argues, what is needed is the realization that "the nature of thought itself must change if it is to be posthumanist" (xvi), then we would add that this change is not enough. Common notions of reason are the result of the intensification of the imagination, of feeling thought's becoming. Thus, aesthetic consciousness alternation is a necessary component of the posthumanist project, one that shifts imaginative vectors from anthropocentric and superstitious to zoömorphic and savage intensities. Here we must emphasize the importance of the imagination in articulating sensation and thought, pre-subjective and post-subjective social forces in order to change the nature of thought. In this sense, Hardt and Negri's struggle to reclaim the monstrous as an imaginative site of anthropological exodus cannot be forgotten.

We can now return to the vampire, the werewolf, and Medusa in order to affirm the generative and productive capacities of monsters. Reclaiming the vampire, Hardt and Negri (2005) argue that this figure offers an "alternative mechanism of reproduction" (193) outside of the immunizing logic of the family and the nation-state, multiplying the monstrous dimensions of social life beyond traditional parameters of property (public and private) and the commodity form. To critique capitalism from the very terrain of the vampire means to simultaneously think how immunization turns into an autoimmune disease, and in turn, how autoimmune deficiency becomes an opening for a new form of collective life beyond the body of capitalism. As Donna Haraway (1997) points out,

> The vampires are the immigrants, the dislocated ones, accursed of sucking the blood of the rightful possessors of the land and of raping the virgin who must embody the purity of race and culture. So, in an orgy of solidarity with all the oppressed, one identifies firmly with the outlaws who have been the vampires in the perfervid imaginations of the upstanding members of the whole, natural, truly human, organic communities. (215)

For Haraway, the vampire is the agent of the uncanny surplus that exceeds the purportedly natural life of communities, revealing the violence of the fantasy of racial purity, sexual chastity, and species homogeneity. Thus we cannot simply abandon the vampire but must recognize within the vampire a new mode of existence emerging from within the very system it infects. We have to think the possibility of a coming community without relapse into immunizing logics that exterminate the stranger/monster in the name of the Same. If the present moment is the moment of the living dead (poised in the state of exception between life and death), then this moment is not simply a moment of devastation and ruin (the end of time) but is also a radical time of action and revolution (the time of the now)—a time of insurgent activity that is viral and global in scope where the vampire stands as symptom of the capitalist system and as a potent figuration of a new relationship between life and death emerging from within the state of crisis and emergency. Indeed, Marx's imaginative use of the vampire as a lone, sovereign predator, feeding off of the life of the laboring masses, is certainly savage. Yet Haraway's collective, insurgent, and revolutionary rethinking of the vampire is zoömorphically connected to a vitality beyond immunization of the community (beyond the life and death of the organism), indicating a thriving that escapes the desire induced by the sovereign command of capitalism's vampiric lust. In short, Marx's savage critique is suddenly surcharged with a renewed zoömorphic vector that moves toward valences of becoming-monstrous through the internal powers of constitution that emerge when diverse life forms across species lines forge demonic assemblages within the transversal commonwealth.

Likewise, we cannot simply or easily transcend the level of the werewolf in order to return to a pre- or post-alienated existence. If Marx's (1978) savage imagination retains the trace of "species-being" (75) to overcome human alienation, we have to question his reliance on an anthropocentric anchoring point to ensure his political teleology.[13] Opening up a different imaginative line of flight beyond humanist species-being, Agamben (1993a) argues that focusing on the barrier between use and exchange value that defines the terrain of the fetish and the fetishist should not lead to fixation on difference (as with deconstruction) but must move toward a new appreciation for *harmonia* as a "laceration that is also a suture" (157)—a notion of harmony that is not about the proper location of the human (and thus the negation of the improper) but concerns proper impropriety toward new forms of becoming that escape measure. In other words, Agamben is attempting to rethink the fetish not in terms of negation (of full presence or as gap or lack) but rather as a productive profanation that plays with improper objects to unleash a certain potentiality in excess of the commodity form. In the open space between use and exchange where we cease to be human, Agamben finds the imagination of the fetishist and the melancholic at work, producing new objects, new subjectivities, and goals. The laceration of the werewolf is not to be transcended to a state beyond the monstrous—a nonalienated, ontological purity of the fully realized human—but is itself a location for imagination to reconceptualize life. Both melancholy and fetishism are strategies for pursuing a presence through a constituting absence, for pressing recognition to its internal limit in order to suspend the criteria that separates and thus sacrifices. As a monstrous excess or surplus, the werewolf dwells, for Agamben, in a zone of indistinction—a threshold creature that ushers in a new game of putting partial objects together in unexpected ways to create new *harmonia* that is no longer human or animal, proper or improper.

Finally, if we live in monstrous times, there is no longer this objectifying distance, and the bestiary must stand on equally monstrous grounds as its object of analysis. The Marxist bestiary is in a sense a form of imaginative reconstruction that must find in Medusa an ally. The monstrous becomes a zoömorphic revelation (rather than simply a savage allegory of exploitation) that embodies the true plurality of Medusa as sublime and beautiful, disease and cure—a figure that opens up a new terrain of monstrous possibilities for revolution and revolt that includes humans and nonhuman animals. We must reclaim the monstrous and thus take back the power of Medusa from the state in order to reenergize insurgent movements for democracy against bureaucracy and state policing. Within the traditional parameters of the nation-state or the community, the monster is dismissed as a form of barbarism (a superstitious imaginative construction that turns Medusa against herself in the name of the status quo). Alternatively, we must recognize within the monstrous another pathway that runs counter to the limits of "belonging to" or "recognition of" the humanist community of the state. Rather than gentrify Medusa through dissection and thus immunize the nation-state against its own internal contradictions, we must think through the paradoxes of a political practice that acts in reverse: returning Medusa to life by articulating her figure with corporeality and the monster with creative powers of rupture and constitution.

In order to multiply the constituting powers of Marx's gothic bestiary we must amplify the savage and zoömorphic dimensions of his monstrous imagination and thereby propel it into the postmodern, posthuman condition of the present. We must recognize that the imagination itself is the faculty of the werewolf—a *harmonia* or resonating field of intensities that challenge proper and improper distinctions or classifications in order to construct new lines of flight or exodus. That social revolt is the revolt of the vampire (as an insurgent multitude of human and nonhuman forces) against the sovereign Vampire of capitalist Power. And that Marxism itself is not simply a shield deflecting the calcifying magic of Medusa's severed head but is rather an imaginative resuscitation of her zoömorphic powers of critique. In short, the monster is no longer shackled to the negation of the law of capitalist separation of the common but rather becomes an imaginative space of invention and creative exodus that suspends the law of capitalist separation or of communal scapegoating and in that moment, enables new natureculture assemblages to emerge. Clarifying and adding to this emerging bestiary is a key goal of this book, and our analysis of the feral child, the alien, and the faery will intensify and extend our understanding of zoömorphic politics.

In addition, what Hardt and Negri's theory of a posthumanist monster enables us to accomplish is a further clarification and extension of exopedagogy. Although they do not directly address the issue of education in their work (see Lewis 2010), we can extrapolate from their scant notes in order to build a bridge between the cultivation of swarm intelligence emerging from within a transversal commonwealth and the function of exopedagogy as a teaching and learning about the monstrous. Swarm intelligence is predicated on an alternation of the senses that allows for thought feelings that do not result in scapegoating, fetishizing, or abandoning the monstrous through anthropocentric privileging or domination. Rather swarm intelligence recognizes that the human is always a becoming-animal against Power, and that the multitude is a viral swarm whose surplus common is the collective product of intense natureculture struggles within the

transversal common that cuts across species boundaries. To cultivate
swarm intelligence, exopedagogy intensifies the zoömorphic and savage vectors of the imagination through imaginative play between the
human and the animal, leading to new political narratives of transformation and invention. If as Hardt (2007) argues, "we have to imagine what structures of local autonomy and democratic participation
today can serve to train the multitude in the necessary capacities for
self rule and, moreover, rekindle the desire for and imagination of a
new, full democracy" (xxiii), then we would argue exopedagogy is a
step in the right direction. Likewise, the theories of swarm intelligence and of the transversal common (as the material and immaterial
basis for the monstrous) both further exopedagogy by providing critical links between the function of the bestiary and the cognitive and
imaginative life of political and economic insurgency.

1

VICTOR, THE WILD CHILD:
HUMANIST PEDAGOGY AND THE
ANTHROPOLOGICAL MACHINE

Civilized life is made by renunciation of the life of nature; it is almost
the snatching of a man from the lap of earth.
> —Maria Montessori, *The Montessori Method*

Each feral moment is valuable.
> —Bhanu Kapil, *Humanimal: A project for future children*

We have all seen or heard of "wild children." From literature we
have the iconic images of Mowgli the abandoned boy-cub raised by
wolves in Rudyard Kipling's famous book of fables *The Jungle Book*
as well as Edgar Rice Burroughs' Tarzan character who was raised by
apes in the African jungle. And Maurice Sendak's iconic book *Where
the Wild Things Are* (1964) presents the story of Max, King of the
Wild Things, who dresses in wolf's clothing in order to cross the
sacred boundary that separates men from beasts. While such fiction-
alized stories document our ongoing fascination with feral humans,
they pale in imaginative scope to the existence of actual cases of feral
children being raised in the wild by a variety of animals. There is of
course the strange case of Kamala and Amala, two girls supposedly
found living with wolves in the forests of Bengal, India, in 1920. More
recently, in Kenya in 2005 a man found a baby girl being nursed by
his pet dog. Apparently the dog had found the baby in a nearby forest,
had carried it home, and had been taking care of the infant for several
days until the man's children heard the child crying and recovered her
(http://news.bbc.co.uk/2/hi/africa/4530423.stm). Even stranger is
the case of the Ukranian "Dog Girl" Oxana Malaya who lived for five
years with a pack of dogs after having been virtually abandoned by
her abusive parents. When found in 1991 at the age of eight she had

adapted flawlessly to her conditions—barking, running on all fours, and so on (Grice 2006). Most recently, a little girl from the Siberian city of Chita was found living with dogs and cats. Like Oxana, she had learned the subtle nuances of nonhuman animal communication but could not speak Russian (2009, http://news.bbc.co.uk/2/hi/europe/8070814.stm). In all these cases, feral children have provided us with imaginative flights of fancy that condemn the moral laxity of parents and "civilization" more broadly as well as important evidence in cognitive and linguistic development. But more than simply fictional characters or obscure scientific research data, feral children are also linked to the question of humanist education. In fact, education is haunted by its own feral children.

On January 9, 1800, a strange young boy was captured in Saint-Sernin in the South of France. Almost immediately rumors began to circulate. Had the boy been raised by wolves in the forest? Was he a savage or a demon? Soon enough, the child, who could not speak and was by all measures of French society considered feral, was soon taken to the Institute for Deaf-Mutes in Paris and entrusted to the tutelage of France's most well-respected intellectuals including Phillipe Pinel (founder of psychiatry) and the renowned educator Abbe Sicard. While Pinel's panel of experts quickly dismissed the child as an idiot and therefore incapable of learning, the tenacious young doctor Jean-Marc Gaspard Itard took it upon himself to civilize the trembling and mute child. Thus begins the story of the wild boy of Aveyron or, as he would later be named, Victor.

Certainly this story is curious and offers a unique footnote in the history of education. Itard is after all considered one of the founders of special education as well as a key influence on the renowned educator Maria Montessori (Ferguson 1987; Shattuck 1980). And although Jane Roland Martin (2007) has argued that educational metamorphoses such as Victor's represent certain ethical and political questions that are central to education, she does not follow through on these questions in her analysis, reducing the complexity and significance of Victor's education to a sanitized philosophical reflection on language acquisition. In this chapter, we would like to take up and follow through on Martin's questions and suggest that the wild boy of Aveyron is not simply a historical footnote from the educational archive, whose relation to the present lies solely in terms of educational techniques. In fact, we will argue here that the trials and tribulations that Itard undertook to educate *homo ferus* (re)enact the primal scene of a superstitious and anthropocentric educational practice, which is predicated on the ban of the proverbial if not mythical figure of the wolf-child. By linking Victor's case history with the broader political discourse on the feral human or the werewolf, we will begin to recognize that education, like society in general, operates through the exclusion of the *homo ferus*—an internal exclusion of the monster as both the necessary backdrop for the production of modern science and French national identity and as dangerous other to be feared. At stake in centering Victor's case as a defining moment in education is a more basic understanding of how education functions as an "anthropological machine" (Agamben 2004) to replace the figure of the feral (as monstrous contamination) with the less threatening figure of the abnormal, thus sustaining a division between human and nonhuman animals by creating a new dyad between the normal and the abnormal. Stated differently, the abnormal becomes the medical attempt to gentrify the disruptive power of the monster and thus transform the exceptional into the exemplary. Yet, as we will demonstrate later, the violence and trauma of this primary division produces a surplus, a residual stain that cannot be fully incorporated into the symbolic order of bourgeois society, thus constituting a melancholic educational subject. If as Bonnie Honig (2003) argues, the community needs the myth of the foreign founder to unify citizens under the law, this unity is also threatened by the existence of the foreigner—or in our case, the existence of the nonhuman animal (creaturely life) as the final residuum of the monstrous stranger.

VICTOR AS WILD BOY

1. From Gesticulation to Gesture: The Immunitary Logic of Pedagogical Exorcisms

Victor began his entrance into the scientific order of things as a grotesque, as a monster, as a wolf-boy. A local commissioner in the village of Saint-Sernin named Constans-Saint-Esteve offered an early description of a boy "captured" in the local woods. As Roger Shattuck (1980) argues, in Constans's letters, we find no mention of the boy as an idiot (8). Rather, this mute, dirty, and inarticulate child was described in premodern terminology as a "boy-animal" or, as the villagers saw him, as a "wild savage." The fact that Victor would gaze longingly at the moon led to further tantalizing speculations that he had been raised by a pack of nocturnal animals. Only when the boy was delivered into the care of Sicard at the Institute for Deaf-Mutes in

Paris was the monstrous subsumed into the natural order by the new scientific language of psychiatry. Although the Society of Observers of Man had entrusted the child to Sicard as a pupil, Sicard failed to work with the so-called Wild Boy of Aveyron. In fact, Pinel's assessment of the boy's cognitive faculties precluded the possibility of education. A panel of esteemed scientists and philosophers proclaimed the child to be an "incurable idiot" and sentenced him to a life of seclusion in an asylum (32). He was not a noble savage or a philosophical embodiment of *homo ferus* but rather a mental case not worthy of Sicard's pedagogical attention. In short, the wild boy became an idiot, and in the course of the examination, the monster was explained as a natural deformity of the mind and the aberration became contained within a medical diagnosis. Here the boy was recast as a clinical case, as a bundle of symptoms, as a defective human rather than an unholy monster. The result of such a prognosis: a life sentence in the asylum. The monster as medically defective was thus quarantined and sealed away from society as a lost cause.

Itard—the founder of otorhinolaryngology or the scientific study of the ears, nose, and throat and esteemed educator of deaf-mutes—began where Sicard gave up. Rather than abandon the boy to the asylum, he decided to educate the child as a *proto-human*. Inspired by the theories of Locke and Condillac, Itard argued that the human is in essence a *tabula rasa* and that education was everything. Whereas Pinel pronounced that the child's life bore a "perfect identity" with incurable idiots, Itard (1972) suggested that the wild boy's current state was due to lack of education (98). Quoting Itard at his most ostentatious and his most sublime:

> Cast on this globe, without physical powers, and without innate ideas; unable by himself to obey the constitutional laws of his organization, which call him to the first hand in the system of being MAN can find only in the bosom of society the eminent station that was destined for him in nature, and would be, without the aid of civilization, one of the most feeble and least intelligent of animals. (91)

Thus for Itard, the Wild Boy of Aveyron became an experiment, an opportunity to prove the validity of Locke's speculative anthropology as well as the profound power of a modern, fully scientific educational methodology. Here the boy was recoded not as a monster to be feared, not as an incurable idiot to be separated from the rest of humanity (an animal who, as Descartes described, is nothing more than *automata mechanica*), but rather as a helpless and defenseless generic *potentiality* for humanization that must be fully actualized through scientific pedagogy. Hence, the boy entered a new problematic—a problematic whose medicine, or whose cure, was pedagogy. The goal: to produce a perfect French citizen, and thus to prove that the bourgeois body could unfold from within nature's own course. In this sense, the project of constituting a cosmopolitan identity based on the particularity of the French, modern subject needed this stranger, this foreigner from the forest, in order to prove its own mythical universality.

A key question remained: How does one teach a pure potential? How can the inarticulate, wild, convoluted, and seemingly subhuman gesticulations of this child be transformed into the controlled and internally regulated gesture of the properly human? In broad strokes, here was how Itard hoped to teach Victor:

1. To attach him [Victor] to social life, by rendering it more pleasant to him than that which he was then leading, and, above all, more analogous to the mode of existence that he was about to quit.
2. To awaken the nervous sensibility by the most energetic stimulants, and sometimes by lively affections of the mind.
3. To extend the sphere of his ideas, by giving him new wants, and by increasing the number of his relations to the objects surrounding him.
4. To lead him to the use of speech by subjecting him to the necessity of imitation.

Altogether Itard hoped to train the body in order to effect the "moral treatment" of the mind. In order to carry out such an experiment, Itard combined teaching with modern medicine resulting in one of the first clear and rigorous descriptions of biopedagogy or a pedagogy whose very purpose is at stake in the training and monitoring of the human body. To regulate this body, medical and pedagogical discourses invented the figure of the "abnormal"—the clinical object of scientific experimentation and observation that replaced the uncontrollable and unobservable life of the monster.

In his work on the production of the discourses and objects that define "abnormality," Michel Foucault locates an important shift between witchcraft and exorcism as a turning point in the examination and training of the body that led to what we are referring to as biopedagogy. The struggle against witchcraft as a monstrously dangerous state of transgression concerned the violent eradication of the body of the accused in a public display of sovereign violence. The witch is tortured and burned in the ostentatious display of the might of the sword as witnessed in the Inquisition. If witchcraft appeared at the fringe of Christianity, then possession resides at its very center. The witch was simply a "bad Christian" who had to be exterminated in order to safeguard the life of the community, but the possessed soul is a much more complex figure that demands close investigation, observation, and above all technologies of confession, for the possessed is a divided, anguished, tormented individual. As a contested terrain, the soul of the possessed is a site of infiltration by the devil but also a site of resistance. This is a complex body that in many ways forms the genealogical backdrop for the body of alien-abductees (see chapter two). Both have bodies written over with secret codes, mysterious signals. Both are bodies alive with the hideous traces of libidinal sensation against which the Church, or as the case might be, the military wage a war of containment and boundary splitting. As Foucault (2003b) writes, whereas the witch's body is concealed by magical powers, the body of the possessed is a "fortress body that is surrounded and besieged" (212), animated by a whole series of convulsions. These convulsions were the "resistance effect of Christainization at the level of individual bodies" (213). To avoid this resistance, the Church invented a whole series of anticonvulsive mechanisms. The mechanisms that Foucault describes include an internal moderator (stylistic and rhetorical procedures to codify the confession), expulsion of the convulsive (here Foucault locates this important historical shift toward medicine), and support from the educational systems (providing precise and scrupulous training of the body). Thus medicine and education took over the convulsive body, which became the prototype of madness in the eighteenth century, transforming into "nervous illness," "vapors," and a host of other "female" disorders of the mind and the body. At the dawn of the twentieth century, the anticonvulsive remedy for the abducted body became psychotherapy, which territorialized the alien narrative through "childhood trauma" or "sexual disturbances." Summarizing, we can say that for Foucault the shift from witchcraft to that of possession signals a rupture between sovereign force (working on the fringes of Christianity) and the emerging technologies, mechanisms, and discourses of biopedagogy that define the boundaries between the normal and abnormal through the abandonment of the monstrous witch.

Yet exorcism does not simply vanish or become a minor, residual phenomenon as Foucault would have us believe. The practice of Christian exorcism as the sovereign decision over life returns as a ghost in Roberto Esposito's theory (2008) of immunization. Whereas in Foucault's work the relation between sovereign power and bio-power remains unclear, Esposito articulates the two poles of biopower through the category of immunization, which he defines as "the negative [form] of the protection of life" (46) or the "fold that in some way separates community from itself, sheltering it from an unbearable excess" (52). As the secularized and medicalized discourse of exorcism, immunization maintains the health of the community through a critical subtraction of an excess (the convulsions or sensations of the monstrous flesh). Imported from a Christian dialectic of confession and convulsion, medical immunization forms the foundational metaphor for modern biopower, creating a horizontal or immanent form of sovereign power internal to political, medical, and educational discourses and practices. Here, Foucault's theory of sovereignty becomes a "meta-immunitary" dispositif where "in order to be saved, life has to give up something that is integral to itself, what in fact constitutes it principal vector and its own power to expand" its "primordial intensity" or constituting powers (59). The corpse as disavowed backdrop for defining the living now merges into a complete "cadaverization of life" wherein life turns against itself in the form of a sovereign decision against the population—the result is what Agamben (1998) would refer to as the replacement of the citizen subject with the figure of bare life, existing between life and death—the ultimate monster who is abandoned by society. As such the sovereign decision is reinscribed into the very heart of the biopolitical and, as we will demonstrate, the biopedagogical through an immunization that turns life against itself in a form of autoimmune disease.

Returning to Itard's pedagogical approach, we would like to highlight the role of education and of schooling in this immunizing project. As we shall see, the inclusion of life into the political, or as our case might be into the pedagogical, is ultimately predicated on the fundamental ban of the nonhuman animal. Itard's holistic pedagogy incorporated the entirety of Victor's biological life from the senses to the cerebellum, but in this exhaustive training on the micro-level, an effective negation was enacted on the pre-linguistic, schizophrenic body of "natural man" as an inarticulate animal whose gesticulations and convulsions had to be exorcized in order to sustain the boundaries of the superstitious and anthropocentric community.

This modern exorcism utilizes the secular technology of biopedagogy to ban the wolf from the human—an exorcism through which possession emerges as an educationally treatable condition. In this sense, educational exorcism becomes one arm of the anthropological imagination of biopower through which "the human" as a raced and gendered construct is separated from "wild beasts" (Agamben 2004). Humanism for Agamben is a particular structuring of knowledge predicated on the centrality of the human as the apex of all measure. Underlying humanism is what Agamben calls the "anthropological machine" that constructs and maintains the superiority of the human by attempting to gain mastery over the divide between the human and the animal. Quoting Agamben,

> Insofar as the production of man through the opposition man/animal, human/inhuman, is at stake here, the machine necessarily functions by means of an exclusion (which is also always already a capturing) and an inclusion (which is also always already an exclusion). Indeed, precisely because the human is already presupposed every time, the machine actually produces a kind of state of exception, a zone of indeterminacy in which the outside is nothing but the exclusion of an inside and the inside is in turn only the inclusion of an outside. (37)

The origin of such a machine is not simply a historical fluke. As Agamben (2009) argues, "apparatuses are not a mere accident in which humans are caught by chance, but rather are rooted in the very process of 'humanization' that made 'humans' out of the animals we classify under the rubric Homo sapiens" (16). What Agamben is attacking here is a certain form of thinking that arises when nature's order is categorized hierarchically in terms of moral or political worth against a biologically defined other. Such thinking emerges within an anthropocentric history that ensures that "human" beings remain at the apex of evolution. Paradoxically the anthropological machine is dependent upon the disavowed zone of indistinction that it attempts to erase (the sphere where the question of the human is held in suspension), thus the infernal repetition of the machine through endless permutations to classify the differences and similarities between human and nonhuman animals. Each permutation of the machine cannot eradicate the surplus common that separates and unites life forms—a remnant that refuses to allow the community of "humans" to fully coincide with itself.

Because society functions through the principle ban on the "wolf-boy" (as a site of indistinction between human and animal both sustained and disavowed by the anthropological machine), education comes to serve as a social machine to institute this split: producing the human as the negation of the animal. As such the following discussion will assert that the ban remains within the biopedagogical through which the subject of education becomes a divided subject (a melancholic werewolf). In other words, biopedagogy is not a break with the sovereign's right over death, but rather is poised on a fault line between the positive power of normality/abnormality and the negative power of sovereignty that defines the immunization paradigm. Modern immunization emerges as an imperfect exorcism of the convulsions of the wolf.

At first it seems curious to argue that the human is predicated on a negation. Itard goes to great lengths to demonstrate that Victor's senses have been deprived in the wild, degraded, and thus must be totally revivified. When first discovered, Victor could not sense the difference between hot and cold. His senses had been so dulled that he could eat boiling hot potatoes without flinching. Likewise, he had no use for clothes, which merely hindered his movements and provided no shelter from the elements. Furthermore, Victor could not distinguish between sounds and could not distinguish between tastes. In other words, he lacked a sensual life and was captivated by the immediacy of animal survival. Yet these are not signs of deprivation (as interpreted by Itard) but rather by an organic immediacy, a surplus of pleasures and intensities written across the body as a deterritorialized zone. Victor, although presumably "deaf," could in fact hear the cracking of nuts with great acuity. In addition, he could tell if an animal carcass was edible just by smelling it. Such observations enter into contradiction with the notion of sensual deprivation upon which Itard justified his pedagogy of the body. In effect, Itard's pedagogy was not so much to imbue Victor with sensation as to territorialize the "body without organs" (Deleuze and Guattari 1983). Or, as Davide Panagia (2009) writes, the goal was to transform sensation/affect (a zone of indistinction and intensities) into sense/emotion (territorialized, codified, and hierarchically arranged strata)—the noise of animal *phone* into the articulate speech of human *logos*. The problem is therefore not a lack but rather an insensible surplus of sensation that is not properly organized. If, according to Panagia, noise is a problem for political discourse (contaminating speech acts and normative proceduralism with its seemingly "irrational" utterance) then so too noise of the animal voice is also a decisive problem for a pedagogy that is predicated on the exorcism of the animal from the human. For instance, Itard had to retrain Victor's hearing to be sensitive to variations in tone, pitch, and emotional inflection of the voice; his sense of touch became increasingly acute, allowing him to feel texture and shape; and his sight began to acquire depth and distinction. Most problematic of all was the domination of the senses by smell. As Horkheimer and Adorno (2002) argue smell is the most mimetic and creaturely of sensations, causing the most peculiar problems for

Victor's "training." Through many biopedagogical efforts, the various sensual modes were folded into a curriculum where sensation became increasingly restricted to specific erogenous zones rather than amorphously dispersed throughout the body and/or written on the body according to the laws of forest life rather than civilization. Furthermore, the wild, convulsive, and often times violent bodily movements of the child were slowly replaced by a more tempered and contained posture, which, along with sense stimulation, rendered his body docile and responsive to localized sensual stimulation.

Key here is that Itard's conception of the body is predicated not so much on increasing the pleasures of the senses as on an operationalization of the organs in accordance with a utilitarian notion of fitness and bourgeois comportment. Thus his pedagogy is not so much Schillerian play as it is the molding of the body into a properly functioning social mechanism predicated on an instrumental and medical understanding of utility. In fact, the experiment through which Victor was reconstructed to be an educated subject was predicated on a medical model whose biopedagogical components included experimentation and observation of results. As such Victor's classroom was stark and sanitized, cleansed of social distractions, isolated from the distractions of social interaction with other children, and reduced to the essential experimental components: subject and object. While Victor's interaction with his caretaker Madame Guerin most assuredly involved play, such activities were not included in Itard's diary, and as such, we can only imagine that they were considered "childish" if not "feminine" or "animalistic" and thus lacking in educational value.

In a way, teaching Victor's body became for Itard a concerted effort to universalize the body of the white, male, bourgeois tutor through the "natural language" of the gesture. There was in Itard's pedagogy a desire to make Victor's body speak the normalistic language of the burgeoning bourgeoisie and thus to supplant the inarticulate and savage body of violent gesticulations with the codified and orderly body of middle-class society. This process of codification results in an "embodied communication" system (Hewitt 2005) in which Itard could "read" Victor, and in turn read himself (as well as his social universe) *through* Victor. The gesture in this sense becomes a way to choreograph movement and thus to syncopate the individual with the broader body politic. Yet as we shall describe here, this embodied communication system—which Itard sees as dignifying Victor to his proper station in the great chain of being—ultimately produces its own surplus and as such is haunted by the excess that it supplants. In this sense, at the very inception of the bourgeoisie, the failure of its class to stabilize the fragility of its body—so well illustrated in Foucault's history of sexual discourse (1990)—inscribes itself in its inaugural pedagogical confrontation between the new science of biopedagogy and the recalcitrant body of the feral child.

Making Victor's body speak (i.e., making the body into a legible text that can be read and in turn read itself) ultimately created a somatic precedence for the later and more complex acquisition of Victor's remedial semiotic skills. In other words, the training of life, or the molding of the body became the organic foundations of biopedagogy and ultimately verbalization. Throughout his teaching, Itard repeatedly stressed the centrality of the spoken word. Dismissing Victor's gesticulating body as "animal," he insisted Victor verbally speak, for to speak was to enter the human and expunge the wolf. Missed here is an opportunity to recognize in Victor's gesticulation a possible language beyond the familiarity of the bourgeois gesture—a language of the body that is neither fully human nor animal but rather a monstrous contamination that moves between hierarchical distinctions that separate voice from noise, gesture from gesticulation.

Andrew Hewitt's analysis (2005) of the paradox of the bourgeois gesture is useful at this point to clarify the dialectic of immunization at work in Itard's biopedagogy. By inscribing the social performance of class and gender into the body via "enfleshment" (McLaren 1999), the bourgeoisie ultimately risked reducing their own subjectivity to nothing more than a ritual of automatic and mechanical movements, of reducing the autonomous subject to the level of the automaton (mechanical imitation). Michael Newton (2002) argues that speech had to replace Victor's "language of action" precisely because the gesture was replicable by the orang-outang—a mute ape in whom the noted philosopher Buffon recognized politeness and courtesy (88). The gesture as a calculated and socially efficient technology of the body might in the end replace the gesticulation, but it must be overcome through verbalization as an expression of "inner spirit" rather than simple conformity to rules of conduct. Hence Itard's obsession with the oral dimension of communication as the needed "proof" that bourgeois subjectivity can externalize itself as the universal. Through Itard's instruction, the bourgeois body demonstrates its inherently contradictory and unstable domain. On the one hand, the gesture must incorporate the unintelligible gesticulation into its repertoire in order to negate its imitative qualities (as such the gesture itself always already verges on the gesticulation). On the other hand, the bourgeoisie must likewise maintain the spontaneity of the gesticulation (now recast as inspiration or spirit) it negates or else the body becomes mere mechanical movement or simple mimicry devoid of the human supplement. The pedagogical project of inoculation injects a kernel of the gesticulation into the gesture in order to strengthen the gesture against its pre-linguistic excess (a hygiene of indistinct sensations), yet in this very procedure, the gesture dialectically verges on collapse. Stated differently, the very fact that the ban on gesticulation includes a necessary mimetic moment (in which Victor overidentifies with the gesture of the civilized, white male through nonconceptual imitation) speaks to the internally barred notion of the universal modern subject whose body is located on a split that must in the end be simultaneously courted and disavowed by the educational anthropological machine. What Itard thought was simply a *tabula rasa* is in the end not a void but rather a cacophony of sensation, gesticulation, and convolutions that cannot simply or easily be wiped clean.

2. Language in Education: From Captivation to Boredom

Here Itard reaches his greatest challenge. While succeeding with simple signs, Victor's linguistic progress was severely limited by his inability to think in terms of signifier and signified. Thus the word "book" could not signify a type of thing but rather a singular object. Through a tortuously slow and arduous process, Victor eventually gained the use of signification and thus entered into a symbolic world. This world gave him access to what Itard referred to as a genuine human capacity: the capacity to invent. Language held within it a key mechanism for reconstructing Victor as a man rather than a beast. As Itard (1972) professes, "I think, that this new way of looking at things, which suggested the idea of putting them to new purposes, must necessarily have forced the boy to step outside the restricted circle of his more or less automatic habits" (162). Here Itard speaks the veritable language of the anthropological machine that posits the human as *animal rationale*: the being that has language and reason as a supplement to mere animal life. Stated differently, language led to surprising inventions and the possibility of abstracting thought that is essential to the maintenance of a humanist and humanizing society. In this sense, language produces innovation precisely by negating the animal within the boy, a negation that produces a certain surplus of affect that cannot easily be cured through the dialectic of immunizing pedagogy. The discovery of language inaugurated a new emotion in Victor: *human boredom*.

Throughout Itard's long instructional sessions, Victor continually lost concentration and threw fits of anger. These were eventually replaced by a much more subdued and somber emotional state through which Victor was somehow transformed. He was in other words rendered bored. As Giorgio Agamben (2004) describes in Heideggarian terminology, the hinge through which the animal and the human are both conjoined and separated is the relation between captivity and boredom. While drawn into the world, the animal is nevertheless closed to the openness of being itself (its unconcealedness), producing a state of captivation. Captivation for Heidegger is essentially the impossibility of apprehending the Being of being and thus lacks a world (only an environment). Yet, according to Agamben's interpretation of Heidegger, this closedness to being is complex, indicating "a more spellbinding and intense openness than any kind of human knowledge...insofar as it is not capable of disconcealing its own disinhibitor, it is closed in a total opacity" (59). Thus it is the very poverty of world the animal suffers that is the zone of indistinction leading from the animal to the human—not as a supplement to the animal as in the model of the anthropological machine, but as an "operation enacted upon the not-open of the animal world" (62). Boredom is the place of this operation where "human openness in a world and animal openness toward its disinhibitor seem for a moment to meet" (ibid.). In other words, when Itard champions the acquisition of verbal language as the supreme accomplishment of human invention, the dialectic of immunization returns in the form of profound boredom—the affective trace of the nonhuman animal. Boredom reveals the human capacity for animal captivation. Thus boredom is the autoimmune disease of the anthropological machine of biopedagogy—the surplus of animality that is disavowed and yet is necessary for the human subject to enter into language and invent.

If boredom speaks to the closeness of the human to the animal, it also reveals a unique difference between the two—a difference that Itard all too quickly glosses over. The anthropological machine of biopedagogy defines the human as the negation of the animal, as a supplementary being whose greatness lies in reason and language. Yet, an analysis of boredom reveals a surprising twist on this narrative. Quoting Agamben in full:

> In captivation the animal was in an immediate relation with its disinhibitor, exposed to and stunned by it, yet in such a way that the disinhibitor could never be revealed as such. What the animal is precisely unable to do is suspend and deactive its relationship with the ring of its specific disinhibitors. That animal environment is constituted in such a way that something like a pure possibility can never become manifest

within it. Profound boredom then appears as the metaphysical opera-
tor in which the passage from poverty in world to world, from animal
environment to human world is realized...The jewel set at the center
of the human world and its *Lichtung* {clearing} is nothing but animal
captivation. (68)

In this complicated passage, Agamben argues that in a state of captivation, the animal is only capable of action in response to the particular disinhibitors or stimuli of its environment. The animal can only
exist as a potential-to-be given a set environment. What distinguishes
the human is, paradoxically enough, the potential-not-to-be, a profound impotence or deactivation of specific possibilities. Summarizing,
Agamben (1999a) writes, "*Other living beings are capable only of their
specific potentiality; they can only do this or that. But human beings are
the animals who are capable of their own impotentiality. The greatness
of human potentiality is measured by the abyss of human impotentiality*" (182). In direct opposition to the anthropological machine with
its hierarchies of value, here the human emerges not as additive but
as subtractive. It is the animal that enables our potential-to-be and
it is the human that enables our potential-not-to-be: thus the site of
indistinction between the two is precisely the location of potentiality
itself (as both the ability to be and not to be). Whereas Itard focuses
on the triumph of the acquisition of language and the immediate
skills of invention that this acquisition gifts to Victor, he does not
recognize the *dialectically interwoven and mutually constituting* relation between the human (invention) and impotence (boredom). Thus
he misses that in language, the human emerges as distinct only in its
paradoxical proximity with the animal—a state that we have been
referring to as the monstrous. If his diary entries gloss over Victor's
boredom as an unnecessary and temporary side-note, we can read
between the lines of his narrative in order to see that boredom is a
new location between the human and the animal and thus a radically new type of openness. If the animal is open to the stimuli of its
environment and the human open to the world, then the monstrous
between opens up to a pure potentiality, a whatever being that is not
simply lazy or exhausted but rather bored. In other words, boredom
is not strictly human or animal but rather is the *inoperative* open that
exists between the two. This is the space that the anthropological
machine cannot confront and must cross out, yet at the same time,
the success of the anthropological machine rests on the continual
production of boredom as the unique accomplishment of human language acquisition.

3. The Violence of the Ban

Here we see two zones of indistinction and contamination emerging within Victor as a result of the anthropological machine's immunizing work: the gesticulation and the gesture (the pre-linguistic dimensions), captivation and boredom (the linguistic dimensions). In each case one of the pair must be banned for the other to assume dominance and thus for the figure of the human to emerge from the internal cut. Yet there are two significant stumbling blocks to this overall process of infernal splitting that we have yet to examine in full: freedom and masturbation. These two splits, unlike the first set, ultimately reveal less about Victor and more about Itard himself as a subject caught within the contradictions of the bourgeois anthropological machine—a subject whose imagination is the product of certain superstitious beliefs in the Power of science to erase the trace of the monster and anthropocentric beliefs in the superiority of the human.

In the first case, the cultivation of Victor's senses over and against his incorrigible sensations resulted in what Itard perceived to be a deprivation or ban of Victor's "natural" freedom in the wild. In one particular passage, Itard (1973) notes the "melancholy reverie" and the "character of sorrow" that pass over Victor's face as he stands before a window on a moonlit night staring at the forest beyond (104). Again, when taking Victor to a rural villa, Itard noticed how the child seemed preoccupied with a desire to run away into the forest. He was in other words, haunted by the "remembrances of a life independent, happy, and regretted" (115). Itard had to make Victor emotionally, psychologically, and physically *dependent* on civilization in order to root out the last remnants of the animal within, to include life through its very exclusion. As such, the regulation of the senses—indistinguishable from the simultaneous repression of the polymorphous, sensational body without organs—ultimately must be transformed into a *desire for regulation* itself through pedagogical intervention. Stated differently, the goal of education became the movement from demand (animal captivation or survival in the immediate throngs of existence) to that of desire (as constitutive of the bored yet innovative subject of education). Itard's own reflections on this process of "liberation" through education make him take pause and seriously contemplate the ethics of Victor's confinement. Thus it is around the notion of freedom through cultured dependency versus animal captivity that freedom begins to acquire a rather ambiguous formulation, and Itard's pedagogy loses its self-assurance. A brief anecdote reveals the success and failure of Itard's strategy as well as his own internal splitting through the process of teaching. On one occasion Victor did manage to escape and flee into the forest. Yet several days later he emerged "doubtless driven homewards by hunger and the impossibility of surviving on his own" (Itard 1972, 170). Is Itard's analysis here correct? As proof of Victor's inability to survive (even though he had lived in the forest for at least six years without aid) and his new love for social comforts, Itard goes to great lengths to describe Victor's emotional joy at seeing Madame Guerin, his governess. Perhaps another reading is possible here. Victor emerged from the forest not because of his desire to return to Itard or because of his inability to care for himself but because of his overwhelming sense of the split emerging within him. In other words, he felt homeless in his lost forest home and as such was estranged from the environment that once held him captivated. In this sense, Victor wandered in the perplexing zone of indistinction between civilization and nature (a wherever place that escapes classification), unable to identify with either, but in the end driven to return to civilization. Why?

This anecdote holds great theoretical value for education. In the zone of indistinction where laws of city and forest are suspended, Victor felt the weight of the split as the awakening of a passionate attachment to his subjected, civilized self. It is an attachment not simply to the conveniences of the social or to love of his comrades as Itard speculates but rather an attachment to subjectivity itself, to his self as Victor. To use Judith Butler's terminology (1997), the psychic life of power through which Victor as a subject was subjugated induced a certain fear concerning this subjectivity: a fear of "desubjectification" through a return of the repressed animal other within (130). Victor, the wild boy, began to sense freedom in the paradoxical dependency on a subjectivity imposed upon him from the outside by the Other. Thus we witness a scene of turning in Victor that complicates Louis Althusser's theory of interpellation in an important way.

When Victor was originally captured and handed over to Itard's care, education was by force alone. Itard was stringent, stern, and demanding. He was also at times reluctantly cruel and violent. For instance, to teach Victor the concept of justice, Itard forced a false punishment on the boy, which leads to a physical confrontation between student and teacher as master and slave. Again, he deprived Victor of physical activity and food in order to develop the functions of his sense organs. As Octave Mannoni (1972) argues, these pedagogical displays of force were due not simply to the cold calculus of Itard's medical orientation, rather they were more directly pulled from the tradition of (cruel and unusual) animal training. As Nietzsche once observed, taming and breeding arise as practices that dominate animality in the name of "humanity" as a superior form of life. Citing Nietzsche (1990):

> To call the taming of an animal its "improvement" is in our ears almost a joke. Whoever knows what goes on in menageries is doubtful whether the beasts in them are "improved." They are weakened, they are made less harmful, they become *sickly* beasts through the depressive emotion of fear, through pain, through injuries, through hunger.—It is no different with the tamed human being whom the priest has "improved." (66–67)

Here, Nietzsche emphasizes the *violence* of taming as an act to overcome animality, to erase the animal so that the human can emerge through its negation.[1] The aggression against natural life causes pain and suffering in the form of weakness—a weakness that exists in the gap that separates humanity from its own animality. While interpellation for Althusser (2001) is precisely a painless act through which the subject turns to the hailing of a sovereign figure, here we see the brute force of a sovereign's ban over and against the animal. It is only because of this moment of constitutive violence that, when alone on the edge of the woods, Victor turns to the faint call of Itard hence forth internalized as a passionate attachment to his own subjectivity. *The primary passionate attachment responsible for Victor's turn was instigated by a relation of force through which something (gesticulation, sensation) was effectively lost.* As such the violence of Itard's pedagogical gesture is effectively redoubled within the emerging educated subject who must initiate a second sacrifice in order to become paradoxically free to choose the city over the countryside. This second order sacrifice is a loss of the loss—a melancholic subject who no longer understands what he or she is searching for, who has lost the coordinates of humanity and animality.

Like the hinge that swings between boredom and captivation, so too this melancholic state exists in a zone of indistinction. For Walter Benjamin (1985), melancholia is "the most genuinely creaturely of the contemplative impulses" (146) as smell is the most creaturely sense. Casting the eyes downward toward an attentiveness to the earth and to the things of nature, the melancholic subject exists in a state of forgetfulness of his or her humanity. Bound to the refuse and ephemera of the earth, the melancholic gaze turns from heavenly redemption, only to find justice in the smallest details of creaturely life. In fact, what makes the subject human is precisely the act of for-getting humanness in the moment of melancholia! Quoting Benjamin (1968), "The righteous man is the advocate for created things and at the same time he is their highest embodiment" (104). For Benjamin, to become a just human (and thus fully realize humanity as a com-munity of belonging and recognition) is, paradoxically, to remember the creaturely moment of melancholia that embodies the uncanny indistinction between the human and the animal—returning us to the trace of the werewolf that is infernally split between presence and absence. Again, it is in Victor's mood that we see the impossibility of achieving the goal of Itard's humanist pedagogy, for whenever the anthropological machine attempts to draw distinctions, the animal restlessly returns to haunt the human subject and thus suspend the law of recognition. In those moments of turning that Itard observes when Victor is poised between world and earth, his own ambivalence as a human is revealed, a moment that calls into question his anthro-pocentric and savage imagination.

Also this secondary ban demonstrates the sacrificial logic of immu-nization that is distinctly different from that offered by Agamben's focus (1998) on *homo sacer* or the sacred man who can be killed with-out impunity. For Agamben, *homo sacer* as a stranger is cast out of the city, thus constituting the city through a fundamental exclusion. Yet as we see with Victor, *homo ferus* as a stranger is *cast into* the city (as the abnormal) in order for the city to immunize itself against exter-nal pathogens (the monster). This shift in movement that blurs out-side and inside forms the two sides of the anthropological machine, both of which produce a remnant that cannot be fully (ac)counted for within the count of the people and yet is the necessary supplement to such counting.

Using this example as a moment for theoretical innovation we could argue that the subject is not simply constituted through a hail-ing, as in Althusser's model, but more importantly through a more principle cut that produces the condition upon which hailing will be recognized as hailing—the cut between the human and the non-human animal, between the wolf and the boy. Through relations of force, external authority became the internal regulatory principle that made Victor pause and turn back toward the city. On the edge of the forest, Victor's self-consciousness—constituted through and by the law of the sovereign's ban—became self-subjugating. Yet it is important to notice in Itard's narrative the speed with which he glosses this episode. For Victor did not so much return with open arms to the town, but rather lingered on its fringe, haunted by a certain unconscious investment in that which had been banned. In this moment of suspension and indecision we might ponder a question that further complicates the apparent distinction between boredom and captivation. Is it not possible that in this realm of limbo, the animal became bored with his surroundings and the human captivated by the call of civilization?

Because of this split, there remained an element within Victor's psyche over which he was permanently melancholic, a wound left by the violence of Itard's pedagogy, a psychic stain of that which could not be fully symbolized. As Butler (1997) would claim, Althusser's model of education as interpellation precisely misses the disavowed kernel of the ban over which the subject remains unable to grieve. Or as Mladen Dolar (1993) argues:

> [T]his sudden passage [from gesticulating creature to a human subject] is never complete—the clean cut [in our case the cut of the sovereign's violent decision over Victor's life] always produces a remainder. To put it in the simplest way, there is part of the individual that cannot successfully pass into the subject, and element of "pre-ideological" and "pre-subjective" material prima that continues to haunt the subjectivity once it is constituted as such. (79)

Hence the subject of education as an anthropological machine is in sum a melancholic subject whose boredom speaks to a foundational lost object inaugurated by the violence of the ban. As discussed in the previous Intermezzo, melancholia is a strategy through which we remain in relation to that which we have no relation. It is the subject position of the werewolf—half-human and half-animal—who embodies a strange sense of justice precisely because of this constitutive split. In attempting to erase the monster (*homo ferus*) with the abnormal, Itard's pedagogy produced an even more monstrous form, an even more monstrous aberration! The monstrous contaminant of the animal returns to haunt the community through its own immunizing strategy in the form of melancholia. Thus the law that exorcizes the monster reproduces the monster *ad infinitum* as the necessary surplus of the ban.

Bearing in mind Itard's memoirs, Jean-Jacques Rousseau's pedagogical model now appears as a naïve romance. As Bonnie Honig (2001) argues, most political philosophy—and we would add educational philosophy—is written as a romantic love affair that ends with the happiness of marriage, social identification, or social unity. In *Emile* (1762), Rousseau argues that education cultivates the human child's natural propensities for democracy, individuality, and civility. As such, education is simply the externalization of the internal possibilities of an inherently bourgeois democratic spirit. Stated differently *Emile* presents the founding mythology of education for the modern world: education as the teleological unveiling of the inner spirit of the human that leads to a community of consensus, harmony, and beauty. It is a story whereby humanity's essence is expressed in reality and thus becomes imminent to humanity's experience of itself—fulfilling the quest to universalize and naturalize a French sense of cosmopolitanism. Yet this "non-coercive" pedagogy is already predicated on the fact that a more fundamental ban has been enacted: a ban that constitutes the human in the first place as the negation of that which is coded as animal. What Victor's case reveals is that education as an anthropological machine is not a teleology but rather an *interruption*, a break, a split—or in its most radical formulation, an exorcism—that leaves a trace of the monstrous within the perfect symmetry of the human (a residual foreignness or creatureliness). This ban is a violent act, a rupture that inaugurates the educated subject as a melancholic werewolf. And it is this ban that is so graphically depicted in the struggles between Victor and Itard. In this silent classroom sealed off in the Institute for Deaf-Mutes, the anthropological machine of education revealed the violence within its functioning that Rousseau's more romantic image of student and teacher repressed. Rousseau denied the necessity of this fundamental split instituted by the sovereign ban and thus misrecognized humankind as a supplemental substance (democratic free spirit) added to animal life rather than a primary impotence whose jewel is the residual stain of animal captivation. Just as Karl Marx (1990) once exposed the myth of political economy as a farce concealing the violence of capitalism's origins, so too Itard's narrative gave a brutally honest early depiction of the violence existing within the very matrix of biopedagogy—an internal ban on the animal that remains as an excess in the psychical economy of the bourgeois individual.

As such Itard inaugurates a new discussion concerning education and its ambiguous relation to the French Revolution's ideals of liberty, fraternity, and equality. If education itself is an interruption, a violent moment in the coming to be of the subject, then what does this mean for freedom itself? While Itard could not answer such questions, he nevertheless felt their weight and momentarily called into question his own motives for educating Victor. In Itard's words (1972),

> At this moment [in Victor's language training] as at many times before, I was only too ready to abandon my self-imposed task, acknowledge as

wasted the time I had spent, ready to wish that I had never known this
child and to condemn the heartless and vain curiosity of those men
who had wrenched him away from a life of happy innocence. (146)

Two issues arise from this quotation. First, through Itard's words we
see a sudden intensification of the savage and zoömorphic imaginative vectors that undermine the hold anthropocentrism has on his
scientific and pedagogical practice. Itard turns to Victor's gesticulating body that appeared free from conventional regimes of value in
order to imagine freedom from the bourgeois body politic, and it is
this space of imaginative difference that ignites a mixture of love and
regret. Second, he exposes the cost of scientific vanity and its contradictory relationship to revolutionary values of freedom and enlightenment. In terms of the former, this is the closest Itard will come to
touching the truth of his own libidinal investment (unconsciously
written in the margins of the text) into the ambiguous nature of
Victor (constructed as both temptation and aberration), and in terms
of the latter, Itard momentarily lifts the veil of enlightenment rationality to reveal a darker dialectic wherein the very freedom of democracy is a form of subjugation to a sovereign ban that inaugurates the
immunizing gesture, the very parameters of the human are constituted by a melancholic attachment to a creaturely surplus. As such,
in the making of Victor as a man, Itard himself, through the pedagogical process, is dialectically remade as a doubting subject whose
absolute faith in science is suddenly shattered and his own ambiguous
desires and fears of the feral revealed. In this sense, Itard's narrative
is not a romance but rather a gothic tale of the monstrous that troubles accepted notions of freedom, science, and national identity. It
reveals the undecidable nature at the very heart of his "humanist" and
"progressive" anthropological machine known as biopedagogy. Here
there is no hero (as in Rousseau's teleological tale) but only a haunted
subject (an antihero) whose inability to become a full citizen leaves
him in a perpetual zone of indistinction between two subject positions: the humanized citizen of the enlightened nation-state and the
animal of the forest. It is Itard's memoir that then must be repressed
within the history of educational philosophy as a curiosity, for it is the
painful yet crucial description of education's relation to the problem
of the modern world.

     Thus, emerging from Victor's many episodes of flight and cap-
ture we see Itard's growing ethical quandary. If Victor had been content to live his feral existence, why had he been captured, brought
to Paris, and why indeed had Itard volunteered to be his tutor? Of

course there are Itard's own scientific reasons—to prove Condillac's theory of human nature—and the injunction of the revolution to care for the sick and the poor in the name of universal rights (Newton 2002). But we would argue that the overcoming of anxiety of the feral was a central motivating factor in Itard's (cruel?) experiment. As Agamben (2004) argues, "the decisive political conflict, which governs every other conflict, is that between the animality and the humanity of man" (80). The biopedagogical is a site where this contest is waged, where the human and the nonhuman animal in the figure of "man" are posed in contestation and antagonism. In the feral child, mastery is at stake, mastery over animality through which the human animal is constituted as an internal ban and through which civilization (or more specifically the universalizing of the bourgeoisie) can be separated from the rabble of nature. Yet perhaps Agamben's analysis did not go far enough and as such needs to be read in conjunction with Freud's theory of the uncanny in order to fully explain the fear of and fascination with *homo ferus*. For Freud (2003), the uncanny "applies to everything that was intended to remain secret, hidden away, and has come into the open" (132). In other words, the uncanny is the repressed that has returned to confront us. The feral human, in this sense, could be read as the uncanny return of the animal within the nonanimal animal of man. It is an obscene double that, like all uncanny doubles, speaks of the death of the human. Rather than a primitive stage having been surmounted in anthropological time, Victor reminds Itard of the possibility that the human is never separate from the animal as a disavowed other. Hence, Itard's apparently "humanistic methodology" is on another level a terrified response staved off by the immunizing technologies of biopedagogy. Yet at the same time, his persistent fascination with Victor and his construction of Victor's forest life as a naïve state of freedom also speak to Itard's zoömorphic longings. In this sense, his romanticization of Victor as the noble savage in the very heart of the French countryside is the result of his own internal division as a scientist and as a teacher. As such, the uncanny return of the other within the familiar is a site of great ambiguity, a paradoxical location that speaks to the limits of enlightenment reason and the great longing for a return to a pre-capitalist, pre-scientific, pre-disciplinary, and organic relation to nature. The uncanny figure of Victor therefore is the object of both anthropocentric and zoömorphic imaginative forces—each vector destabilizing the other within the larger matrix of social, scientific, and political relations to Power. In short, a close analysis of the relation between Itard and Victor enables us to begin to theorize the role of the uncanny in pedagogy—a topic that has itself remained repressed by the mythological consciousness of figures such as Rousseau. Exposing the uncanny dimension of Itard's fear/ love and their inscription onto Victor's body as a text thus reveals the primal scene of humanist education: a technology of the anthropological machine that is held in sway by the very state of indistinction that it attempts to continually overcome.

4. The Sexual Surplus of Education as an Anthropological Machine

Finally after five years of this tug of war between the animal human and the nonanimal animal of man, the limits of Itard's biopedagogy were reached when Victor entered puberty and the primary issue became his polymorphous perversity in the form of public masturbation and obscenity. At first Itard held great hopes that puberty would expand Victor's moral horizons, yet the result was somewhat different. As Itard (1973) writes,

> I have awaited this moment with great keenness, envisaging it as a source of new sensations for my pupil and of fascinating observations for myself, watching out carefully for all the preliminary phenomena of this moral crisis; every day, I waited for a breath of that universal emotion which stirs and stimulates all creatures, expecting it to move Victor in his turn and enlarge his moral existence. (175)

While Itard might have thought that human nature was unnatural in the sense that it lacked an essence and was defined solely through education, he nevertheless appeared at this stage to believe that sexuality or attraction to the opposite sex was "universal" and hence above the need for instruction. As Foucault (1990) has argued, sexuality is an invention and as such is a pedagogical matter. Yet Itard adopted the passive gaze of the clinician and simply observed Victor's frustrating sexual development. In other words, Victor was left to teach himself the uses and abuses of the body, revealing a polymorphous sexuality all too disturbing to Itard.

Rather than attraction to the opposite sex, Victor was given over to "desires of an extreme violence" without purpose or direction (Itard 1972, 175). Most importantly, as Julia Douthwaite (1997) points out, when Victor's sexual violence was directed at women, Itard simply observed the unfolding of events that increasingly seemed to resemble rape (195). In fact, it remains uncertain whether or not Itard himself set up such encounters as sexual experiments. Victor's sexuality was in this sense viewed through the eighteenth-century stereotype of the savage man's libidinal voraciousness at the expense of the female as catalyst to transform Victor from wild boy to civilized man through the conduit of sexual development. And yet in the end, the constant state of restless frustration and anxiety produced in the boy did not in fact accelerate his learning process but rather hindered it further until the pace of advancement almost stopped completely. Here we see the return of the animal gesticulation, which the codification of Victor's body had meant to replace. The body itself remained in excess of its textualization and the gesture revealed its unstable performativity despite the most aggressive forms of immunization.

In the end, Itard (1972)—perhaps driven by his own sexual anxieties concerning Victor's wild gesticulations—realized his failure, and in a moral quandary posed the problem thus:

> I did not doubt but that if I had dared to reveal the secret of his anxieties and the reason for his desires to the young man I would have reaped an incalculable benefit. But on the other hand, supposing that I could have tried such an experiment, would I not have revealed to our Savage a need which he would doubtless have sought to satisfy as publicly as his other needs and which would have led him into acts of great indecency? (178)

In other words, Victor could not enter fully into the patriarchal sexual contract, could not imitate Itard's body as pedagogical model—further demonstrating the instability of the bourgeois body and its norms. Certainly this episode demonstrates the impossibility of gendering the feral, yet what concerns us most is the devastating effect this has on the very notion of education as a biopedagogy of the body. As long as sex remains outside the sphere of immunization, the entire enterprise of humanist education grinds to a halt. Thus Victor offers a startling test case in the development of a central preoccupation in Western European education.

Over the course of the century, sexuality steadily became a concern for the burgeoning fields of psychiatry and education in France. As Foucault (2003b) argues, the relation between desire and instinct created a "pedagogical medicine of masturbation" that came to define the terrain of the economically useful body by the end of the eighteenth century. Itard's concerns demonstrate the limits of his own approach and signal the advent of a unique field of pedagogical science: How to control, police, train, and observe the sexuality of the child? How to transform what Freud (2003) would refer to as the child's "infantile sexual research" (57) into the sublimated search for knowledge in a wider sense? These questions come with the stark realization that what makes us human—our sexuality—is also what makes us most like the animal. In other words, sexuality becomes the zone of indistinction or state of exception where relations of inclusion and exclusion are suspended. Itard recognized the link between animal sexuality, morality, and education but could not find the biopedagogical technologies to harness this potential and thus sublimate it into a socially productive form of expression. The result was the ultimate termination of Victor's formal education. After five years of instruction, Itard bid Victor farewell, and they parted ways.

Ultimately Itard (1973) summarized Victor's overall progress as follows:

(1) that following on the almost total absence of speech and hearing, the young man's education is still and always will be incomplete; (2) that because of their long period of inactivity, his intellectual faculties can develop only slowly and with difficulty and that this development...is here the slow and arduous result of an active education where the most forceful methods have been used to obtain the slightest results; (3) that the emotions, emerging with equal slowness from their long torpor, are subordinated in their application to a deep feeling of selfishness and that puberty instead of effecting a tremendous emotional development seems to exist here only to prove that if there exists in man a relationship between the needs of the sense and the emotions of the heart, then this sympathetic harmony is, like most great and noble passions, the fortunate fruit of man's education. (178)

Stated simply, although great advances had been made in civilizing the wild boy, Victor's instincts had been severely "retarded" in growth. They were not biologically defective as Pinel had originally suggested, but rather stunted, stuck in a state of arrested development that was both miraculous in itself but also a great failure when compared to Itard's anthropocentric imagination. As such, Itard moves Victor from a field of mental illness into a field of abnormality as the study of instinctual disorders and nonmedical conditions. Education had rendered, to use Foucault's language (2003b), "the great monstrous ogre" into the everyday "abnormal Tom Thumb" (109). With this ban on the wolf, Victor could be rendered (ab)normal. Likewise, Itard's enthusiasm waned—his medical and pedagogical gaze no longer viewed Victor as a wonder (both frightening and desirous) but as a regrettable abnormal. The work of the ban performed through the anthropological machine (which divides the human and the animal by perpetually circling the disavowed remnant of animality) of education produced a new field of normalities through which Victor became ranked on a scale of competencies, efficiencies, and productivities that all function within the parameters of a humanist discourse. Just as Pinel erased the monster with the discourse of mental retardation and congenital idiocy, Itard (1973) placed Victor within a field of normality via a discourse of infantilism and the (limited) technology of immunizing biopedagogy. With this last move, Victor was squarely inserted into an episteme triangulated between "pleasure-instinct-backwardness" (306), which is the matrix that has come to define education in the twentieth and twenty-first centuries.

In having to ban the wolf in a literal sense, Itard's pedagogy thus encapsulated the project of humanist education as such, exposing the internal mechanism of the anthropological machine at work on the subject of the feral. But the ban itself remains operative in the residual moment of melancholia or boredom in which the animal returns as surplus of normality—revealing that at the very heart of the human is the exorcized animal, at the heart of the law of the abnormal remains the stain of the monstrous. These sudden eruptions are not so much glitches in the anthropological machine that can be "fixed" through more refined techniques of biopedagogy. Rather, it is in relation to sexuality that the gesture can no longer mediate the body and the body politic, the sensual and the ideological. Thus the central difference between Victor and other French pupils: in the latter, surplus becomes a form of surplus-value (a generic potential-to-be) that is socially useful whereas in the former, surplus remains inert, a pure abandonment to an invisible life suspended between the fully humanized French citizen and the call of the wild. The "successful" French student and Victor therefore form two halves of truth that are severed by the anthropological machine. To be free in Agamben's formulation is to remain im(potential), capable of being or not being this or that. As it stands, neither Victor nor the "typical" French student can be free, and thus neither can participate in the creative production of the surplus common. If Victor is the just man (Benjamin's melancholic subject) then it is a justice that remains in the deconstructive moment of the split (of melancholic longing) rather than the joy of a new *harmonia* where, as Agamben (1993a) argues "the laceration [of the ban] is also a suture" (157). As Honig (2001) writes in relation to the biblical story of the immigrant Ruth and the Israelites, the melancholia of the stranger "gets in the way of the closure this community seeks to attain through her *and* in spite of her" (71). Such is the fate of Victor's perpetual melancholic abnormality—no longer the prize of French, bourgeois society, he is effectively pathologized through an immunological and anthropocentric pedagogy that cannot erase the stain of the monstrous stranger. And it is precisely through this stain and in spite of it that the community attempts to maintain an ontological purity. The project of the anthropological machine outlined in Itard's diary did not die with Victor. In fact, it spread its domain, and with the discourse of normality the anthropological machine fully ingratiated itself into the schooling apparatus of modern Western civilization. As Licia Carlson (2003) argues, there is a long running history in popular and scientific discourse of equating women, certain ethnicities, certain races, and disabled groups with the animal. That which had to be banned in order to construct the human as mankind returns in the form of a psychological projection onto the other as degenerate. Read as a political allegory, Itard's anthropological machine could be seen as a pedagogical attempt to constitute the population of a nation-state (homogenous, regulated, hierarchically organized) out of the resistive and "feral" multitude, which, as Antonio Negri and Michael Hardt (2000) argue, is always coded as monstrous. This formula certainly had a profound impact on early education reform in the United States, and we can hear echoes of Itard's final abnormalizing pronouncements in this 1894 report from the committee on compulsory education: "Careful research into the history of pauperism and criminality seems to show that the child's bent is fixed before his seventh year. If childhood is neglected, the child will mature lawless and uncontrolled and the final end will be the jail or the poorhouse" (quoted in Tyack 1974, 70). Here the feral becomes projected onto the racialized urban immigrant population whose children are "lawless" animals and whose intellectual, moral, and civic growth will be permanently rendered infantile without the function of the bureaucratized, centralized, and standardized anthropological machine known as the U.S. common school. To educate is not simply to regain order over the disorderly but to render human that which borders on the animal—to replace the monstrous with the banality of the abnormal. Or as the case might be, if the "animal" cannot be considered totally exorcized because of skin color, then he/she is to be abandoned as *monstrous*. Such a case is found in the medical (if not pedagogical) writings of Dr. Robert Bean who wrote in 1906 that the adolescent Negro will develop an increase in sexual energy coupled with a degeneration of mental growth. As such, without "proper guidance" the Negro for Bean would revert to a state of nature, becoming, if you will, completely feral. In sum, the wolf-boy comes to haunt twentieth-century American biopedagogy—as a pedagogy concerned with the pleasure-instinct-backwardness relationship of the immunization paradigm—in a newly racialized form. If Agamben (1998) is correct and—within the present historical moment—the state of exception has extended its terrain thus conflating the citizen with bare life, then the extension of the feral to youth *as such* is now a pressing problem. As Republican Bill McCollum declared, "Violent juvenile crime is a national epidemic," and "today's superpredators are feral, presocial beings with no sense of right and wrong" (cited in Ayers 1997/98). The threat of the feral as a "presocial being" and thus outside the social contract now extends to youth in general, further demonizing and criminalizing a population already deprived of political voice. As Foucault (2003b) has described, the abnormal is an everyday subject defined by his or her "condition." These conditions are not medical states per se nor are they to be feared as violent and destructive. The "monster" on the other hand is violent, disturbing, and often seen as a contaminated site between the human and the animal. If the discourses surrounding the wolf-child attempted to replace the monster with the abnormal, the monstrous cannot be repressed for long without returning. Thus, for instance, the rise of the discourse of the monster is seen in popular publications such as *Time*, whose cover story concerning the Columbine High School shootings read: "The Monsters Next Door." The shadow of the wolf-boy is long, revealing the anxieties produced by an anthropological machine that attempts to immunize the human against the animal through a variety of criminalizing procedures, control mechanisms, and social scapegoating. What is at stake is not simply community but rather a *human* community set against the wolf-boy as a "presocial superpredator."

BEYOND THE BAN AND INTO THE OPEN

Two modes are represented by Victor: the ban and the process of immunization through the anthropological machine of education. When the logic of the ban meets with normality in the moment of biopedagogy, the subject as abnormal appears on the fringe of the educational machine. Thus what is important to note here is that both techniques function *together*. Whereas for Foucault and Althusser, there is a historical shift from brute force (the force of the sovereign) to subtle and noncoercive techniques of normality through hailing and/or technologies of the self, the case of Victor reveals how the sovereign ban exists at the heart of education as inaugurating a necessary split upon which further distinctions can be made concerning the student. As such, normalistic education includes a violence that is denied by both Foucault's strictly disciplinary theory and Althusser's description of interpellation into the common sense of belonging that defines the parameters of community life. They each miss the principal function of the ban through which the notion of humankind emerges within a tension between the nonhuman animal and the nonanimal animal.

To end these processes, education must be detached from the imaginative matrix that defines the limits of the anthropological machine. To do so is no longer to think the figure of the human as the evolutionary or teleologically inscribed goal of perfection via education or the animal as the pejorative other to be mastered or dominated. Rather than construct the split between the human and the animal, education must think the zone of indistinction, the hinge through which the human-animal and the animal-human oscillate. To imagine this zone of indistinction is no longer to think the human or the animal (terms constituted within the anthropological machine) but rather to think *life* as such. In the space of the open, life "is no longer human, because it has perfectly forgotten every rational element, every project for mastering its animal life; but if animality had been defined precisely by its poverty in world and by its obscure expectation of a revelation and a salvation, then this life cannot be called animal either" (Agamben 2004, 90). As such pedagogy of life cannot be concerned with constructing yet another (and this time more authentic) articulation of the human animal. Rather, a radical pedagogy of life must explore this zone of the hinge where the nonanimal animal and the animal-animal do not so much collapse into one another (and thus return to an imaginary pure state before the fall often valorized as a schizophrenic moment of deterritorialization) nor simply become abandoned but rather become suspended and thus rendered inoperative. The self-suspension of the ban that underlies the anthropological machine opens up a field of free use, of infinitely creative involution that moves beyond the human and the animal and thus reclaims the indistinction that is a monstrous ontology.

So if we were to imaginatively rethink Victor's education in relation to the open, what would it look like? What if Itard's anthropocentric imagination were to become a zoömorphic imagination that does not separate the surplus common from the nonhuman animal? Whereas Itard predicated his education on a series of bans, he could have perhaps exposed his own knowledge system to the unique epistemology of the feral (Mannoni 1972). For instance, Itard never asked how Victor had survived in the woods alone for upward of six years. By opening himself up to Victor's environment he would not have seen a lack of knowledge, but rather a wealth of knowledge linked to survival within his environment. Thus Itard might have recognized the zone of indistinction that joins and divides the human and the animal, nature and culture, thus letting the anthropological machine idle. Itard would have had to become Victor's pupil in the forest, overturning the implicit hierarchies of value and immunizing logics of biopedagogy and suspending the divisions of sensibility and rationality that define the humanist project. Or perhaps even better, they could have explored the threshold between metropolis and forest together, in mutual abandonment to the world where categories and concepts familiar to both are rendered strange. It is in this zone of proximity and distance from each other where student and teacher no longer know who or what they are that *life* itself emerges. This threshold is the real state of exception—a biopolitical point of contact where politics and life enter into a zone of indistinction that no longer has to be exorcized but rather seized upon as a productive, generative surplus. This is the location of a *coming community* that exists in a state of limbo between the city and the forest. If, as Heidegger (1995) argues the origin of philosophy is a sense of homesickness and exile, then it is here in the in-between zone of contact and separation that Victor and Itard engage in a new and strange form of imaginative creativity that lacks a specific grammar—a zone between logos and phone, between voice and signification, a pure potentiality to be and not to be this or that—a true dirty home. This is the zone where Itard and Victor meet as strangers, as foreigners to each other and to themselves where the coordinates for inclusion and exclusion are rendered inoperative and they must become friends without recourse to recognition or belonging—the sublime beauty of exodus.

What if Itard's pedagogy was not so much the scientific study of humanity's coming into being through the negation of the animal (a ban on the monster) as it was a playful quest in the open of life? What if, rather than starting with a predetermined notion of the human that must be rigorously analyzed through tests and measurements within a clinical, sterile space of the classroom, he began to play with Victor and thus invent new games? As Agamben (2007) argues, play is a space of suspension of the ban, a zone of free usage. Play preserves the law only in suspension, and by making the law inoperative, play "deactivates the apparatuses of power and returns to common use the spaces that power had seized" (77). In play, the child's relationship with toys troubles the very distinctions between the proper and the improper that Itard's humanist pedagogy holds as the law. Children have a fetishistic relation to toys, which are "suspended between this world and the other" and thus "belong neither to the internal and subjective nor to the external and objective spheres" (Agamben 1993a, 57–58). Toys are a pure potentiality to be this or that, and thus express a form-of-life beyond the sovereign ban. In the work of Gregory Bateson, Cary Wolfe (2003) has importantly emphasized how play is a zone of indistinction where preverbal, nonhuman communication and human communication pass through one another, creating a temporary zone of indistinction that troubles binaries between species—an opening to the transversal commonwealth (see Intermezzo).[2] When M. Guerin plays with Victor in the garden, she is enacting a moment of learning and teaching that is properly beyond Itard's scientific method, a new exopedagogy that is out of bounds of an anthropocentric imagination. Play is a *profanation* of educational immunization, thus suspending the fundamental dialectic that transforms life into death, investment into abandonment, and citizenship into bare life. It no longer is predicated on a fundamental sacrifice and thus divides itself from the division that constitutes *homo ferus* as a sacred individual.

In other words what is needed is an exopedagogy beyond the anthropological machine. Here, exopedagogy adds to Esposito's affirmative reconstruction of biopolitics in a significant way. For Esposito, key to overturning the limits of immunization is the movement from inoculation to mutation or, monstrous metamorphosis. Drawing on Nietzsche, Esposito argues that life must rejuvenate itself—and thus escape the cadaverization of life—by tapping into the excess or surplus that is disavowed through inoculation. Life must, in other words, define itself not in terms of limits but in terms of its overcoming of limits through a Dionysian moment of perpetual transformation and transvaluation of all values.[3] Rightly, Vanessa Lemm (2009) demonstrates that Nietzschian becoming is fueled by a return to the dreamworld, the sensations, and the instincts of the animal. This Nietzschian ethic of life affirmation enables a deconstruction of the sovereign-immunitary dispositif and thus a new notion of generative life —life that is immanent to its own form as both a potential to be and not to be this or that. This is a concept of life wherein norms are no longer held above and outside the body but rather perpetually constituted by the body as a measure of its own constituting powers. Quoting Esposito (2008): "Completely normal isn't the person who corresponds to a prefixed prototype, but the individual who preserves intact his or her own normative power, which is to say the capacity to create continually new norms" (191). Innovation rather than exorcism becomes the dominant organizing principle of becoming as a process of involution (as a mutual exploration of artifactual natureculture assemblages). Exopedagogy is thus, to use Niezschian terminology, a "gay science" that says yes to the multidimensional and constituting powers of life to invent new values through living labor and no to the logic of the ban. The gay science is an experience of life as sovereign to itself, as life giving itself to itself as its own gift. In the chapters that follow we will explore this new zone of potentialities opened by a variety of exopedagogies that do not attempt to gentrify the monstrous but rather engage with it through imaginative practices of play.

2

THE REPTOID HYPOTHESIS:
EXOPEDAGOGY AND THE UFOTHER

The problem with Itard's humanist pedagogy as explored in chapter one basically revolves around the question of recognition—both of self and of the other within the presupposed framework of the "human." Indeed, the first question asked by doctors and educators when faced with the wild boy was: Is he human, or capable of being humanized? This opening question jumpstarts the anthropological machine, which always defines the human as a surplus of the animal or as the negation of animal sensation, gesticulation, sexuality, and so on. The traces of the feral must be hunted down and exorcised in order for the immunization of the human to be complete. But what if Itard started with another question, a question that did not begin with predefined notions of recognizability predicated on common and good sense? What if he did not begin with an assumption about what it means to be fully human? What if he walked with Victor into the beastly place between forest and city where all are strangers to each other and to themselves? In this paradoxical no-man's-land is it not possible to attend to the appearance of an uncanny wonder that suspends the divisions of the sovereign decision over and against Victor? What if Itard decided to play, and thus abandon himself to the abandonment of a zoömorphic and savage imagination out of bounds of his humanist science? To ask such questions is to inaugurate the first steps of an exopedagogy as a pedagogy that profanes the humanist subject of education by learning from the exceptional and monstrous profanation of the human in order to let the animal, the unconscious, the creaturely, and the body speak. We must risk the open space between human and nonhuman animals that emerges when we let the anthropological machine idle, and in this sense produce a new educational machine—a "zoontological" (Wolfe 2003b) machine.

In this chapter we will examine the monstrous imagination of David Icke's "reptoid hypothesis." Through a close reading of Icke's alien conspiracy theory, we will demonstrate the waxing and waning of the zoömorphic and savage imagination as it attempts to form new narrative forms for combating the humanist assumptions of Itard's pedagogy. While giving a brief glimpse of a posthumanist, coming community that resists the lure of the anthropological machine, Icke's opus ultimately demonstrates the difficulty of remaining within the terrain of the monstrous without lapsing back either into nascent forms of residual anthropocentrisms or overly romanticized versions of posthumanist becomings. In other words, Icke's imagination returns too easily to the recognition of tried and true narratives of human/animal relations while at the same time dipping too close to capitalism's own euphorically intense affective structure.

THE REPTOID HYPOTHESIS: LIONS AND TIGERS AND ALIENS, OH MY!

> I am the lizard king. I can do anything.
>
> —Jim Morrison

Alien reptilian invasions, blood-sucking, pedophilic Illuminati agents acting as totalitarian world leaders, trans-dimensional alien-humans interbreeding to support a program of cosmic imperialism on an unimaginable scale—no, this is not an episode of *X-Files, Primeval,* or *Doctor Who,* neither is it an undiscovered Philip K. Dick or H.P. Lovecraft novel, nor is it the latest Hollywood science fiction spectacle. Rather, it is the real-life and ever-evolving conspiracy theory of the self-proclaimed "most controversial speaker and author in the world," David Icke. Icke, one-time British soccer star turned BBC sports personality turned UK Green Party spokesman, is now today's most (in)famous proponent of what we are calling the "Reptoid Hypothesis"—the idea that alien lizards conspiratorially control the Earth and with it human destiny. Inasmuch as the reptoid, a figure of radical difference—what we will refer to as "UFOtherness"—also takes on decidedly animal overtones, we will seek in this chapter to examine how Icke's narrative stands today as representative evidence of a popular dystopianism that projects onto the animal (as cause) the sum total of the fear and discontent that have arisen around contemporary issues. Yet, a closer investigation of Icke's theory also suggests that savagely zoömorphic readings of his work are possible in which it is theorized that the end to global domination can be arrived at only via the formation of new human/reptoid alliances toward peace. In this chapter we will attempt to unravel these various layers of ambiguity, arguing that Icke's theory simultaneously represents a progressive desire for the construction of an alternative posthuman/animal future and a reactionary retreat from the potentialities of this critical/aesthetic move. In other words, the savage and zoömorphic imagination that Icke exhibits is inhibited from the inside by counterforces of a humanistic and/or superstitious nature.

While those unfamiliar with Icke and reptoid discussions may wonder if this is a discussion worthy of the non-lunatic, we want to caution against relegating Icke's work to merely fringe status. Rather, Icke is representative of a major countercultural trend that is indeed global in proportions. For instance, Icke's webpage purportedly received over six hundred thousand hits in its first year alone, and for over four years he has been invited to lecture in at least twenty-five countries (Cowley 2000). Icke's most recognized publication—the massive 533-page Rosetta stone for conspiracy junkies, *The Biggest Secret*—has already gone through multiple re-printings since its release date in 1999, and his latest conspiracy/ufology testament, *Alice in Wonderland and the World Trade Center Disaster*, passes for vogue amongst American, British, and Canadian audiences as well as in non-Anglo international cultural arenas such as South Africa (where the book has been an enduring Top 5 seller). In fact over two thousand people attended Icke's lecture at London's Brixton Academy, a performance that was later turned into the DVD entitled *Freedom or Fascism: Time to Choose*. The demographic breakdown of his audience is, in and of itself, an interesting phenomenon. Icke appeals equally to bohemian hipsters and right-wing reactionary fanatics. As regards the latter, in England the British Nazi Group Combat 18 supports his writings, and in America the ultra right-wing conservative group Christian Patriots often attends his lectures (Crumey 2001; Taylor 1997). But they are just as likely to be sitting next to a sixty-something UFO buff, a Nuwaubian, a Posadist, a Raëlian, or New Age earth goddess.[1] Thus, Icke has an expansive popular appeal that cuts across political, economic, and religious divides, uniting a wide spectrum of left and right groups and individuals under his prolific and all-embracing meta-conspiracy theory.

Icke's rise to international fame is not in and of itself an anomaly. In fact, his theory is part of a larger alien conspiracy culture that began its ascendancy as a post–World War II Cold War phenomenon (Jung 1959; Peebles 1994), and since the *X-Files* series and movies, asserted itself as a popular aspect of a global media culture (Kellner 2003b, 126; Pritchard et al. 1994). Following an alleged crash of a UFO craft in Roswell, NM, in 1947, a new genus of so-called contactee literature sprang up, and newspaper reports thrilled to the idea that aliens filled the skies (Dean 1998, 40). While many associated the alien invasion with the Communist threat (Mars the red planet equaling the Soviet Red Army), those in contact with the aliens reported differently, finding instead that the aliens were in fact here to help humankind survive global crises such as world war and nuclear weapons (Clark 2000, 133–135). However, by the 1970s, with scandals such as Watergate and the Vietnam War suggesting to an increasingly paranoid public that governments can act in defense of their own powerful and secret interests, numerous reports of alien abduction made it clear that intruding aliens might very well have their own (potentially harmful) agenda (Keel 1970, 290). While television shows such as *Star Trek*, *Outer Limits*, and *The Twilight Zone*, and films such as *Star Wars*, *Alien*, and *Close Encounters of the Third Kind*, all helped to cement the connection between aliens, politics, and entertainment in the popular imagination of the 1960s and 1970s, the 1980s continued the alien craze with the creation of a new set of narratives that began to continue alien themes with conspiratorial ideas. The year 1982 brought *The Thing*, which—like 1979's *Alien*—suggested the analogy to political conspiracy through its portrayal of an alien life form that infects and gestates within its human hosts; and in 1983, the GenX television miniseries *V* offered a compelling, literal version of the Reptoid Hypothesis for Reagan's "trickle down" America, with imperialist reptiles plotting the take-over of the top fifty world capitals. *V* was quickly followed in 1985 by the immensely popular *Enemy Mine*, a movie in which all-American fighter pilot Dennis Quaid first hates and then learns to love his Draconian lizard counterpart Louis Gossett, Jr.; and in 1988, *They Live* dramatized how a new optic (literally: sun glasses) could help a human resistance movement to perceive that freedom was a lie created by a highly managerialized society run solely for alien domination and exploitation. Meanwhile, Whitley Strieber arguably inaugurated contemporary alien fandom in literature with a series of books detailing his own abduction story, and in 1989 Strieber's best-selling "autobiographical" novel *Communion* was also made into a Hollywood movie.

With alien conspiracy already at a fever pitch, the rise of a potential New World Order on the sociopolitical stage in the 1990s appeared only to intensify such thoughts in the public's imagination. Hollywood released a steady stream of blockbuster movies that focused on the topic, with *Fire in the Sky* (1993), *Independence Day* (1996), *Men in Black* (1997), *Contact* (1997), *Alien Resurrection* (1997), and *The Faculty* (1998) as just some of the films that sparked the collective alien craze during the decade. While perhaps not reaching the pitch of the 1990s, alien films still function in Hollywood as symptomatic expressions of social, political, and economic fears. For instance, M. Night Shyamalan's 2002 film *Signs* and the Oscar nominated *District 9* (2009) offer political allegories of the relationship between communities and alien monsters "threatening" boundaries between inside and outside.

On TV, unprecedented audiences tuned in to watch the series *Dark Skies* (1996–1997), and the widely popular, award-winning, extremely ambitious television opus *X-Files* (1993–2002). The mantel then passed to the visionary TV series titled *4400* (2004), which explored the strange phenomena and powers surrounding a returned group of abductees from a comet/time-capsule that crashed into earth. This is not even to mention the innumerable alien-themed pseudo-documentaries—including the now debunked alien autopsy—that were broadcast on stations ranging from Fox to the Discovery Channel. Even more recently there have been a number of UFO "reality TV" programs such as "UFO Hunters" that utilize various historical/archival, sociological/psychological, and scientific methods of investigating E.T. phenomena. Finally, while aliens flourished on the big screen and small screens, the Internet has become the most significant arena for cultivating and expanding alien conspiracy subcultures. Scattered throughout the Net, an unfathomable number of alien conspiracy sites arose, including UFOU: Earth's First UFO University (http://www.ufou-visiblecollege.com/), the Alien Press (http://www.alienpress.com/), and of course, Icke's own website (http://www.davidicke.com/). The grandfather of alien media in all its variegated forms is irrefutably the late night conspiracy theory staple *Coast to Coast AM* with George Noory. This strange talk show delves into all things paranormal, extra-terrestrial, and unidentified, and people love it. According to Timothy Lavin (2010), *Coast to Coast* is the most popular overnight show in the continental United States, and has "helped set a tone that, both thematically and rhetorically, now pervades American media" (68).

Outside of the culture sphere, the allegory of the alien has also taken decisively political and scientific overtones. Perennial interest in the alien within global capitalism is symptomatic of what Jodi Dean (1998) refers to as "the familiarity of strangeness" (157), which disrupts any attempt by communities to maintain consensus through a politics of recognition. Diagnostically transcoding fears concerning destabilized boarders and the loss of security, "aliens" speak to the very real experiences of insecurity in a post-9/11 world where invasion, contamination, terrorist subplots, and so on monopolize media as well as the popular imagination. Likewise, Richard Doyle (2003) argues that alien arrivals are symptoms of an overall economy of the sample (from DNA to DJ) pervasive within the information saturated landscape/cyberspace of postmodernism. For Doyle, the endless proliferation of alien abduction stories replicates the model of sampling precisely because of their citationality and iterability. The citational quality of informatics blurs boundaries between the proper and the improper with the proliferation of mutant strains. Thus for Doyle, the question of alien experience is the question of communication and information distribution in a postmodern political world. Drawing on Deleuze and Guattari, Doyle argues that sampling is ontological, revealing the "capacities for transformation" (195) that constitute strange and uncanny becomings without the attending criteria for recognizability as friend or enemy, self or other. Aliens open portals to other worlds that dissolve tried and true boundaries dividing community from the radical outside just as easily as those navigating cyberspace point and click their way through endless virtual realms. Becomings populate the media world we live in as well as the cyber-universe most of us vacation in—or perhaps inhabit permanently.

Debbora Battaglia (2006) furthers Dean's argument, finding in alien-enthusiasts new forms of knowledge construction that cross disciplinary boundaries (contaminating science, philosophy, spirituality, and folklore) in order to stay attentive to the appearance of those moments in our lives when common sense breaks down and sensation breaks through (events such as strange lights in the sky, vague memories of abductions, the peculiar feeling of lost time, the strange sensation of a foreign implant just below the surface of the skin). In the face of the strange, new knowledge systems break with the conventions of science, producing utterances whose truth value or verifiability require tools and intellectual mappings that have yet to be invented. Often dismissed by "expert scientists" such utterances pose questions that complicate what counts as evidence, who is a credible witness, and what source confers legitimation. In this sense, there is a profound epistemological shift from an emphasis on the regularities of natural systems back to the early modern natural philosophy of "strange facts"—marvels that were, as Lorraine Daston and Katharine Park (2001) point out, "conspicuously detached from explanatory or theoretical moorings" (237) precisely because they "contradicted everyday expectations, fragmented the categories meant to contain them, and repelled explanation" (246). In this sense, E.T. culture's postmodern science of wonder is really a return to the early modern concern for the monstrous particular, exceptional, and anomalous detail.[2] Like the alien experience, the strange fact of the early moderns resisted quantification and empirical verification, often failing the principle of independent corroboration. Furthermore, "E.T." cultures "do not require the encompassing value of a coherent cultural system of belief" (Battaglia 2006, 3) in order to form new practices and rituals of contact that provide surprisingly imaginative responses to the inadequacies of common sense and preexisting epistemological frameworks. In fact, Battaglia argues that E.T. culture is defined by its *"contact consciousness"* (ibid.), which is more concerned with becomings, mixing, and disorganizing the social and the scientific rather than forming coherent doctrines or finding final solutions to the interminable problems of strange facts. E.T. cultures are bound around mysterious traces rather than substantiated identities—traces of affect that linger in dreams and vague memories, traces of enigmatic signs inscribed on the flesh, traces of displaced time/space, and traces of communication with shadowy others. These are communities that are related through shared questions, confusion, wonder, and awe at inexplicable events and strange facts that suspend disbelief. In sum, the alien offers a taste of the "foreignness appropriate to lived experience beyond comprehension and our zones of comfort and visibility" (10). The condition of E.T. culture is the condition of the monstrous state of exception as such—a condition that lacks stable coordinates for inside and outside, self and other, fact and fiction. Indeed, E.T. culture is more than simply a fringe interest, it offers a momentary glimpse of the beautifully sublime nature of the state of exceptional culture, politics, and science that defines the present.

Underlying these domains of alien exocultures is an exopedagogical moment whose resource for navigating this terrain is the uncanny UFOther. Resting in an imaginative zone that is neither strictly a common notion of reason nor a random sensation, the UFOther is a suspension that exists betwixt and between (dis)orders and (dis) identifications. The UFOther, then, opens up new possibilities precisely because of its tenuous location between worlds—an image that is always in excess of itself, a thought that is always becoming different from itself. This is a close encounter of the nth kind, which according to Doyle (2003) is "the encounter with alien thought, the thought of an alien as itself a consequence of the informatic character of the universe…a signifying exteriority of thinking, the sampling and being-sampled that thought entails" (215). A close encounter of the nth degree is an imaginative connection with the outside (pre-subjective, pre-individual sensation) within thought (common sense). Instead of an exorcism, the practice of exopedagogy is a close encounter that enables us to neighbor the uncanny beyond the limits of predetermined common sense, constantly inventing new languages, modes of research, and sensitivities in order to articulate the strange facts of a life out of joint within exceptional times.

These UFOthers are like the assistants from Kafka's novels. For Giorgio Agamben (2007), these helpers are half-formed creatures of the imagination. Supposed to be "helpers," these incomplete monsters "have no knowledge, no skills, and no 'equipment'; they never do anything but engage in foolish behavior and childish games" (29). Their cryptic, "inconclusive gestures" speak to a coming community that escapes understanding yet ignites the imagination. They are both "eternal students" and "swindlers" (30) who represent that which has been lost and potentially that which is to be redeemed. In this sense the UFOther (an unpronounceable incantation) is an inoperative term for an inoperative, imaginative companion poised on the very edge of thought's becoming in the face of strange facts where human and animal, inner and outer spaces, and familiar and wondrous dichotomies are suspended.

While our intention here is to explore the efficacy of Icke's Reptoid Hypothesis as a particular instantiation of exopedagogy and UFOtherness and not the intricate varieties of the myriad competing visions of alien life and conspiratorial intrigue that now exist worldwide, we want to make clear that our interest in Icke is primarily in interpreting his work as an iconic representation of this ubiquitous global exoculture outlined here.[3] We hope to illuminate some of the ways in which the figures of global conspiracy and the alien—*qua* reptile (i.e., animal)—signify important contemporary hopes and fears about alterity and animals generally. While others have emphasized how the alien represents an imaginative projection of racialized fears and anxieties (see Roth 2005), we will focus on how the UFOther is an imaginary manifestation of contact consciousness that enacts (de)stabilizing intensities between humans and nonhuman animals within the imaginative space of the transversal commonwealth. The animalization of the UFOther indicates certain fears of the humanist subject that are constituted through the logic of the anthropological machine (an anthropocentric and superstitious imaginative narrative about contamination of the ontological purity of human existence) but also could offer new entry points for rethinking kinship relations that cross species boundaries, challenging who we are, where we come from, and where we are going as a species and as a life form (a radical form of zoömorphic and savage narrative that opens up a space for increasing the swarm intelligence of the multitude). In other words, we feel that a critical analysis of a newly emergent global phenomenon like David Icke is itself part of a larger utopian project that hopes to locate resources for exopedagogy to create new, imaginative bestiaries that explore the ambiguity of the struggle between multitude and capitalism.[4]

THE TALE BEHIND THE TAIL: TOWARD A REPTOID HISTORY

The fool doth think he is wise, but the wise man knows himself to be a fool.

—William Shakespeare, *As You Like It*

We want to begin by presenting an overview of Icke's reptoid hypothesis.[5] Much of his writing on aliens reveals an homage to the "ancient astronomer" literature—founded by the controversial cuneiform translator Zecharia Sitchin—that finds in the text of the oldest extant creation story, the Mesopotamian Enuma Elish, reasons for suspecting that extraterrestrial beings created humanity as a sort of primordial biotechnology experiment. According to both Sitchin and Icke, rather than having evolved on their own according to Darwinian natural selection, humans are in fact the result of a genetic experiment carried out by a race of reptilian aliens called Anunnaki (Icke 1999, 1–17)—a type of artifactual selection. In short, it is claimed that the Anunnaki produced humans as a slave race by inter-splicing their genetic material with that of Homo Erectus (7). While Icke draws upon Sitchin's "ancient astronomer" theory—thus endorsing a rather paternalistic narrative of indigenous people and their inabilities to create technological innovations without a superior colonizing force guiding them—he does develop some surprising insights into contemporary capitalism through the reappropriation of this myth. Whereas Sitchin (1995) had hypothesized that the Anunnaki of the twelfth planet came to Earth in order to mine its rich mineral base of gold and other precious metals (22), Icke (1999) believes that the Anunnaki reptoids desired to mine mono-atomic gold (30–38). This mineral supposedly has the ability to increase the carrying capacity of the nervous system by ten thousand times and so, when ingested, the Anunnaki would be able to process vast amounts of information and accelerate trans-dimensional travel. Icke also postulates that the Anunnaki live off human fear and anxiety. In this monstrous narrative, Anunnaki are emotional vampires.[6] Given that the source of capitalistic expropriation is no longer strictly labor-power (flesh and blood work in the factories) and instead the immaterial labor of the multitude that to a large degree is composed of affects, Icke's alien vampire that lives off our anxieties is a much more accurate allegory for capitalism than Marx's own vampires. And given that capital has taken on increasingly virtual forms, it is no surprise that Icke's savage imagination allegorically shifts from terrestrial monsters to virtual monsters from outer space in order to depict the alien nature of our capitalist, global system. Down through the ages, Icke believes, such Anunnaki have initiated numerous blood rituals and human sacrifices. During these rituals, human victims release large amounts of negative energy, which is then absorbed by Anunnaki waiting in the fourth dimension, their preferred stomping ground. To quote Icke: "Thus we have the encouragement of wars, human genocide, the mass slaughter of animals, sexual perversions which create highly charged negative energy, and black magic ritual and sacrifice which takes place on a scale that will stagger those who have not studied the subject" (40). In this sense, the centrality of the human as the apex of the evolutionary ladder is deconstructed, and human laborers are revealed to be no more than an enslaved animal workforce for far superior alien beings, opening up a window through which humans can potentially reidentify with the suffering of other nonhuman animals within bioproductive networks.

With a satisfactory labor force accounted for, then, Icke claims that the Annunaki still faced the problem of who would rule on Earth as overseers of their human slaves. Thus, Icke imagines that the Anunnaki interbred with another alien race to produce earthling slave masters. Icke refers to these other extraterrestrials as the "Nordics" because of their blond hair and blue eyes. The resulting "super-hybrids" are none other than the Aryans (Icke 2001, 251). This strain of alien hybrids retains many of the central reptoid traits, including "top-down control, emotionless 'cold-blooded' attitudes, an obsession with ritualistic behavior, and so on" (275). This reptilian state of consciousness characteristic of the Aryans is, for Icke, a "lower level of development" in spiritual evolution, and is directly related to fascist militarism, technocratic rationalism, and racism (19, 251). Because of their close ties to the original Anunnaki, the Aryans can also shape-shift (transform themselves back and forth between human and alien bodies) and some can even control weaker, human minds. This shape shifting can be captured through special film processes that reveal the indistinct "aura" of the reptoid that always surrounds these figures (see, for instance, Icke's analysis of images of George W. Bush).

Mirroring a number of claims made by the political far-right, Icke asserts a standard conspiracy-culture line that the pure Aryan blood-line has ruled the planet throughout history, though he is unique in developing it in an exocultural direction. In Icke's mind, Aryan lizards have been Sumerian kings, Egyptian pharaohs, and, in more recent history, American presidents and British prime ministers. According to Icke, forty-three American presidents, including George Washington and George W. Bush, are direct reptoid-lineage descendants, and the Queen Mother herself was "seriously reptilian" (79). In fact, it is at this point that much of Icke's work has its most enduring interest, by providing historical critique that is at once trenchant political analysis mixed with what reads like an over-the-top satire in the tradition of Jonathan Swift.[7] In this respect, Icke's work includes any number of accountings of how world leaders and other famous personalities, in order to satiate their reptilian bloodlust, take part in ritualistic sacrifices and pedophilic activities that include kidnapping, hedonistic drug parties, and brutal murder. Icke himself theorizes that such obscene acts as these typify the difference between alien-kind and humanity and that they are necessary else the Aryan-reptilians lose their temporary human form and revert to their original reptoid physiognomy. Again following the prevailing exocultural explanation, Icke claims that in order to maintain their position of world domination down through the centuries, the Aryan lizards have created a secret society known as the Freemasons or Illuminati. The Illuminati are the grand historical puppet masters, presiding over all human activities through indirect channels of control and manipulation. From the innermost secretive "Round Table," a handful of reptilian masterminds directs the course of human events via a network of international organizations such as the Council on Foreign Relations, The Trilateral Commission, The Bilderberg Group, the IMF, World Bank, and the United Nations (339). The plan is quite simply "to complete their financial control of the human race" (345).

In order to maintain their anonymity and deflect attention away from their ubiquitous presence in international finance and politics, Icke believes that the Illuminati are very interested in mind control. The media and the Internet are two powerful tools that they have developed to achieve mind control over the general populace. In

Icke's conspiratorial schema, "The media, in turn, get their 'news' and 'information' overwhelmingly from official sources, which, like the media itself, are owned by the reptilian bloodline" (260). Commenting on the Internet conspiracy, Icke writes, "The Internet is an Illuminati creation and only exists because of military technology…It allows for the easiest possible surveillance of personal communications through e-mails, and the websites visited by individuals give the authorities the opportunity to build a personality and knowledge profile of everyone. It's about control" (415). The Internet, then, is just another step toward perfect surveillance of the human race. The "most important goal of the Illuminati is," according to Icke, "a micro-chipped population" (368). Once a microchip is inserted into the human body, each individual will be tracked using a global positioning satellite. Thus in the twenty-first century the reptoids have gone digital, inventing and deploying new information technologies that will further suppress the truth, expand the scope of surveillance, and restrict individual freedoms.

So what can humans do to liberate themselves from the tyranny of our shared oppressors? Icke ends each of his books with a kind of sensual program for emancipation that can often be found in all manner of New Age communities. As opposed to the rational discourse of science, which is a "fascist club," Icke suggests that we realize and manifest multiple, overlapping realities in our lives through an aesthetic multiplicity of becomings. These multiple, even contradictory, interpretations of the real are not simply misunderstandings but the results of our differing positions within an overall energy field of various intensities. Thus, each narrative of reality is in fact united on a deeper level by our "multi-dimensional infinity" (406) or "vibrational wholeness" (399) set against "the five sense prison" (Icke 2002, 462) of fascism. Rather than subjectively fragmented and biologically finite beings lost in a sea of "cosmic accidents," Icke asserts that we are all part of a unifying, trans-dimensional force: love. This force unifies all life in the galaxy. In fact, Icke argues, "We are the reptilians and the 'demons' and, at the same time, we are those they manipulate because we are all the same 'I'" (Icke 2001, 424). In the end, therefore, it is not clear whether Icke is in fact suggesting that reptoids are simply psychic projections and that his numerous treatises are little more than an elaborate allegory or if he actually believes that reptoids do literally exist outside the human imagination. Things get even more complicated when he states, "If the reptilians and other astral manipulators did not exist, we would have to invent them. In fact we probably have. They are other levels of ourselves putting ourselves in our face" (423). Yet this *uncanny* ambiguity is productive. The reptoid emerges as the ultimate UFOther, neither here nor there, material or psychical, real or simulation, self or other. They are the trace of an imaginative testimony that bears witness to the nonhuman in the human and thus prevents their separation (human versus animal) or simply their collapse into indistinction—rather each is rendered strange... a contact that is always and already an uncanny distance. If Itard's biopedagogy was an attempt to exorcize the animal and thus reconstitute the dialectic of inside and outside, then Icke's exopedagogy is an attempt at a close encounter that suspends divisions that mark the human and its spatial/temporal coordinates. The UFOther in Icke's treatment is a suspension of the categories that partition the sensible order of a superstitious and anthropocentric imagination, and thus the reptoid troubles the order and clarity of the human community by insisting on the viability of a contact consciousness not restrained by common sense but rather imaginatively exploring the exceptional zone of indistinction that resides beyond the boundaries of the anthropological machine. Whatever Icke says about the reptoid, it is this exploration of a monstrously profane being where human and animal are rendered strange through the UFOther that is the most fascinating and perplexing aspect of his theory. Thus, his latest books end by declaring that his future work will no longer take on the air of conspiratorial critique, but rather present solely a positive vision of multidimensional love—love for the uncanny otherness of the self—that exists in the dislocated location of the fourth dimension of his zoömorphic and savage imagination (Icke 2002, 479–86).

ICKE'S LOVE BIOGRAM TO CAPITALISM

> The only difference between myself and a madman, is that I am not mad.
>
> — Salvador Dali, *Diary of a Genius*

In an imaginative attempt to manage the disorienting complexities of present age "virtuality," the rise of a global media culture, the explosion of new information and biotechnologies, and the seemingly infinite expansions of transnational capital, conspiracy theory is—as Fredric Jameson (1992) has argued—a populist form of cognitive mapping that attempts to represent the unrepresentable totality of these seemingly disparate yet interconnected social, political, and economic transformations. Expanding upon Jameson's model of cognitive mapping, Douglas Kellner (1995) argues that contemporary alien conspiracy theories represent a form of "pop-postmodernism" that constructs new modes of representation suitable to the uncertainty, (dis)organization, and fragmentation that often characterize the cultural logic of the present age (156). While Jameson argues that most conspiracy theories are in fact "degraded" or ideologically mired products of an information underclass, such cartographic attempts to trace the topography of the postmodern landscape offer an aesthetic/pedagogical strategy for combating the effects of global capitalism. Because postmodern society is often bewildering and disorienting, it can, for Jameson, lead to political paralysis and nihilistic confusion. Thus, in order to regain a sense of political agency, an "as yet unimaginable new mode" of representation and narrativization must be constructed with the ability "to grasp our positioning as individuals and collective subjects [within the space of transnational capital] and regain a capacity to act and struggle" (Jameson 1995, 54). Conspiracy theory characterized as an impoverished form of cognitive mapping has gained widespread popularity in critical theory, becoming the starting point for thinking through a variety of conspiratorial narratives (see, for instance, Knight 2002).

Although it might be tempting to argue that Icke's conspiracy is a cognitive map, we would like to emphasize how Icke's work demonstrates the limits of Jameson's theory. As Brian Massumi (2002a) argues, cognitive maps are "visual forms grouped into fixed configurations" (179) that privilege three-dimensional Euclidean space, visuality, and conscious organization of coordinates. Key to the cognitive map is the function of the landmark that offers a stable position around which we can organize our movement. In other words, the cognitive map functions within the parameters of the gaze and its privileged relation to critical reason. While there are certain features of Icke's map outlined earlier that certainly contain such elements, we would also argue that his map exceeds this model in important ways, pushing us to the very edge of political coordination.

Icke's is not so much a mapping of fixed configurations as it is dynamic zones of sensual becomings and cosmic vibrations that escape three-dimensional models of space, pole-vaulting us into alternative dimensions. In this sense, the reptoid hypothesis is a "*poetic* production" that constitutes a "structure of feeling" (Lepselter 2005, 265), unsettling the bearings of human animals as members of a species, a planet, a solar system, and on into infinity. What is critical here is that Icke's reptoid hypothesis emphasizes topological becomings (vibrations) that are, as Massumi (2002a) would describe, "continuous and multiple" (184), thus privileging movement and intensity without recourse to "superior" coordinates. Rather than a cognitive map, Icke provides what Massumi aptly names a "biogram" that orients us through pre-individual, pre-subjective, and pre-conscious sensations that blur distinctions between personal inner-space and public outer-space. If Jameson's cognitive map functions to "grasp our positioning as individuals," then Icke's topological measuring of intensities and morphological becomings resists the temptation to make action dependent on the visualization of localization and individuation. Thus emphasis is placed on "frequency ranges" (Icke 2001, 382) rather than fixed points, and agency is collectively cultivated by overcoming thresholds of "low-vibration" (390). In this sense, if cognitive mapping is an aesthetic pedagogy of locational points within a gridded network of three-dimensional space mastered by the gaze of critical reason, Icke's biogram is an exopedagogy of the affective surplus outside the five sense prison, which challenges any hierarchical privileging of individual cognition, visualization, and calculation over embodied and embedded orientation in four-dimensional space.

More than anything else, he constructs alternative visualizations, new auditory sensitivities, and new tactile relations (all "impossible perceptions" as Jameson would say) in order to give imaginary life to uncanny expressions of global capitalism and their effects on the stability of relations between self and other, nature and culture. For Massumi (2002a), the biogram is not predicated on cognitive mastery through vision but rather through synesthetic forms that are "dynamic," "diagrammatic" (186), and thus embodied and embedded in sensorial systems. Biograms privilege movement over fixity, connection over compartmentalization, equality of sensations over hierarchical ordering. In this sense, the biogram is synesthetic. As an "intersensory hinge-dimension" (188) synesthesia is a condition normal to infantile perception as well as nonhuman animals. Massumi draws indirect parallels between synesthesia and a homing pigeon's abilities to orient flight. Also, Daniel Heller-Roazen (2007) argues that synesthesia as a "thinking-with" demonstrates the inability to separate perception (a purely animal faculty) from self-perception (the "exclusive domain" of the human animal). Rather than simply "degraded" forms of cognitive mapping as Jameson would imply, Icke presents us with a biogram of alternative synesthetic orientations to a world of intensive vibrations rather than fixed landmarks, and sensorial deformations and contaminations rather than visual cognition. Indeed, we would argue that syesthesia is the ultimate form of E.T. contact consciousness. It is in moments when Icke privileges seemingly degraded forms of narrative description on the edge of cognitive mapping that he is most posthuman, that his imagination is most zoömorphic. Creatively critical paranoia fuels this bewildering, biogramatic project. In his book *Media Spectacle*, Douglas Kellner (1995) makes the distinction between a reactionary "clinical paranoia"—a mindset that has dissociated itself from a reality principle and retreated into a world of occult fantasy—and a much-needed, progressive "critical paranoia" that is suspicious and inquiring of the politics of media culture (140).

To the degree that one interprets Icke's biogram of transdimensional, body-morphing reptoids literally (as a mimetic representation of external reality), it would be classified as clinically paranoid and thus symptomatically dystopian. And yet Icke's analyses of events such as the dubious media portrayals surrounding the Gulf War and 9/11 and his overall critique of our growing hi-tech surveillance society would appear to qualify as "critical paranoia" as well. Yet, we would argue that Kellner's positive conception of paranoia must be read so as to include the type of novel syntheses and imaginative perceptions that characterize Salvador Dali's technique of "paranoiac-critical" activity that figures the dynamic constitution of uncanny sensation, hybridic monstrosities, and heterogeneous powers. In Best and Kellner's own discussion (2001) of the paranoid imagination at work in the literature of Thomas Pynchon, they have written of a "creative paranoia" (27, 55) that we believe is much akin to the sense given by Dali—a synesthetic implosion of sights and sounds in the form of fourth-dimensional portals and intergalactic vibrations (where flesh becomes scales and nails become claws). As Margot Norris (1985) demonstrates, zoömorphic writers, scientists, and philosophers from Charles Darwin to Max Ernst utilize the aesthetic of surrealism (as a mode of creative paranoia) in order to convey the "infinitely plastic" nature of life that "conform[s] to no a priori logical or conceptual categories" (42) and thus ruptures identity, recognizability, and belonging. Norris argues that while Ernst might have been inspired by a gothic aesthetic (akin to Marx's use of the gothic outlined in the Intermezzo), his zoömorphic imagination ultimately abandoned the gothic attempt to narrativize irrational events. We would like to suggest that this movement from gothic to surrealist aesthetics is not so much a negation as an *intensification* of certain elements found within the gothic genre—a heightening of its posthumanist elements according to a creative paranoia pressing up against the outer rim of the ego. While the full flowering of a critically creative paranoia might be interpreted as dystopianism at its worst, it is interesting to note that Ernst Bloch, the progenitor of contemporary utopian theory, argues that paranoia "reacts to the traditional powers with querulousness and persecution mania, but breaks them at the same time with adventurous inventions, social recipes, heavenly roads and more besides" (ibid., 93). Consequently, it appears to us that Icke's biogram could be analyzed as a form of "pop-Pynchonism" (Kellner 1995) that is not dissociated from a reality principle so much as it is working to produce an entirely new one through the synesthetic touching of strange facts that resist explanation or capture by the five sense prison.[8]

Whereas Donna Haraway (1997) argues that posthumanism must avoid the extremes of either paranoia or denial (7), Icke reveals that exceptional modes of aesthetic imagining might be necessary in order to critically and creatively orient the swarm intelligence arising from the monstrous state of exception. And if Deleuze and Guattari (1983) once argued that paranoia is a reactionary territorialization of schizo desire back into a modern notion of the unified subject, then we would argue that critically creative paranoia has a more progressive valence: one that does not foreclose on the possibilities of a zoömorphic narrative of the monstrous dimensions of life while at the same time pressing the subject-supposed-to-know to the limits of recognizability. Fran Mason persuasively argues that while others might be quick to dismiss paranoia, the divisions between critical thinking (as endorsed by cognitive mapping) and paranoid fantasy (as endorsed in conspiracy theory) often deconstruct themselves. In Mason's analysis (2002), both critical and conspiratorial thinking exist in a paradoxical (dis)location between the radical inside and outside of society and between the total fragmentation of the postmodern self and the coherent unity of a modern construction of self. For us, paranoia is the emotional and cognitive expression of the current state of exception where laws have been suspended ushering in a permanent crisis between self and other, and ultimately self and world. We cannot abandon this monstrous terrain for the "safety" of critical theory and the assurance that it brings—such a retreat would merely mystify the paradoxical ambiguity that Mason points out between self-reflection and self-delusion. While clinical paranoia aligns itself with a superstitious and anthropocentric imagination predicated on fantasies of individual autonomy and control, a critically creative paranoia can be productively rerouted through a zoömorphic and savage imaginative reconstruction toward a posthumanist future. Remaining inside the ambiguity and dangers of critically creative paranoia enables us to navigate the terrain of the monster without lapsing into the equally fantastical delusion that the gaze of critical theory can outsmart madness once and for all. In fact, we would argue that it is when Icke's biogramatic thought feeling most closely approximates the features of a cognitive map that the clinically paranoid tendencies of his imagination become most acute, providing surprising evidence for Mason's claims. This is precisely why we have chosen to highlight the affective surplus or vibrational synesthesia of Icke's surrealist narrative. These intensities and energistic extensions of consciousness beyond consciousness and sense beyond sense tip the conspiratorial hat from paranoia to joy—not as a negation but as an amplification of inherently zoömorphic proportions.

In this sense, paranoia is a location that contains many ambiguities best illustrated by Icke's own reptoid hypothesis. To think the present crisis we must remain immanent to this monstrous location where savage and zoömorphic imaginations fold into one another and where superstitious and anthropocentric imaginings return with brutal force. The reptoid—as a whatever creature, a UFOther, neither fully external nor internal, corporeal nor incorporeal, human nor animal—becomes a central figuration for our bestiary of the current state of exception. The reptoid attends to the perplexing sensation of both radical alienation of nature (nature as a personified alien abductor) and uncanny doubling of the self within this radical exteriorization (the reptoid is, in the end, nothing more than a valence of the human). The UFOther provides a model of a contact consciousness that demonstrates the impossible synthesis of nature and culture—where they are held in intimate union precisely because of their irrevocable split.

Ultimately, Icke's (2002) creatively critical paranoia gives way in his books to a utopian examination of monstrous being where life itself emerges as a transdimensional or "multi-dimensional infinity" (456). His utopian vision of quirky oddities and idiosyncrasies living together in a surreal cacophony is well summarized in the following quote:

> We must let go of the fear of what other people think of us and start living and expressing our own uniqueness of lifestyle, view, and reality. When we do this we step out of the herd and if enough of us do it, there is no herd...We allow everyone else the freedom and respect to express their uniqueness without the fear of ridicule and condemnation...No one seeks to impose their beliefs or reality on anyone else, so always respecting the freedom of others to make different choices. (Icke 2001, 426)

Here is a synesthetic world of mixing, difference, and strange contaminations that cannot be easily reconciled with a politics of order, efficiency, and control. Rather than deviations from a Platonic ideal, Icke's description (1985) of monstrous differences suggests a new political ontology that privileges what Norris refers to as the "unself-conscious arena of the modern beast" (139) to constantly invent, create, and germinate new modalities of life. It is a world organized no longer in relation to immunizing logics or common sense recognition but rather by contact consciousness where all are strangers and thus potential friends. His repeated emphasis on "vibrational wholeness" shifts analysis from sense to sensation as the new, pre-rational, pre-subjective ground for a coming community that does not have preconceived notions of belonging or of identity and that exists outside of the tyranny of a sovereign decision over whose lives count within the consensus of the community. Politics becomes an intensification of the these flows and imagistic excesses of the spectacle pushed to their very limit in order to become something other than human, something other than a political community with determinate and determining boundaries—a properly profane state of existence. If Jameson (1995) argues that the "waning of affect" is a symptom of late capitalism's deterritorialization of the subject (giving way to subjectless intensities and political paralysis), then for Icke, as with Deleuze, this symptom is also a gateway or threshold toward a new understanding of the coming community.

Within an Ickean utopia of trans-cosmic diversity, community will be unable to restrain burgeoning permutations of existence from expressing themselves in increasingly complex formations through the collective labor to produce the surplus common. According to Icke, these re-productions of selfhood, in tune with a vibrational wholeness and multidimensional infinity above and beyond the cultural and political status quo, will no longer be judged as deviant or abnormal but rather simply as concrete expressions of our collective awareness of an ever-present universalizing strong force: love. This Ickean utopia might be considered as an example of what Deleuze and Guattari (1983) have written of as a "deterritorialized zone," a place of pure affective production (319–322). Icke's imaginative utopian vision receives its best political reading as a form of populist articulation of a Deleuze and Guattarian nomadic body—a synesthetic body without organs that becomes liberated through its self-involvement with an endless creative process that effects new valences of difference (Deleuze and Guattari 1987, 381–384). As Icke (2001) states, each individual is in fact "many people" (423), and this internal multiplicity is accomplished—as with Guattari's concept (2000) of "heterogenesis" (69)—through the pulverization of the centered, unified, Oedipalized ego,

a process by which the contradiction between the liberal self (predicated on private property, individual agency, and control) and its relationship to the larger community begins to disappear. In this sense,
it is in the posthuman turn freed from the constraints of biopower
over and against life that Icke's conspiratorial paranoia becomes intensified into a pure desire, pure schizophrenic multiplicity of affect, a
pure joy in multiplicitous invention and generation. Indirectly, there
is reason not to dismiss Icke (2001) when he asserts that in his utopia
of free-thinkers and actors "we are all one," united across differences
by love itself—love of our collective joy in the very production of singular novelty (423). Icke's wholeness and his emphasis on the One of
collectivity is not reducible to democratic liberalism (in that it is not
predicated on recognition) or to fascism (which sacrifices the singularity as a scapegoat for an absolute identification of self and collective)
or to romanticism (which posits some type of natural wholeness from
which humanity has fallen). Rather, we read Icke's gesture as a posthumanist invocation of a monstrous life—a life without prior identities,
a life full of involutions across divisions. It is on this expansive domain
that Icke forges a new swarm intelligence all his own—an intelligence
predicated on synesthesic contamination, affective amplification, and
multiplicitous transformations without end.

   Yet the question remains, has this euphoria of free flowing affect
really escaped the separation of the surplus common from the multitude? Or is it not in the end the ultimate fantasy of transnational
capitalism? Any politics of affect today simply must confront the
growing reality of transnational capitalism that, as Hardt and Negri
argue (2000; 2004; 2009), is itself predicated on an immaterial,
affective economy. While there are savage moments in Icke's conspiracy theory, it is in the last utopian turn that we find a lack of
ability to distinguish between becoming-multiple and becoming-
capital. Thus Icke's grand utopian vision leaves behind the critical
capacities of the savage imagination, and in the end fetishizes affect
as a post-capitalist escapist fantasy. To the degree that Icke's reptoid
hypothesis can be read positively as a clarion call to reconfigure new
selves that implode traditional dualistic hierarchies such as human/
animal, human/alien, and self/other, we find that the lack of a suf-
ficient theory of capitalism in his work may only serve to lead prac-
titioners down the commodified road of New Age neo-shamanism
(Noel 1997). As Hardt and Negri (2000) warn, postmodernist theorists often miss the mark when they assume their enemy consists of
Enlightenment reason or modern forms of sovereignty that constitute community through binaries of Same and Other. The problem

is that within the present moment, "the affirmation of hybridities and the free play of differences across boundaries...can even coincide with and support the functions and practices of imperial rule" (142), which is rhizomatic, multiplicitous, and deterritorializing. Read in this light, Icke's own utopian vision of an alternative transdimensionality is sustained by the monocultural transnational capitalism that functions as its disavowed anchoring point. To this end, Icke himself is at his worst when he interprets his notion of the infinite "I" in a humanist direction of a pluralist, liberal anthropocentrism (Icke 2002, 483). By doing so, he thereby undermines the radical impact and political efficacy of his vision by reducing the brutalities of human-induced oppression to a mere game of a clinically paranoid consumer self. Icke (2001) states, "It's just a game. It's just a ride" (427). If play worked to potentially undermine the anthropological machine in Victor's case (see chapter one), the historical modality of community and capitalism have shifted significantly to the point where play is now internal to an affective economy. As Agamben (2007) points out, the spectacular phantasmagoria of capitalism both unleashes the nonutilitarian excess of play while also capturing it in circuits of exchange. In this case, where the monstrous is the law—and thus the distinction between profanation and sacrifice melts into thin air—an alternative form of militancy is necessary that is never *simply* a game of self-invention or reinvention. And, if it is all just a game, Icke does not recognize how his own media-saturated identity as guru of the reptoid hypothesis and his political clarion call to play new games of involution are caught within highly exploitative and superstitious circuits of the capitalist imagination. Thus at the crucial moment, his biogram is decoupled from a truly savage understanding of its own function and topples into a love letter to capitalism.

IDENTITY IMPLOSIONS: ALIEN/HUMAN/ REPTILIAN HYBRIDITY AND THE RETURN OF ANTHROPOCENTRISM

Man is an enigma to himself...The possibility of comparison and hence of self-knowledge would arise only if he could establish relations with quasi-human mammals inhabiting other stars.
                                        —Carl G. Jung, *The Undiscovered Self*

Research involving contemporary representations of alien/human/ animal hybridity is related to large-scale changes being affected by

new technologies and capital—post–World War II technocapital—and
is part of posthumanist critical theory. Such literature points in two
directions: historically, toward the analysis of a past discourse of primarily Western humanism, and, imaginatively, toward a reconstructed
future in which the oppositions and hierarchies that characterize such
humanism are suspended. There has been a bevy of writing that problematizes the hallmark of Western humanism—an anthropocentric
liberal subjectivity—by demonstrating the variety of ways in which
it is predicated upon the dichotomous notion of self and imaginary
other (Sargisson 1996, 117–27), culture and nature (Horkheimer
and Adorno 2002), and human and animal (Bleakley 2000; Noske
1997). While some science fiction writers such as William Gibson
represent the absolute abolition of nature and the animal, reducing
them to the binary zeros of a technocultural hallucination, other SF
writers from H.G. Wells (Best and Kellner 2001, 164–71) to Octavia
Butler (Sands 2003; Stillman 2003) have centered the dystopic threat
represented by the alien figure of non-anthropocentric human/
animal hybrids. As a sort of allegory for immediate political concerns
like the explosion of biotechnology as a primary future economic
direction for world markets, dystopic SF hybridity symbolizes that
new technologically produced life forms in lab test-tubes destabilize
traditional notions about humanity through their transgression of
boundaries. Furthermore, such narratives challenge existing animal
communities and the ecosystems that support them in a rather violent and unsolicited manner. By contrast, theorists such as Haraway,
Deleuze, and Guattari (1991) celebrate the possible utopian dimensions of undermining what Derrida has called the liberal subject of
"carnophallogocentrism" (112). In particular, Deleuze and Guattari
(1987) have called for the politics of a "becoming-animal," in which
a new aesthetics of multiplicity and the ecology of difference is prac-
ticed and in which the history of humanism's hierarchical and self-
valorizing theory of evolution must give way to a theory of creative
"involution" (233–239).

    The iconic drama of the reptoid versus human battle for the fate of
the planet in the work of David Icke speaks directly to these critiques
of the liberal humanist tradition, though we want to argue that it
does so ambiguously, containing both positive and negative vectors of
imaginary invention. In his figure of the Aryan/reptoid nobility, Icke
conjures an image of the alien/human/animal hybrid as the ultimate
representation of modern evil—global leaders are lizards, then, in the
same manner that Dr. Jekyll's madness for power resulted in his being
revealed as the "hardly human" and "troglodytic" quasi-animal named

Mr. Hyde (Skal 1998, 68–69). In combination with this image, Icke (2000) further describes the enslaved rest of humanity as a passive "herd" of "sheeple," or sheep people (13–17). In this respect, Icke's portrayal of the carnivorous alien lizards, who rule cruelly and mightily over a kingdom of domesticated human-sheep, is both complex and contradictory in its over-coding and universal application of the animal image to denote the radical difference of a fourth-dimensional species of space colonialists. As with similar science fiction narratives such as *The Planet of the Apes*, Icke's theory utilizes the textual device of critical (Kumar 1991) or cognitive (Suvin 1980) estrangement, in which the image of the alien-animal-other serves to create the necessary distance by which we can criticize and examine current human norms *vis-à-vis* their relationship to Otherness generally. In this sense the representation of the reptoid could be considered savage, as it associates evil with contemporaneous notions of fascism, assimilative capitalism, hierarchy, war, and carnivorousness. Yet the castigation of these human-all-too-human behaviors comes at the expense of the vilification of reptiles (and other animals), and so the animal image in Icke becomes an icon upon which human vice can be projected and so sacrificed.[9] Additionally, in a similar manner, Icke (2002) decries the defining image of herbivorous and pastoral animals, which serves here to represent under-realized human potentials (14–15). In this sense, Icke's savage imagination appropriates the animal in a similar manner to Marx's own gothic imagination—both turn human systems of production into monsters via the vilification of animals. The representation of the animal in Icke's work, then, becomes an ambiguous code that represents human over (and under) development on all sides. Lacking any possibility of a positive valorization in and for itself, the image of the animal serves only to underwrite a savage, but ultimately heroic, narrative about distinctively human possibilities and futures—even if these humans are "schizos" and their communities are asynchronous. In other words, Icke's use of the allegorical animal to describe various states of human evolution is merely an anthropocentric imaginative turn upon which human foibles and fears are projected onto the UFOther, which acts as a phantasmatic screen for reenacting the very fears of the feral that fuel the anthropological machine. The problem here is that Icke has not become monstrous enough, and thus the appearance of difference is caught within a matrix of common sense assumptions about animals projected into human dramas. His paranoia dips back into a clinical level of superstitious myth-making in the name of humanist domination over and against the threatening other.

His call for reconception of unlimited cosmic Otherness based on the unlocked potentials of human love also seems too anthropocentric. As such Icke appears to move in the utopian tradition of other theorists of universal love such as Charles Fourier, who thought that cosmic harmony would necessitate the development of a new relationship between humans and nature such that novel animalities would arise. However, where Fourier imagined the possible existence of "antilions," "antisharks," and "antiseals" that would be friendly to humanity, he didn't imagine a correlative problem with the astronomer Lalande's "peculiar desire to eat live spiders" in the new amorous world (Geoghegan 1987, 20–21). This need to negate an image of radical animal differences—while simply expanding human liberty—speaks to the implicit inequalities of such a vision, and we believe a similar mistake occurs in the work of Icke.

If there has been a shift in the popular representation of aliens from the alien hatred of the 1950s (invasion narratives) to the alien love of the 2000s, Icke's pop-postmodernism seems to deconstruct binaries between these narratives. What appears to be a violent opposition between us (the human) and them (the alien-animal other) turns out to be an intergalactic love-fest where self and other implode through the unifying strong force of love. The gesture is ambiguous and could be read as an overcoming of hate by love, or one could see this as proof-positive of Neil Badmington's thesis that the turn to alien love in the 1990s is a repetition of alien hatred—both of which ultimately reinscribe the traditional humanist binary opposition between the human and the extraterrestrial. As Badmington (2004) writes, " 'Alien love' is a kind of humanism; 'alien love' is Alien Chic" (11). Alien Chic is therefore nothing more than an attempt to salvage the human from within the posthuman valorization of alien love.

Through his decisively anthropocentric projections, a deep anxiety is revealed in Icke's writing concerning the unknowable and unsymbolizable sensation of UFOtherness, captured by the reptoid. Icke's reptoid is ultimately a reactionary and conservative icon, and it seems to represent a future characterized by the "fifth discontinuity" (Best and Kellner 2001, 164–165), in which a superior species enslaves and perhaps destroys humanity. Hence, the reptoid can be read as an emblem of dystopian warning about limit transgression, and while the Ickean universe is one in which hybridity reigns, his final message ironically appears to be a caveat about courting monstrosity unabashedly. In other words, as a model for exopedagogy, his work ultimately caves in on itself. While superficially embracing the rhetoric of love as a unifying strong force, which crosses species and other boundaries, Icke is reluctant to truly engage the radical ambiguity posed by difference on its own terms and thus enter into the indeterminate zone of whatever being between human and alien and human and animal. Thus, the reptoid, as the figure of irreducible UFOtherness outside our decisively human common sense, is conveniently domesticated in the end. The great potential for dissensus is lost in the attempt to translate his close encounter with the UFOther into both a rousing historical narrative and a political clarion call that rehabilitates a recognizably humanist project. A real ethic of reptoid difference would have to face the terrifying possibility that a close encounter with alien love—if we can even call it such—may disgust, baffle, or horrify our human sensibilities. Interestingly, UFO folklorist Thomas Bullard (2000) notes that such a conception is presently gaining favor amongst UFO abductees, who are advancing a notion of "The Change": a "time when hybrids and normal humans coexist in a world of extraordinary beauty. Yet this coexistence will be altogether on alien terms. Their paradise is a soulless alien realm that snuffs out the uniqueness of humanity and leaves little hope that we can avert its coming" (182). Without an embrace of this change, Icke's imagination topples into an anthropocentric and superstitious form of clinical paranoia concerning the safety of humanist boundaries inside of capitalism rather than beyond it. Therefore, Icke's final utopian call to love the reptoid-within does not go far enough. The reptoid-within must be allowed to transform or, as the case may be, mutate the sensations of love as such, otherwise the reptoid becomes a trained alter-ego that crushes the transgressive and revolutionary power capable of producing new valences of love in the surplus common between human and animals, earthlings and space creatures.

CONCLUSION: REPTOIDS OF THE WORLD UNITE?

Irresistible and bittersweet that loosener of limbs,
Love reptile-like strikes me down.
                              —Sappho

David Icke's project is twofold: to provide a searching and devastating critique of the mainstream (the savage imagination) and then to offer an alternative, love, as a positive vision that might replace that which he has previously annulled (zoömorphic imagination). Yet, as we have suggested earlier, this call for love is ambiguous, merely reinforcing a traditional, humanist subject and complying with the affective economy of global capitalism. In fact, Icke's entire project ultimately is reduced to sustaining the integrity of the autonomous human subject who is interested in transforming the world into a metaphor for self-understanding and self-realization—a classically superstitious and anthropocentric narrative structure. For Icke, the process of personal awakening unfolds, then, as follows: fascism negated by a complex of paranoid conspiracies that is then doubly negated by the personal awareness of what the Upanishads refer to as "*Tat tvam asi*"—"Thou art That" (*Encyclopaedia Britannica*)—a final move that is not the radical desubjectification that he seems to desire. In other words, his notion of love does not completely break with the "five sense prison" of the human anthropological machine and can be read diagnostically as the truth of what Badmington calls "alien love" in general, which is nothing more than a restaging of alien hatred.

The famed ufologist Jacques Vallee seems to chart out the terrain missed by Icke's exopedagogy, remarking upon how states of non-ordinary consciousness may be connected to experiences of alien conspiracy:

> I am going to be very disappointed if UFOs turn out to be nothing more than visitors from another planet...I think the UFO phenomena [*sic*] is teaching us that we do not understand time and space...At this level, it does not matter whether or not UFOs are real. If people believe that something is real, then it is real in its effects...Could the UFO phenomenon be manipulating us? Could it be a teaching system of some sort? Perhaps something that we are creating ourselves...Or, could it be manipulated purposely by people who have the technology to simulate UFO sightings?...There is another way of thinking about this. We are at a time of crisis on earth. We have the means of destroying the planet, which we have never had before in human history. It may be that there is a collective unconscious. Perhaps we are creating the visions we need to survive, in order to transcend the crisis. Perhaps there are no UFOs in a manufactured sense. (Qtd in Mishlove 1993, 184)

Vallee here clearly recognizes the exopedagogy of UFO phenomena. The "teaching system" professes a powerful lesson: that our world is trapped in a five sense prison, and thus limited in our ability to hear, to see, and to feel the appearance of difference within time and space. It is the appearance of the UFOther as a complex natureculture production not reducible to subjective fantasy alone that is necessary to survive and thrive against the separation of the commons from an interplanetary germinal life force that blurs distinctions between human/alien/animal.

More recently, John Mack, the Harvard psychiatrist vilified for his positive studies of UFO abductee experiences, has spoken of the need to transcend "the dualistic mind" that erupts in self/other relations that underlie warfare and terrorism. Conclusions such as the following again attempt to move beyond Icke in order to realize his own goals for an education out of bounds of the five sense prison:

> Humanity seems to be at a turning point. We are experiencing a kind of race to the future between the forces of destruction and creation. The preservation of our lives and possibilities will come not from the strategies of terrorists, nor from the bombs of the self-righteous. This can happen only through a great awakening, a worldwide shift in consciousness that can transcend the habits of dualism, and enable the citizens of the Earth to become a genuine family of people and peoples, in which each of us can come to feel a responsibility for the welfare of all. As Gandhi once said, "We must *be* the change." (Mack 2002, 17)

But, as is the fate of all attempts to represent the unrepresentable such utopian visions ultimately fall back upon themselves, stagnating under the pull of an anthropocentric and superstitious imaginative tractor beam. Mack once again insists on a preexisting humanity that is on the verge of a change or turning point. Rather than see humanity as always already alien, Mack locates himself decisively within a humanist problematic at the very moment when he is attempting to overcome humanism by emphasizing the progressive possibilities of alien abduction. While it might be argued that in calling for a redeemed version of "love thy enemy" Icke presents an allegory that promotes a necessary and renewed attention to the appearance of animality and Otherness, Icke's stereotypical images of the animal as unreasonable, emotionless beyond fear, and concerned only with basic survival instincts serve as reactionary themes within his work that reinstate the hierarchies defining humanism. Indeed, upon reading his voluminous alien conspiracy theory as an allegory, one senses that the reptoid serves at the level of narrative as little more than a foil for a romance about the potential heroism dormant in today's humanity—the larger community of liberal subjects for whom play is just play and a game is just a game.

In light of this paradox, perhaps it is appropriate to end this essay with our own clarion call for a new exo-revolution that re-incorporates—as part of a larger whole—Icke's reptoid ethos into the ongoing struggle against the forces of capitalism. We are unwilling to give up on the utopian aspects of Icke's imagination and the project of exopedagogy more broadly. Icke has tapped into the strange sensations of disquietude and dissimulation that perturb the present historical moment. Right-wing fanatics,[10] leftist conspiracy buffs, New Agers, college students, and an increasingly dissatisfied and questioning multitude the world over have found something deeply provocative in Icke that cannot simply be explained away as manifestations of a collective false-consciousness, clinical paranoia, or, as Freud would say, group hypnosis. Icke's politics are more complex than such characterizations, as is his contradictory relationship with capitalism and media spectacle. It is our conclusion that theories such as Icke's can be utilized to point us in a direction in which the exopedagogical imagination envisions new forms of whatever life that suspend the anthropological machine. With recent reports of ever-increasing rain forest destruction—this despite over two decades of global concern and education—the idea that the future hopes for existing endangered flora and fauna may in fact depend on letting idle the problematic of humanist pedagogy that always teaches the lesson of human identity set against the animal other.

In this respect, Icke's call to awaken to the greater cosmic significance of love and the univocity of the One—with his implied insistence that the non-awakened shall be committed to the spectral Hades of a growing military-industrial complex purgatory framed by dire poverty and extinction of hell, on the one hand, and the Hollywood Hills of heaven, on the other—strikes us as the lasting impact of his exopedagogy. As capitalism violently transforms the world in opposition to ecologies of place, the world stands in need of a massive transformation in a counter-direction. Icke's notion that such transformation may be effected through the emblem of transgression, in which we signify our commitment both to the locality we inhabit and to the larger forces of life through the invention and deployment of new savage and zoömorphic aesthetics, represents a sort of utopia that moves beyond the merely fanciful, and it is exactly this sort of thinking and practice that is unfortunately missing within much of the presently more secular and materialist-oriented antiwar and alterglobalization scene.

3

FAERY FAITHS: ALTERMODERNITY
AND THE DIVINE VIOLENCE
OF EXOPEDAGOGY

the earth we pace
Again appears to be
An unsubstantial, faery place;
That is fit home for Thee!

—Wordsworth

The subjective spirit which cancels the animation of nature can master
a despiritualized nature only by imitating its rigidity and despiritual-
izing itself in turn.

—Adorno and Horkheimer

In this chapter we will further develop the central concepts that define the practice and theory of exopedagogy. In particular we will look more closely at the aesthetic dimension of the UFOther and argue that all critical pedagogical practices must begin with a sensorial alternation—an opening beyond what Icke describes as "five sense prison" into the disfiguration of the monstrous. We will also argue that sensorial alternation is not simply a *redistribution* of the sensible, but at its most radical a *rupture* of a new sensorium that attempts to suspend the logic of sense underlying contemporary power relations. In particular, we will argue that the UFOther of the faery is a particular zoömorphic and savage imaginative threshold for touching upon the enigmatic kernel of monstrous life that disturbs the economy of death defining current biopower, thus opening up a location for what Walter Benjamin describes as the "creaturely." Here creatural life is an ethical and aesthetic response to overcoming the boundaries between the human and the nonhuman sustained by the anthropological machine (Hanssen 2000).

Our choice to focus on fairy faith is far from arbitrary. Rather fairies are "creating a pop culture wave" (Dunnewind 2006) worth billions of dollars to the media industry of spectacular-democracy. Major films such as *The Spiderwick Chronicles*, video releases such as the Barbie Fairytopia series (which has now also been turned into a hit musical for the stage), best-selling books such as *Fairyopolis* and the *Artemis Fowl* collection, and Nickelodeon's hugely popular television show The Fairly OddParents have quickly become vital cultural capital for many kids, thanks in large part to mega-corporations such as Disney and Mattel moving to turn the fairy into *the* childhood commodity of the early twenty-first century. With sales increases of fairy-themed products up as much as 40 percent since 2005, the marketplace is becoming increasingly saturated and adorned by shimmering little people with colorful wings, wish-granting magic, and a kind of gentle sweetness that is very much the antithesis to our larger sociopolitical climate of genocidal war, ecological catastrophe, and ubiquitous greed.

Of course, fairy tales that appeal to idealizations of childhood innocence are nothing new. Great similarities exist, for instance, between the present moment and the form of popularity that fairies enjoyed throughout Britain after World War I, when a major cultural spectacle was generated over the possible pastoral existence of the Cottingley fairies[1] and items such as Cicely Mary Barker's Flower Fairy books became national bestsellers. There is, then, perhaps a kind of universal cultural logic at work in both cases—confronted by the blight of imperialism and industry that is the modern Mordor, people tend to find happy, fairy-filled fantasies of Tolkien's shire appealing and eminently consumable.[2] Those of us who are not ourselves the masters of capital can still at least clamor for the verdant peace of our own private Hobbiton, an imaginary place in which we tarry merrily and so let the horrors of the day slip into reveries that the world remains ever as it has been and social crisis is not worthy of our vigilant alarm. In this sense, the moral injunction of Solomon's "This too shall pass" has been transformed into a kind of fairy pedagogy for capitalism akin to the "We're making progress" of George W. Bush. Both serve to opiate the masses' suffering in favor of a form of spiritual equanimity that really amounts to little more than the attempt to fashion people to work as placated agents for the monetization of hedonism.

Ironically, then, in their disturbing complicity with mendacious capitalist agendas, today's fairies are not so dissimilar from present ruling class interests. Indeed Jack Zipes (1997; 2002), a careful social

critic of fairy tales in both their old and new varieties, has illuminated
how the genre, far from serving as a sanctuary from pathological values and norms, has almost always served to reproduce them in easily
digestible ways for children (as well as adults) and should thus be
considered as a socializing tool.[3] Relatedly, W. E. B. DuBois (1968)
has commented on how people "allow their children to learn fairy
tales...which in time the children come to recognize as conventional
lies told by their parents and teachers for the children's good. One
can hardly exaggerate the moral disaster of the custom." What is the
tooth fairy after all but a creation of American post–World War II
affluence (Tuleja cited in Narváez, 1997), and a child's first ritualistic
initiation into the commodity form? As folklorist Tad Tuleja states,
"the unstated subtext of the Tooth Fairy ritual is 'produce and sell' "
(416). Are fairies, then, just stooges for the status quo?

  We believe that this is not necessarily the case, but a distinction
is therefore demanded. In this chapter, we would like to differentiate between "fairy," as in fairy tale or fairy-themed commodity
products, and "faery," a paranormal, supernatural phenomenon
associated with spirits and magical experiences of creatural life.[4]
By our account, the fairy is a cultural artifact whose force is con-
sonant with image-capitalism and spectacle while the faery is an
indigenous, psycho-spiritual[5] becoming-animal that implicitly challenges social domination and oppression by erupting into unques-
tioned and rigidified hierarchical orders of the industrialized global
North.[6] While fairies are the ornaments of a world jailed by disenchantment—Max Weber's "specialists without spirit, sensual-
ists without heart" (1958, 182)—in our view faeries can represent
savage and zoömorphic transgressions of contemporary forms of
anthropocentric domination and destruction of complex natureculi-
ture assemblages. Opposed to the immunizing dialectic of health
and death where life of the polis is predicated on the exclusion of
natural life, we therefore posit "faery" as a rupturing element—a
UFOther—that can potentially serve as a beacon of resistance in
the ongoing defense of life against the logic of the anthropological machine. Stated differently, the fairy is a form of superstitious
imagination (commodification and reification) whereas the faery is
a violent force of the savage imagination (the power of the common)
that intensifies and revitalizes the constituting powers of a form-of-
life that escapes measure. In what follows, we shall attempt to chart
how the fairy and faery converge and diverge within a biopolitical
and biopoetic matrix. It is important to remember that although
the fairy can be seen as an immunized version of the faery, the

inoculating trace of the faery remains a utopian promise that can produce counter-imaginings from within the commodity form. In other words, the fairy cannot be simply or easily reduced to a mere ideological distortion of the faery, nor can the apparent dichotomy be strictly sublated through dialectical movement. Rather the two are specific biograms of feeling though emerging from within particular political, environmental, cultural, and economic contexts.

Drawing on our analysis of the reptoid in chapter two of this book, we would like to further examine the imaginative practices of contemporary faery subcultures, with a specific focus upon how these utopian communities can shed light on alternative educational and political forms of creatural life. Through an exopedagogical approach to these faery countercultures we hope to produce novel theoretical and imaginative tools for thinking both in and against dominant forms of biopower that have had an increasingly destructive effect on the natural world and on human and non-human animals.

FAERY PEDAGOGIES

> Imagination alone tells me what *can* be.
> —Breton

While researching faery subcultures, we were struck by the overt relationship between those interested in the fey and the theme of education. It turns out that there are entire organizations, such as the Fairy Congress, that conduct annual conferences, and that invite international representatives from both the human and faery worlds to attend. Indeed, the Fairy Congress frames its charter directly in terms of a dialogical educational mission to bring faeries and humans together to learn from one another and foster better relations between the two worlds.[7] Other noted faery scholars such as R. J. Stewart also argue that the interaction between faeries and humans is one of learning or re-education (we would say) against oppressive forms of contemporary education that de-legitimate indigenous and mythical forms of knowing the world (www.rjstewart. org/irish-faery.html).

But what exactly is distinctive about faery pedagogy? What are its methods, and what is it trying to convey? The method and curriculum of faery pedagogies are varied (Bloom 1998; Helliwell 1997; Hodson 1982; Maclean 1990; Morgan 2009; Steiner 1992). Perhaps it is in the works of R. J. Stewart that we find the most comprehensive instructional guide to contacting the faery realm. Describing his own faery workshops, Stewart (1995) writes,

> In faery workshops we use traditional themes, images, and techniques· to change individual and group awareness. We also enter (literally and in full awareness) the faery realm and encounter faery beings. In the more advanced stages of this type of work a dialogue is developed, a relationship in which the human and faery beings act as allies, and this alliance is gradually extended to other orders of living creatures. (12)

The pedagogy is composed of two interrelated methods. First there are energy techniques that attempt to transform the body (make the nervous system itself receptive to the shocking sensation of the UFOther) and second there are visual and imaginative techniques that work on the mind (that intensify these sensations through various forms of visualization or narrativization). Combining meditation, narrative story-telling, and dream work, Stewart suggests that the human student can enter into an altered state wherein new alliances between humans, faeries, and other nonhuman beings can join forces against ecological degradation. Here Stewart highlights the differences between his own faery pedagogy and other forms of New Age mysticism.[8] New Ageism often is, despite its aura of Aquarian spirituality, detached from the land[9] and traditional knowledge systems (Aldred 2000), and thus it leads to forms of consciousness that are increasingly otherworldly and globalist (which is the fantasy of the liberal humanist subject [Hayles 1999]). Linking spirituality and philosophical thinking to the land and with material forces of life through faery cultures is for Stewart (1992) "one method of restoring the land to health," thereby providing for the re-energization of compelling forms of ecological activism (7). For him, faery pedagogy is therefore not a form of retreat from catastrophic realities (as the fairy of media culture or New Age celestial transcendence would suggest) but rather a biopolitical and ecological mind/body practice that warns against the dangers of abandoning our ancient places. Yet if alliances are built, these alliances are not strictly on human terms, for the faery remains elusive, a trickster, whose forms and shapes are often frightening figurations of an uncanny other decisively at odds with human aspirations and potential good intentions—"assistants" (Agamben 2007a) that nevertheless subvert human expectations for helpful friendships. As Stewart wisely points out, "Many of the occupants [of faery worlds] are friendly towards their human cousins, but not all. Which is hardly surprising, when we consider how blindly destructive we have been. So maybe we need some caution and respect in this realm, rather than romantic wishful thinking?" (http://www.dreampower.com/faery.html).

Stewart suggests repeatedly in his writings that learning from faeries is ultimately learning how to relate to the land and to nature more generally in a different, less aggressive, and less exploitive manner. As Stewart (1995) writes, "revival of our [contemporary] contact with the faery realm is an environmental and even global issue...This contact between human and non-human beings, once shunned and rejected, is now sought actively as a potential source of re-balance in a time of environmental crisis" (8). In such passages, Stewart argues that the Enlightenment tradition has transformed nature into mere raw material and submitted it to a means-end paradigm of utility that destroys imaginative links that otherwise serve to bind humans to the land through ethical practices of respect and admiration, but also fear. Such critique could be seen as a popular incarnation of what Adorno and Horkheimer (2002) referred to as the dialectic of enlightenment—yet with a surprising twist. While Stewart would agree that enlightenment has currently been transformed from a liberating to an oppressive practice, he would nevertheless refrain from the general stigmatization of the premodern storyteller inherent in Adorno and Horkheimer's approach. For Adorno and Horkheimer, myth contains within itself the seeds of enlightenment's domination of nature, but for Stewart it also contains—in another set of dialectical reversals—the potential zoömorphic and savage imaginative resources for overcoming of these destructive potentials. Thus, while a critical theorist such as Habermas (1982) can be interpreted as attempting through his work to save reason (as an historical project and goal) from the snares of Horkheimer and Adorno's analysis, a faery pedagogue such as Stewart importantly articulates the complementary second half of this rehabilitation process: saving myth from the jaws of rational instrumentality. As such, Stewart is akin to Walter Benjamin's storyteller (1985), who uses the faery tale to "shake off the nightmare which the myth had placed upon its chest" while retaining the implicit "liberating magic" of myth that instrumental reason lacks (102). In other words, storytelling is, as Agamben (2007) might argue, a "profanation" of myth—its return to common or free usage beyond the sacrifice that always adheres to the sacred. The faery tale is, in other words, a state of exception between pure information and mythical repetition—an altered state populated by strange facts resistant to capture by the five sense prison and open to new thought feelings. It is a particularly savage form of imagination that is not reducible to superstition (which binds us to the Power of capitalism and the nation-state) but rather recognizes the explicit need for lines of flight or exodus from commodification and domination.

The knowledge that Stewart suggests is therefore not simply the remnant of an irrational antimodernity (as Horkheimer and Adorno would suggest) nor is it a linear return to an indigenous belief system that is premodern. As Hardt and Negri (2009) argue, there are differences between various articulations of the antimodern—those that are decisively territorializing (a return to the force of the sovereign) and those that invent "new rationalities and new forms of liberation" (97). Of course there are destructive forms of antimodernity such as the Nazi movement, but this historical fact should not act as precedence for acknowledging the equally rich traditions of liberatory antimodernity found in peasant revolts, workers' movements, and a variety of postcolonial and ecological struggles that discover within traditional knowledge systems and ecological ways of being powerful resources for living out of bounds of nation-state control or capitalist biopower. It is this history of revolutionary insurgency set against all hierarchies and all dialectics of inclusion and exclusion that transforms antimodernity into what Hardt and Negri refer to as the savage imagination of "altermodernity," which is "defined not by opposition but by rupture and transformation" (104). Altermodernity is not a return to the roots or origins of a timeless indigenous past where humans were at one with the earth through mythological wholism. Rather it is a state of becoming-faery that constantly invents new forms of natureculture relations, constantly discovers the potentiality of various "morphisms" as an interactive and dynamic zone of multiple, parallel, and most of all monstrous struggles for liberation. To use Deleuze and Guattari's language (1983), faery culture is not merely a return to a tribal social body that attributes productivity to one or more of the enchanted regions of the earth and in turn, territorializes organic and inorganic flows through geographical limitation. At the same time, faery culture is not the radical deterritorialization of material flows under capitalism—flows that abstract the knowledge systems tied to specific places and landscapes. Rather the altermodernities of faery cultures side with the local, insurgent force of natureculture artifactual relations to combat the destructive intensities of capitalism on a global scale—thus finding synergy between singularities and the commonwealth.

As Stewart himself suggests, resurgence of interests in faeries is not an accident, but is related to current perceptions of climate change, global warming, and massive biological devastation—that is, the global zoocide that marred the twentieth century (Kahn 2005; 2006). According to Agamben (1998), the principal object of thanatopower is not the administered, regulated, and homogenized human body as such but *zoë* (natural or nutritive life), drained of its immanent powers and thus reduced to a passive form of bare life. If the thanatopower of the sovereign is predicated on the production of life as bare life, then Stewart's imagination attempts to reconnect with life as an indistructable, generative, and plentiful vitality and thus *active ally* against capitalism. This notion of *zoë* as indestructible is perhaps best seen in the epic image of the earth elemental's death in the movie *Hellboy II: The Golden Army* (2008). When Hellboy "kills" the gigantic elemental, its humanoid form gives way to a sprawling green oasis of living green vegetation blanketing the urban landscape—an image of the rhizomatic power of the life of the multitude to recompose itself even in its moment of monumental destruction (moving from an organized body to a body without organs, where the organs themselves are deterritorialized through decomposition and recomposition of parts). It is precisely the inability to contain and organize life (and thus dictate its form and function) that is so frustrating for immunization and its infernal dialectic of bio/thanatopowers. Through acts of sovereign decision-making that immunize *bios*—the agency that founds the ordering of society—*zoë* is included only through its excommunication from the political sphere (an included exclusion). As the earth elemental suggests, this reduction is never complete, bare life is never truly bare. Rather there is an immeasurable (non-quantifiable) power within *zoë* that cannot be regulated—a multidimensional and multiplicitious realm of life that pervades both organic and inorganic matter. While those inspired by deconstruction often characterize life as fragile, finite, and vulnerable (Derrida 2002), we would instead argue that life is monstrously productive and resilient, containing in it immense power of invention and generation—a "germinal life" with "tremendous inhuman force" (Ansell-Pearson 1999, 10) . In this sense we agree with Donna Haraway who argues that Derrida's emphasis on shared suffering and the ethic of pity are important but too limiting. Shifting questions, Haraway (2008a) asks: "What if work and play, and not just pity, open up when the possibility of mutual response, without names, is taken seriously [between species]..." (22). Through work and play (forms of bioproduction), monstrous life (which does not have a name) emerges as a "living-in-common" of the multitude. Thus, we would argue, the stumbling block for immunization is the very source of power and insurgent force of the biopolitical multitude. We call for a shift in the politics of life from an ethical identification with the fragility and suffering of organisms to an alliance with the power of germinal life as a vast field of organic and inorganic involutions.[10]

It is the struggle between the productive magnitude of germinal life—the unruly flesh of human and nonhuman bioproduction—and the seemingly infinite destructive capacity of capitalism that forms the matrix from which Stewart's faery imagination amplifies its monstrous dimensions and becomes politically insurgent. In our view, faery pedagogy hopes to teach a new relationship between *zoë* and *bios*, in which *zoë* is no longer transformed into "bare life" as the sacrificial object of sovereign force. Here we reach the aim of faery pedagogy: the rupturing sensation of the power of *zoë* through a new practice of biopoetics. Stated differently, through faery close encounters the unimaginable dimensions of *zoë* can enter into the sphere of biopower as a radical eruption of an altermodernity, whose logic is immanent to life rather than held above it in judgment. In this way, the faery holds a unique location as an imaginary other poised in a zone of indistinction between the subject and object where the faery, much like the reptoid, is an uncanny presence that disturbs the partition of the sensible between what can and cannot be imagined.

Stewart, in particular, consciously side-steps the issue of the "reality" of faeries (www.rjstewart.org/irish-faery.html). Instead he focuses on the *sensation* of the UFOther as a material disorganization of the superstitious imagination. For Stewart, the superstitious imagination acts as an obstacle to faery encounters, cramming the mind with preconceived clichés that prevent a close encounter of the *n*th degree. His meditative practice is an attempt to disconnect the senses from representational figuration of the imagination and become immersed in the multidimensional sensuality of the multitude as a natureculture network or assemblage struggling against destruction and domination of Western industrialization. Citing Deleuze (2003), we would argue that the fairy is a *figuration* (a representation that has been reified and incorporated into the dominant narrative of Western expansion and cooptation of ecological difference), whereas the faery is a *Figure* that is the "master of deformations" (32). If the imagination in its common sense articulation focuses on recognition and identification and thus is complicit with an anthropocentric and superstitious narrative, then the Figure of sensation marks the event of exodus from this order—a creative and generative dismantling of pregiven signs of alien chic. Rather than abstract, the Figure for Deleuze is concrete, linked specifically to nerves, bodies, and forces. Likewise for Stewart, the faery is not to be understood as having been reduced to a mere subjective product of the liberal humanist imagination—and thus a unilateral and highly anthropocentric projection onto nature. In his descriptions, the faery is more properly conceived as a set of indeterminate sensations arising from our attention to the forces of nature that exist in excess of figuration. This is particularly the case when the practitioner encounters giants and titans whose scale and power exceed measure, entering into a dimension beyond the five sense prison. Thus Stewart's imagination is not simply savage but also zoömorphic, recognizing that creativity arises when the human *animal* speaks, when the world of animal life and natural forces are upheld as creative and regenerative forces (Norris 1985). For example, Stewart's concept (1992) of the "underworld" is a presentation of the "unknowable" that lies "beyond expression" yet nevertheless finds a Figure, through our reconstruction of ancient faery storytelling in light of pressing, very real ecological problems (101). Importantly, this conceptualization of the underworld stands as a provocative inversion of Plato's cave. Against Plato's rejection of the cave as a house of shadow and delusion, Stewart encourages us to return from the disembodied forms of reason/spirituality (as represented by New Age practices) into these subterranean spaces where imagination once again connects the nerves of the body with the flows, intensities, and convulsions of an earth that is being pushed to its limits. Likewise, Gaelic scholar John MacInnes suggests that faery hills are "a metaphor of the imagination" (pers. commun., in McIntosh 2005)—a zone of indistinction where musicians or poets would fall asleep expecting to awake either mad or inspired. As such, the faeries represent the situated interface of a potent form of natural and human cultural creativity—a wherever location, an affective biogram of imaginative becomings that exist not only beyond the subject's unconscious but also beyond the boundaries of the subject's body. In this sense, Stewart adequately describes the imagination not as a purely *subjective realm* of fantasy so much as a site of presubjective and post-subjective flows and intensities—the seat of the transversal commonwealth (see Intermezzo) between natureculture assemblages.

This location of the faery betwixt and between nature and culture is a no-man's-land or exceptional state where cultural and natural histories bleed into one another. In other words, Stewart is calling for a reconceptualization of history that is no longer anthropocentric or anchored only in the cognitive faculties and concerns of the liberal humanist subject. Stewart as a contemporary storyteller is, as Benjamin describes, interested in the remnants of traditional wisdom and ecological experience lost to the contemporary, information/data driven world of utility, calculation, and measuring/ immunization. For Benjamin, the storyteller gains authority not through exhaustive explanation or cataloguing but rather through his or her relation to natural history. Thus, in a story by the writer Philip Philopovich, Benjamin (1968) highlights the centrality of "the voice of nature" (105), which supersedes the voice of the human characters to articulate the hidden truth of the narrative, thus calling for a new respect toward the inhuman, subhuman, or creaturely element that exists in excess of humanistic logocentrism. Storytelling—as a profanation of myth—deconstructs the hierarchy of being that is erected through the exclusivity of the sovereign decision over life. In Leskov's story "The Alexandrite," Benjamin notes how "the mineral is the lowest strata of created things. For the storyteller, however, it is directly joined to the highest" (107). It is through the lifeless and inert qualities of the stone chrysoberyl that Leskov tells the story—transforming that which appears static and unchanging (nature) into the temporal unfolding of world history while also demonstrating the static qualities of that which appears dynamic and self-determining (the eternal return of oppression and domination that scars the human world). Thus the storyteller enters into a zone of indistinction that troubles the privileged qualities of the human (as hierarchically superior to mere nature) and of human history (as the teleological unfolding of freedom and self-determination) though a concentrated effort to study the creaturely. This is a new profane history told through openness and attentiveness to the forgotten and seemingly mute surface of nature that nevertheless speaks a language of things predating human logos. For Beatrice Hanssen (2000), Benjamin's insistence (1968) on natural history is "characterized by a radical openness to the creaturely—that is, an alterity that surpassed the confines of the merely human" (6). The faery that Stewart describes is precisely the creaturely excess in the human—the monstrous dimension of the human captured for a fleeting moment in the ruptural nature of the UFOther. It is the sensation of this paradoxical and conflictual meeting point between nature and culture, social and natural histories that breaks down common sense barriers between human and animal policed by the anthropological machine. If the faery is a Figure, then, as Deleuze (2003) argues, it is the location of "a *zone of indiscernability or undecidability* between man and animal" (20). In other words, it is the site of creaturely becomings that are then translated into new narratives of altermodernity that challenge the logic of sense defining biopower and its internal relationship with sacrifice and domination of the natural world.

While many faery pedagogues emphasize the centrality of joy in the close encounter with the sensation of the UFOther, the emotional register of these relations are more precisely characterized by a haunting melancholia. For the faery spiritual guide Catherine Morgan (2009), faery encounters are decisively melancholic: "You see the living tree, by extending its roots into the Earth, extends also a network of understanding, anchoring in place a great database of knowledge and wisdom. Much of that has been lost, torn away in the tragedy that is also known as human evolution . . . we [the guardians of the woods] weep in the silence of the night" (43). The incorporation of the lost object (Morgan's "great database of knowledge and wisdom") causes a breakdown of signification, leaving traces of the profound psychical sensation of a haunting. Summarizing Freud's theory of melancholy, Agamben (1993a) writes that melancholia is an imaginative capacity that "succeeds in appropriating its own object only to the extent that it affirms its loss" (20). The lost object cannot be expressed, cannot be fully worked through, and yet, for Freud, this is precisely the seat of critical agency. The subject refuses to give up (to mourn) on lost causes, traumatic events, compromised ideals, broken promises, and so on. In other words, the subject remains faithful to a loss, does not give way to that which has been sacrificed, and as such refuses to "move on" or "get over it." As Ranjana Khanna (2003) argues in her postcolonial analysis of melancholia, "One could, to some extent, say the structure of haunting would be similar in any group entering into a liberal democracy that was based on their exclusion: women entering into full citizenship in postcolonial contexts, or indeed otherwise, could similarly experience melancholic haunting" (263). In other words, it is the violence of colonization that returns to haunt generations and thus prevent the total assimilation of the subaltern into the political identity of the nation-state. The melancholic gaze, as argued in the Intermezzo, is a creaturely gaze that opens a state of exception between the human and nonhuman animal. The faery is the trace of this creaturely haunting—neither fully self nor other, speaking to both a proximity to the natural world as well as an immanent cleavage from this world. Rather than simply a passive acceptance of the scar of the sovereign decision against life, melancholia can become an active feeling for accelerating a savage and zoömorphic imagination.

Within our current state of highly standardized education, then, faery pedagogy represents a form of decisively political poetics that can open up new configurations of the order of things, scramble ideological codes, create new sensory experiences that lie beyond naïve empiricism or degenerate science, and establish new spiritual connections with the exocultural as a cradle for reimagining a wide range of extant nature/culture dichotomies and hierarchies. In its most radical formulation, exopedagogy is not simply yet another biopedagogy but is rather *a struggle to disrupt the underlying sovereign decision* that inaugurates and sustains the thanatos of biopower: the ban against the constitutive and generative powers of life itself. Rather than simply another becoming-animal of capitalism (Shukin 2010), or another organization of the sensible within a given police order (Rancière 2006), the faery is a strike against the fundamental dialectic of immunization that is always predicated on a sovereign decision over life. For Stewart, the sensation of the UFOther that is the faery offers a new line of flight into an altermodernity that lies parallel yet is irreducible to the fundamental and inaugural ban that *is* the nomos of the contemporary Western biopolitical order. It is a disfiguring aesthetic gesture of animal-becoming that deforms the body of the human (opening its sense organs to new valences of experience) but also deforms the collective body of the community that sacrifices the faery at the altar of the fairy commodity. In short, faery pedagogy is not simply a redistribution of the senses, but at its most savage, it strikes a blow to our superstitious reverence for the sovereign law and its sacrifice of the monstrous.

Such pedagogy also differs from critical pedagogy, as defined by Paulo Freire (2000), when it aims to transcend naïve or magical thinking in favor of critical consciousness. However, it is not clear that all variants of critical pedagogy assume a hierarchical taxonomy of consciousness types. For instance, the critical pedagogue Peter McLaren (1999) writes inspirationally of the disruptive power of the Exú spirits in Brazilian folk religious practices such as Umbanda, Macumba, or Quimbanda that can provide the "grain of insanity...necessary to challenge the power of capital" (lxvii). McLaren's comments are suggestive but incomplete. Here we would like to further this line of thought and suggest that faery pedagogy is not directly concerned with the production of critical consciousness but rather with modes of sensorial *alternation* that can open up a new field of imagination to affects barred from what Icke referred to as "the five sense prison." In other words, it reconnects the savage imagination with the radical biopoetics of a monstrous form of life. The state of the faery is quite literally an altered one (Grof 1985). Just as the work of art in the aesthetic regime according to Rancière (2006) "throws off the pre-constituted political modes of framing" (64) so too does faery pedagogy train the eye to look beyond the given and to revision our relations to nonhuman life. While the critical pedagogy tradition importantly exposes the underlying reality of exploitation beneath ideological mystifications, then, a faery pedagogy of sensorial alternation apprehends utopian possibilities by working to multiply and intensify the doors of perception on a sensual level of what can and cannot be seen, heard, and so on (Blake 1994). Such an alternation ruptures the determining force of the five sense prison through a synesthetic mixing of nature/culture dichotomies within a savage and zoömorphic imagination. If biopedagogy hails the student ("Hey You There!") and gives a mandate to assume a recognizable subject position, then the hailing of the faery is to flee ("Fly Away With Me In the Night!"), an exodus to new horizons of the natureculture continuum—a wherever place of disappearance, desubjectification, and monstrous, open-ended becomings that privilege life over the economy of death. In other words, such pedagogy tries to alter the aesthetic unconscious out of which versions of critical appraisal are themselves produced. Without a new emphasis on sensorial alternation, Freire's critical consciousness remains within the partitioning of the sensible set in motion by the anthropological machine of education (even if that education is in the name of "liberation"). The fear in other words is that cognition (as a human faculty of judgment) will become detached from the creaturely world of sensation, resulting in what Daniel Heller-Roazen (2007) has described as the "common insensitivity" of "the anaesthetic animal" (289). Thus sensorial alternation works on the affective in order to return the anaesthetic animal of critical pedagogy to its savage and zoömorphic imagination.

To be clear, we are not advocating here for the replacement of one pedagogical form with the other but rather see critical consciousness as the result of an aesthetic disorganization and synesthetic reorganization. Just as the primordial faery is easily mistaken for New Age and corporate fairydom without a recognition of the structural forces of political economy that currently strive to banish zoë in all its variations save for "bare life," those who seek a project of conscientization need to recognize the utopian possibilities in cultivating alternative modes of sensual awareness. If there is new interest in Walter Benjamin's "Theses on the Philosophy of History" (1985) perhaps it would not be inappropriate to argue that critical pedagogy must recognize that behind the puppet of historical materialism is not the hunchbacked dwarf of theology but the winged faery of Neopaganism who once against disturbs common sense through a heightened awareness of the sensation of difference and disfigurement that is creatural life. Stated differently, *sensorial alternation is the incubation of a new and monstrous swarm intelligence, the feeling of thought's narrativization of altermodernity beyond the sovereign ban over life.* Gregory Cajete (2000) carefully documents how indigenous epistemologies offer a rich alternative tradition for science in which humans and nonhumans (including celestial beings that can take the form of the Trickster) learn and communicate with one another as part of a universe of interdependence. Likewise, Ivana Milojevic (2006) has insightfully argued for a need to incorporate alternative utopian visions (beyond the merely critical) into a predominantly neoliberal educational discourse. Such "edutopias," she suggests, include feminist pedagogies, indigenous epistemologies, spiritual enlightenment, peace education, and ecological perspectives. In our opinion, the figure of the faery and the practice of biopoetics include all these elements and as such produce unique aesthetic opportunities for imagining impossible perceptions and narrating new forms of altermodernity without recourse to species or genus distinctions.

Sensorial alternation is therefore an affective *excitation* of the self when confronted with the monstrous, which is both familiar and strange, neither proper nor improper. Sensation excites, but it also ex*sights*—opening up a sight that is beyond the bounded sight of the police order (the motto of the police is, as Rancière reminds us, "Move along, there is nothing to see here!"). It also ex*sites* in the sense that it opens the subject up to wherever as the indeterminate and creative nexus of nature and culture in the form of an ecologically expansive and expressive multitude. Thus excitation is the aesthetic foundation of the exodus that characterizes exopedagogy from Icke's five sense prison. In other words, excitation is the sensation of a persistent melancholia becoming a *joy*, which is the affect of an increase of our collective powers of creation and invention central to the democratic insurgencies of the multitude.

From Elf Shot to Arson: Faery Cultural Politics and Direct Action

Beltane, 1997
Welcome to the struggle of all species to be free.
We are the burning rage of this dying planet...Our greatest weapons are imagination and the ability to strike when least expected...We take inspiration from Luddites, Levellers, Diggers, the Autonome

squatter movement, the ALF, the Zapatistas, and the little people—
those mischievous elves of lore. Authorities can't see us because they
don't believe in elves. We are practically invisible...Many elves are
moving to the Pacific Northwest and other sacred areas. Some elves
will leave surprises as they go. Find your family! And lets dance as we
make ruins of the corporate money system.

—Tara the Sea Elf in Pickering 2003

As we have described, faery experiences have been commonly documented within Pagan spirituality, which can be interpreted broadly
to include both indigenous cultural traditions and reconstructionist
(nonindigenous) variants of Neopaganism that have developed over
the last two hundred years in North America, Europe, Australia, and
elsewhere. With the development of the New Age movement over
the last few decades, Neopaganism has blossomed impressively as a
subculture, though it remains highly marginal when placed in comparison with the demographics of mainstream society. Andy Letcher
(2000) has further distinguished between two categorical tendencies
amongst Neopagans—Eco-Paganism and "virtual" Paganism. As a
group, Eco-pagans manifest a radical, direct action environmental
politics based on spiritual insights into the world as unfolding from
the interconnectedness of nature. "Virtual" Pagans, meanwhile, lead
a ritualized Pagan lifestyle of one form or another but do not proceed
to politically engage with global society as a result of their spiritual
connection with the land or nature.[11]

However, by drawing upon the research of the Birmingham
School of Cultural Studies, which attempted to read working-class
subcultures of "resistance"—such as Teds, Mods, Rockers, Skins, and
Punks—*politically* as symbolic challenges to the dominant order"
(McGuigan 1992), virtual Neopaganism[12] can be seen as evincing
styles of counterhegemonic cultural politics. In this respect, the faery
manifesto by Young (1991) is particularly articulate, although it gestures to a counterculture of individualist outsiders. By contrast, of
specific importance to us is the Neopagan penchant for collective
gatherings in which alternative experiences of time, space, place, and
identity are afforded that epitomize subversive ideas such as Bahktin's
carnival (1993) and the differentiated communitas outlined by Victor
Turner (1995). Such festivals also feature pedagogical faery workshops or other informal curricula focused on faery, and aspects of
community building regularly occur through event volunteerism,
communal food preparation, common living areas, and interactive
performance sections (Davy 2007). A diversity of perspectives can

be found within any gathering including: exotic forms of dress/costume and ritualized nudity, religious chastity and uninhibited exhibitionist sex, recreational drug/alcohol use and the spiritual use (or abolition) of medicinals, feminist Wiccans and Druids who worship the Horned God, vegetarians/vegans and carnivores, silent participants and those who favor boisterous behavior, as well as gatherers who seek more interaction and those who desire private experiences. Crucially, struggles over the normative aspect of these preferences do occur within the festivals—sometimes known as "witch wars"—as participants attempt to negotiate and organize their various meanings and denominational ideologies as part of the process of constructing an alternative social institution unbound by the laws and regulations of the dominant division of labor. Here we see the multitude attempting to maintain its internally differentiated flow of singularities while also organizing these singularities according to altermodernity logics of the witch wars.

An annual outdoor Neopagan gathering named ELFest, initially sponsored by the Elf Lore Family (ELF)—now renamed Elvin H.O.M.E. (Holy Order of Mother Earth), a 501c3 religious organization—typifies both the resistant, utopian, and more limited, socially reproductive forms of superstitious imagination that structure such events. ELFest occurs in nature sanctuaries such as Lothlorien, taken from Tolkien's name for "the enchanted land of the wise and ancient elves" (Pike 2001). It costs approximately twenty dollars per day to attend, not including whatever fare is bought from its vendors or the on-site café. Importantly, while ELFest is hardly a thoroughly commodified experience, many of its key features have been successfully reintegrated into capitalism. Therein one can find emergent sustainable technologies and attempts at green living, but companion animals are not allowed; there is only limited recycling and small RVs can be as prevalent as personal tents. Moreover, as is common at many Neopagan festivals, there is considerable iconographic attention paid in both clothing and other merchandise to fairies of the small, winged, and sometimes highly commercial variety. For instance, a visit to the Starwood Festival—billed as the largest Neopagan gathering in North America (and possibly the world)—will reveal attendees such as Tripsy the fairy, a "sky clad" (save for his sandals) Neopagan who was photographed wearing fairy wings and firing elf shots from his tiny bow and arrow handmade from twigs and string.[13] Importantly, Tripsy draws upon the use of faery as a Neopagan form of aesthetic resistance (Letcher 2001; 2004). Yet this resistance is highly ambiguous. Tripsy represents a figuration of the fairy as cliché, as fairy chic appropriated for a countercultural usage. Rather than a becoming-faery (which arises through the "unnatural" exchange of affects that elevate or amplify intensities of individuating differences), Tripsy falls back on the imitation of reified representations of commodified images—dawning prosthetic wings rather than *growing* new, virtual appendages that speak to new natureculture configurations. Yet at the same time, we could argue that Tripsy is deterritorializing the fairy, thus attempting to recompose the cliché as a Figure of the faery (busting apart the commodity from within its fetishized form). In this sense, Tripsy represents the internal complexity of the imagination as a space of zoömorphic and savage becomings as well as anthropocentric and superstitious commodifications. We therefore agree with Keith Ansell-Pearson (1999) who argues that "Part of the difficulty with Deleuze and Guattari's approach stems from a failure sufficiently to acknowledge and make clear the specific character of becomings-animal of the human, such as the cultural contexts in which they take place and which can make them intelligible" (188). Without situating Tripsy's aesthetic resistance within the framework of the commodified Starwood Festival, we would not be able to adequately tease out the various imaginative vectors that inform his performance of the faery.

   Not all Neopagans are content with the limited framework in which New Age faery culture manifests at gatherings. Some have made their presence felt in the alter-globalization movement through the development of gender-bending, fairy-costumed armies that represent a Pink Bloc, which has been known to adopt slogans from pop music, hurl teddy bears at police, and tickle them with feather dusters at global meetings of the G8/WTO (Graeber 2002; Harding 2001). Here Pink Bloc utilizes the fairy as an ironic symbol of its own disenchantment. Rather than simply a form of false-consciousness, the fairy becomes a location for the inscription of its own powerlessness, its own reification, which is now paraded as a counter-factual logic to capitalism. However, perhaps the leading alter-globalization and antiwar Pagan is Starhawk—an Eco-Pagan witch of the Reclaiming tradition and best-selling author of books such as *The Spiral Dance* (1999)—who has repeatedly been jailed for leading ceremonies on the front lines of some of the major protests of the last decade. Vitally, Starhawk has attempted to use her activism as a form of critical faery exopedagogy in response to the cultural contradictions of Neopaganism, a spiritual pedagogy of the body that typifies Eco-Paganism (Harris 1996). In discussing her move toward movement politics, Starhawk's critique (2003) of Neopagan de-politicization is explicit:

> We don't ideologically believe in the separation of spirit and matter, but in practice, we still tend to think that things that are too material, too real-life, are somehow not as spiritual. So a trance to Faery is perceived as "spiritual," whereas a trance to a Brazilian favela slum is not. We can argue about the reality of Faery, but the favela is undeniably real. If we truly believe that our spirituality is about deep interconnectedness, maybe it's more important for us to grapple internally with the reality of the favela than to dance with the faeries.

Likewise, Eco-Pagans, hailing from either the Anti-Roads movement or the Earth First! and Green Anarchy traditions of radical environmentalism, have also attempted to resolve the dichotomy between direct action politics and faery culture. In this, they undoubtedly draw upon a long-standing indigenous tradition amidst Celtic countries of not disturbing faery homes or other paths that appear to be for their travel (Evans-Wentz 2002), a tradition that continues in small villages in the United Kingdom up to the present day (McAlpine 2005). Notably, it was probably this tradition that American artist George Catlin had in mind when in the 1830s he spoke of the tallgrass prairie biome of the Great Plains as a "fairy land" that required preservation (Spence 1999, 10), and hence it is in this way that the emblematic deployment of a militant leprechaun by the late 1970s American militant group, Environmental Life Force, becomes sensible. In the 1990s, another underground militant group bearing the acronym ELF formed the Earth Liberation Front, which drew from the "green spirituality" (Taylor 2005) and primitivism of Eco-Pagan activist groups such as Earth First! and Green Anarchy to manifest a direct action politics of faery vengeance on behalf of all species and the Earth—once again articulating world history through the natural history of the land and of the rocks. In considering the growth of the faery trope in recent direct action environmentalism, Derek Wall (2000) writes, "The noun 'elf' and the verb 'elving,' sometimes mutating into 'pixieing,' evolved from the acronym ELF. Elves aim to do more than manipulate symbols; rather than seeking to embarrass or win over authority, they believe in directly and physically dealing with the ills around them" (86). In the case of the ELF, this belief has resulted in the tactic of arson. This type of violence against the sovereign ban is distinct in that it attempts to embody what Benjamin would describe as "divine violence" (or what we might like to call faery violence) as a rupture with the fatalistic repetition of mythical violence that founds and sustains the law of the nation-state. Divine violence sets itself the task of destroying the violence of the sovereign decision. Paradoxically, Benjamin (1978) writes, divine violence "as a pure means" is "nonviolent" (291). Stated differently, Benjamin argues, "Mythical violence is bloody power over mere life [a sovereign decision over and against bare life], divine violence is pure power over all life for the sake of the living" (297). It is in other words a type of violence that is beyond the opposition violent versus nonviolent. Nor is it simply a means to another end (i.e., sustaining the rule of law), but is rather a pure means, manifesting in itself a transformed or altered way of life that escapes the sovereign ban over the constitutive powers of germinal, monstrous life. Importantly for us, Benjamin notes that divine power is an "educative power" (ibid.). In the act of divine violence, the law is not destroyed so much as de-activated, rendered inoperative so that the very language, symbols, and signs of common sense can be reconfigured for a new, revolutionary purpose (in an act of free play). Thus the distinction between mythic and divine violence is the *pedagogical function of the latter* that throws into relief the machinery of anthropocentrism through its suspension, opening up a space for a coming community. Mythical violence lacks this pedagogical dimension because it mystifies itself, and does not demonstrate the nature of the law it upholds. Mythical violence is supported by a superstitious imagination that does not know its own cause whereas divine violence embodies the aesthetic rupture of the savage imagination as it struggles to overcome the immunizing logics of biopower in the name of an open future potentiality. In fact, mythical violence is, for Benjamin, predicated on a guilt that can only be attended through sacrifice, and as such endlessly reenacts Odysseus's trial (see the introduction). The critical question for ELF is thus: Can the overtly violent actions that it endorses prove to be educational?

Alongside the ELF, the UK Anti-Roads movement—which brought Eco-Pagans out in vast numbers to demonstrate against the extension of highways such as the M3, M11, A30, and Newbury Pass through ecological and archeological sites—was possibly the most powerful grassroots political movement in the world during the 1990s (Letcher 2001). Here free-form gatherings were literally unfolded in the face of construction teams, as combinations of eco-magic and nonviolent civil disobedience (including property destruction) were enlisted toward saving sites such as Salisbury Hill and Twyford Down. As in Neopagan festivals, witch wars also manifested in the direct action protests with camp lines drawn between "fairies" who favored nonconfrontational Neopagan ritual and nature worship, and "trolls" that sought to physically oppose threats to the gathering while engaging in rowdy and aggressive forms of ritual (ibid.). Yet, in a sign of the times, Davey Garland (2006) has explained how tee-shirts that revealed a winged fairy undertaking the destruction (i.e., pixieing) of a bulldozer were printed. Therefore, we should recognize that both Neopagans and various sects of Eco-Pagans have equally drawn upon representations of fairies to serve faery politics in both its cultural and direct action modes. In sum, such movements find within the figuration of the fairy, the imaginative resources necessary for communicating their own biopolitical struggles. In other words, within the savage imagination, the privatized and commercialzed commonwealth can be once again incorporated into the multitude's swarm intelligence as part of a critical bestiary.

In their militancy, Eco-Pagan groups such as the ELF attempt to demonstrate a form of faery pedagogy that teaches that there are limits to capitalist growth and development that are transgressed only at one's peril. While their communiqués may call attention to certain socio-environmental issues, working as anonymous elves means that the ELF's actions require the ability of others to critically articulate their meaning and message in order to reveal the full educational power of their faery violence (Kahn 2006). Lacking this, militant Eco-Pagans only capture the superstitious imagination of the corporate state, which has itself responded in the form of a highly repressive, neo-McCarthyist, and counter-revolutionary "Green scare" designed to put an end to what it has branded as "ecoterrorism" (Best 2006b). Should Eco-Pagans prove unable to overcome this development, those espousing a guerilla-form of faery pedagogy will prove historically untenable and thus remain within the very logic of law creation and law preservation that faery violence attempts to surpass.

Faery is a force of both dark and light. While the ELF and other groups have identified with the dark aspects of faery, important developments have also taken place within groups exploring lighter aspects. The United Kingdom's Dragon Environmental Network (DEN, founded in 1990) deserves to be more widely studied in this respect, having been successful in its political organization via direct action, lobbying, public outreach campaigning, and forms of Neopagan ritual such as eco-magic (Letcher 2004). Part of the group's success is undoubtedly its educational mission. As Davy

(2007) describes, besides offering Council of All Beings workshops, DEN offers coursework in both eco-magic, which entails contacting local spirits for Earth protection, and bio-magic "that involves the study of woodland ecology, of coming to know trees, and of developing spiritual relationships with them" (178). The overarching purpose of their activist exopedagogy is to teach the continuum between the human body and nature through various morphisms that defy categorization, and that there are points of resistance that can be occupied within the "flow of power" (Letcher 2004) in both physical and symbolic dimensions. In this way, DEN articulates a faery pedagogy that espouses, "the body is not merely a vehicle for departing from social norms, for escaping from the strictures of moral codes. It is, in its positive aspect, the grounds for configuring an alternative way of being that eludes the grasp of power" (Radley 1995, 9). In other words, the body becomes a site for ex*sitation* with the overtly political possibilities of a creatural life that escapes the separations of the anthropological machine that separates the multitude from the common and the nonhuman animal from the human.

CONCLUSION: EXOPEDAGOGICAL AMBIVALENCES AND INSURGENCIES IN FAERY CULTURES

Come away! O human Child!
To the woods and waters wild,
With a fairy hand in hand,
For the world's more full of weeping than you can understand.
—Yeats

To reiterate a major claim of this chapter: faery pedagogy is a particular manifestation of exopedagogy as a pedagogy that is set against the codification and regimentation of the sensible according to empirical verification, military force, and economic utility, which only have room for *zoë* as an exclusion. While sharing certain tenants with critical pedagogy in its critique of the sovereign decision over and against life, exopedagogy is also distinct in that it attempts to bridge the gap between the knowable and unknowable, the visible and invisible, the auditory and the inauditory, and sayable and unsayable through the acknowledgment of the UFOther. Attending to the appearance of the UFOther produces a new narrative of altermodernity from within the savage and zoömorphic imagination. Exopedagogy is in other words a monstrous pedagogy that, as Antonio Negri (2008) would argue, unfolds within a "boundless ontological becoming" (66) that scrambles the division of the sensible binding the constituting powers of imaginative labor to the thanatopower of the sovereign decision—returning us to our creatural excitations, our becoming-animal (a becoming that ultimately is a becoming-imperceptible of both the human and the animal in a pure moment of monstrous involution). It is this excess that is the productive motor of the multitude in the attempt to reconstruct culture/nature dichotomies through new kinship filations militantly opposed to the underlying dialectic of death and life that define thanatopower.

Especially due to the pervasive failure of the New Age movement to recognize its cultural complicity with dominant capitalist and colonialist logics, those who would perform exopedagogies that promote aesthetic alternation of consciousness need to ensure that their biopoetics remain savage and thus critical of Power. As Elizabeth Povinelli (2006) describes, there is a complex relationship between Radical Faeries—a movement that attempts to overcome the presumed "spiritual nihilism" of gay men by reconnecting them with pre-Christian forms of Neo-Pagan faery practices and beliefs—and indigenous cultures that is "at best insensitive and at worst a form of cultural genocide" (120). Povinelli writes, "What initially seems harmless, even fun [playful], when gay men are just being gay men, becomes fascist and genocidal for Abe [an indigenous critic] when they *express* this gayness through ritual appropriation [of indigenous spirituality]" (120). In other words, the very work of profanation enacted by the "contact consciousness" of the radical faeries reenacts the trauma of colonization—a form a mythic violence that revivifies the stain of melancholic loss. In this sense, all attempts to strike at the heart of the sovereign decision over and against the creative and multiplicitous flows of life topple over into a reassertion of a colonialist narrative—an act of faery chic that remains a form of superstitious antimodernity.

Previously we extolled the faery work of R. J. Stewart (1995). However, in Stewart's visualization exercises, the door to the faery world is considered permanently open for those who know how to search for it. Likewise, Reiki specialist and presenter at the Fairy Congress, Catherine Morgan's (2009) vision quest into the dwarven realm concludes with a sentimentalist image of eternal hospitality: "Now, with your dwarven guide, you may return to the dwarven realms any time you wish" (81). Yet this could lead to imperialist outcomes in which humanity can essentially "invade" the faery realm as they see fit, thereby turning it into a mere resource for human needs, a policy that does not serve the faery well regardless of peoples' good intentions or simple curiosity. In this scenario, the relative autonomy of the faery world is potentially compromised by human-initiated interactions that could support forms of exploitative faery tourism, if not worse. While Stewart repeatedly argues that proper rituals must be followed and a pure heart (a disinterested interest *a la* Kantian aesthetics) maintained when entering such realms, it is the very act of entering uninvited that we are calling into question—an unchecked voyeurism that relies on the faery world to produce in us a sense of "lost harmony" with the natural (thus repressing the *uncanny* home of exopedagogy). In other words, could it be possible that faery hospitality is not always open to those humans who have learned proper faery etiquette? Is it not possible that the trickster faery is intentionally opting for misrecognition as a lesson for human visitors—introducing the shock of the monstrous that upsets our expectations for recognition? All too often, harmony and connection are emphasized in faery literature that replaces the uncanny strangeness of these close encounters with a de-politicized utopianism that substitutes the utopia of wherever with the myth of origins or roots (Kristeva 1991). In other words, Stewart, Morgan, and others unknowingly perpetuate the connections between education, recognition, belonging, and community that a more radical—and thus violent—faery pedagogy would call into question. Pedagogies promoted by the presumed faery allies could have a negative effect, uncritically reinscribing the modern paradigm of the domination of nature as well as replicating logics of cultural and political homogenization that have been historically brought to bear upon marginalized peoples the world over. In this sense, faery pedagogy would not embody the savage imagination so much as a superstitious fear elevated to a metaphysical plane, thus inhibiting a friendship with the faeries that can only emerge from within the articulated distance of the exopedagogical home.

Perhaps the most egregious example of the superstitious imagination at work in faery culture is the recent workshop held at the 2010 Fairy Conference by David Spangler who advocates that humans have to learn not only to partner with faeries but to "alchemize faery gold into human coinage" (http://fairycongress.com/fc2010/2010_presenters.htm). With a profound sense of fear inflicted from the recent economic recession, Spangler turns to faeries for help to "repair" the very economic system that has worked to destroy and ravage the commons populated by a multitude of plant, animal, and faery folk. Such logic is not so much an anomaly, but rather manifests the insidious infiltration of the savage imagination by larger structures of capitalism rendered not only natural but *supernatural*!

Exopedagogy is not simply a set of rituals and rites that enable us to "access the faerie world" or to recognize the needs and interests of our faery brothers and sisters. At its most revolutionary, exopedagogy is a space of exodus from recognitions, a space of becomings and of trickster doublings beyond measure. All too often the contact consciousness of exopedagogy is mistaken for recognition across differences. In our formulation, contact consciousness is not so much contact with the familiar but with an uncanny surplus common that exists in the outside of the inside of common sense. It is in other words a contact that induces a shared distance or dislocation within the surplus common that forms the matrix of natureculture assemblages and transversal communications. To break with the fundamental sovereign ban that separates and divides life against itself (thus separating the common from the multitude) is, as we have seen, difficult at best.

Difficult, yes, but not impossible to imagine as long as we stay within the immanent logic of altermodernity. In the recent film *Pan's Labyrinth* (2006)—the closest examination of the faery world to date in global media culture[14]—the main character, a young girl named Ofelia, mediates her relation with an oppressive fascist political system through the ancient lore of rural faery cultures in Spain. Far from a vulgar notion of escapism where the human finds peace and harmony, her imaginative flights into the faery world act as a fantastical reconstruction of both the dire realities of Ofelia's family life under a fascist tyrant as well as the very real political possibilities of the resistance that hide in the nearby ancient forest. The lesson of critical-consciousness against the order to obey an oppressive father, the nationalist propaganda, or a mythical faun is learned by Ofelia through the dual axes of political activism and imaginative play that continually intersect and reinforce one another throughout the film. This results in a consciousness that equally rejects the extremely negative logic of fascist disciplinary punishment as well as the demand for complete subservience to the mystical "trickster" authority of primeval lore (i.e., Pan)—reestablishing the long-lost relationship between premodern witchcraft and modern exorcism (Foucault 2003b). As such, we find that the movie depicts Ofelia's resistance to indoctrination of any kind as indicating that sensorial alternation and critical consciousness are symbiotic functions that develop an aesthetic sense of radical political activism capable of opposing sovereign acts of thanatopower that reduce *zoë* to bare life. Against the power to take life (or make life die), Ofelia sides with the utopian possibilities inherent in the "natality" of life as such. Her final gesture of refusal to sacrifice her newborn baby brother to either her fascist stepfather or the mythical faun that instructs her indicates her ultimate development of a unique ethical position: to guard emergent life forces from worldly victimization, on the one hand, and cultivate an imaginative relationship to the world based in the hope for its ultimate renewal, on the other. In other words, she sides with the nonviolent violence of the divine as opposed the mythical violence of fascism. As such, *Pan's Labyrinth* is the perfect embodiment of Benjamin's fairytale in that it rejects both the "nightmare" of mythology and the instrumentality of information, opening up a wherever place where politics find a new articulation. The faery is utilized in this film not to retreat into a fantasy of perfect harmony and belonging (a myth of origins or roots) but rather to gain a critical comprehension of the present political moment.

In this sense, *Pan's Labyrinth* presents a visionary counterexample to Freud's rather anemic depiction of fairy tales in his essay on the uncanny. For Freud, fairy tales are unable to provide a sense of the uncanny because they openly accept the possibility of imaginative worlds and thus lack any clear tension between reality and fantasy. Citing Freud (2003),

> The world of the fairy tale, for example, abandons the basis of reality right from the start and openly commits itself to the acceptance of animistic beliefs. Here it is impossible for wish-fulfillments, the existence of secrete powers, the omnipotence of thoughts, the animation of the inanimate—all of which are commonplace in the fairy tale—to produce an uncanny effect, for, as we have seen, a sense of the uncanny can arise only if there is a conflict of judgment as to whether what has been surmounted and merits no further credence may not, after all, be possible in real life. (156)

Perhaps Freud's description holds true for the superstition of *fairy tales* but not for *faery tales* that exist in the zone of indistinction between sensation and cognition and therefore retain a certain fidelity to the shock at the sudden appearance of the other/difference within our everyday spaces. In this sense, we agree with Donald Haase (2003) who argues that in times of war—or, in our case, in exceptionally monstrous times—such tales reposition the concept of "home" as an uncanny spatial location both familiar and unfamiliar, both intimate and immediate and yet out-of-time. As an uncanny home, the faery tale is savage precisely because it opens up to a future free from the sacrifice demanded by the sovereign decision over and against life, and as such charts the emergence of a new, monstrous, multitudinous altermodernity—a profane possibility where nothing is sacred and thus nothing is sacrificed. In this sense, the faery tale can be juxtaposed to Spangler's appropriation of faery gold, which merely transforms particular historical relations into another mythology, and capitalism into a spiritual alchemy of shared interests. In opposition to Spangler as well as others who fail to learn the lesson of exopedagogy, the suspension that characterizes the savage imagination opens up to an uncanny dwelling where the secret of history lies in its repressed alliance with the magic of the storyteller, and in turn history once again emerges as a real possibility for the location of political struggle.

Emma Goldman (1934) writes in her autobiography that she came to political consciousness by affirming her self-conscious desire to dance with reckless abandon in the name of everyone's right to freedom, self-expression, and "beautiful, radiant things" (56). In this, her critical ecstasy embodies the sort of faery exopedagogy that we hope will become more prevalent amidst the educational and larger political left. These are dark and terribly sad times filled with monumental challenges if we are to create a successful movement for peace, justice, and radical sustainability. The death pall of global capitalism more and more shadows every place under the sun, utilizing capitalism to inject and infect rapacious forms of domination and zoöcide into the everyday lives of human and nonhuman beings. There are no foxholes, or even faery portals (Young 1991), in which one can find shelter from today's perpetual war and be liberated from life's contradictions. Thus, exopedagogy of the faery variety echoes the sentiments of Nietzsche (2004), when he wrote that he would rather be a Dionysian satyr than a saint under social conditions in which "Around the hero everything turns into tragedy; around the demigod everything turns into a satyr play; and around God everything turns into—what? Perhaps 'world'?" (Nietzsche 2002). The attempt to overcome the deadly dialectic of bio- and thanatopower sends us all off on multiple utopian quests for the grail that can provide a final resting place for our collective inquiry. Faery exopedagogy is the ongoing chronicle of one such quest. Yet, to the degree that scholarship on pedagogy does more than just chronicle it (Cook 2003), but partakes of and proffers it likewise, scholars too must learn to listen to the pipes of Pan and uncover new orders of eurythmy that accord with exocultural experiences.

Maybe exopedagogical scholarship is just a faery tale, but if indeed exopedagogy only amounts to a kind of escapism, then at least it is not idle. Instead, such pedagogy troops along to faery *slaugh* songs in pursuit of the wild hunt.[15] Our escape is thus an "exodus" (Virno and Hardt 2006) from capitalism on the field of altermodernity itself, opening up the floodgates of the imagination in order to transform the distribution of the sensible beyond the exclusions of a sovereign decision against life. In this, we happily concur with Tolkien (2001), who wrote:

> I have claimed that Escape is one of the main functions of fairy-stories, and since I do not disapprove of them, it is plain that I do not accept the tone of scorn or pity with which "Escape" is now so often used. Why should a man be scorned if, finding himself in prison, he tries to get out and go home? Or if he cannot do so, he thinks and talks about other topics than jailers and prison-walls?

For Tolkien, escape is an imaginative exodus that redistributes places and beliefs, disorganizing the locations of freedom and imprisonment. Drawing on Agamben (1999a), we would further argue that such exodus is an expression of *impotential freedom* summarized by the phrase "I *prefer not* to recognize these bars as a limitation of my freedom." Stated differently, the prisoner might persuasively see the prison "as not" a prison and bars "as not" bars. If jailed, then Tolkien's prisoners utilize a zoömorphic and savage imagination to subvert the performance of imprisonment, refusing to accept the logic that has assigned them to a specific place—refusing the decision of the sovereign over life even as it weighs down on them. It is through the UFOther that, in a paradoxical shift, the very delusions of paranoia become indistinguishable from the powers of freedom, and it is here that new passions and new affects are cultivated that challenge the fundamental coordinates of a thanatopower over life.

Conclusion

A MONSTROUS LOVE AFFAIR: THE
ETHICS OF EXOPEDAGOGY

In a true fairy tale everything must be marvelous...everything must
be animated. Each in its different way. The whole of nature must be
mixed in a strange way with the whole of the spirit world. Time of general anarchy—lawlessness—freedom—the *natural state* of nature—
the time before the *world* (state). This time before the world brings
with it as it were the scattered features of the *time after the world*—as
the state of nature is a *strange picture* of the eternal kingdom. The
world of the fairy tale is the *absolutely opposite* world to the world of
truth (history)—and just for this reason it is so *absolutely similar* to
it—as *chaos* is to *accomplished creation*. (On the *idyll*).

In the *future* world everything is as it is in the *former*—and *yet everything is quite different*. The *future* world is *reasonable* chaos—chaos
which penetrated itself—is inside and outside itself—*chaos* squared or
infinity.

The *true fairy tale* must be at once a *prophetic representation*—an
ideal representation—an absolutely necessary representation. The
maker of true fairy tales is a prophet of the future.

In time history must become a fairy tale—it will become again what
it was in the beginning.

—Novalis

I want to learn more and more to see as beautiful what is necessary in
things; then I shall be one of those who make things beautiful. *Amor
fati*: let that be my love henceforth! I do not want to wage war against
what is ugly. I do not want to accuse; I do not even want to accuse
those who accuse. *Looking away* shall be my only negation. And all in
all and on the whole: some day I wish to be only a Yes-sayer.

—Nietzsche

Michael Hardt and Antonio Negri (2004) have argued that the
"political project of the multitude...must find a way to confront the

conditions of our contemporary reality" (352) and that this project is characterized by love—one that is capable of creating a "new science" (353) of life for a radical earth democracy, which also entails the revelation of what they term "a new race" or "new humanity" (356).[1] In *Education Out of Bounds* we have attempted to demonstrate that the material, intellectual, and aesthetic turns necessary to more fully realize a new science of the multitude constitute a fundamentally *educational* vocation—a bestiary of the politically, socially, and ecologically monstrous. As Ché Guevara (1965) put it, "Society as a whole must be converted into a gigantic school" (202). Of course it was in this same famous letter in which Ché described how a socialist revolution desires the ever-birth of "the new man and woman" in terms of both emancipated consciousness and material practices that he also importantly mused, "At the risk of seeming ridiculous, let me say that the true revolutionary is guided by feelings of great love" (215).[2] But what exactly is the nature of this "great love"?

Rather than the superstitious love for the sovereign leader, the capitalist love of profit, or the many other forms of socially antagonistic sado-humanist loves that are reproduced every day through media spectacle, we want to argue that it is legitimate to retain hope for a coming community capable of seriously fulfilling an inherited promise of zoöphilia—the affective and effective physics that animates all zoömorphic and savage imaginative materializations.[3] Such would be a re-enchanted altermodernity of peace, biodiversity, and expanded freedom across species divides, a virtuous state of being that could significantly heal (if not resolve) the historical terrors of industrialized capitalism that unfolds into the endgame of genocide, ecocide, and zoöcide respectively when revitalized organizations of *zoë* and *bios* are popularly absent (Kahn 2010). Yet, if this monster of capital is the condition of our contemporary reality it means that outpourings of zoöphilia today are always limited and contradictory. Still, the ancient goddess/god of love[4] was also the lover of war (Burkert 1991). While this delineates exactly our contradictory problem in one respect, it may also be the wise oracular truth that beckons us toward the necessary acceptance of the present moment's revolutionary fate (*amor fati*).

In previous chapters we have outlined the alternative aesthetic registers of "posthuman" cultural figures—such as the feral, the alien, and the faery—in order to reveal how they demonstrate monstrous tendencies alive within the larger public's "common" sense that should be taken seriously by those who presently work for absolute democracy surging through the ontological potential of the multitude. On the one hand, these imaginaries are positively anticipatory of a destabilization of humanist superstitions and anthropocentrisms in which ideological boundaries are politically reconstructed over and against a multitude that is the evolving "mangle" (Pickering 1995) of earthlings with each other and the planet in the potentiality of a monstrous life. On the other hand, a failure to critically interrogate these cultural forms by the public-at-large potentially allows for the terrible return of the repressed elements within such exocultures resulting in a cataclysmic social threat—perhaps as an anthropogenically induced mass extinction event or via nature's cultural re-appropriation by Power in the guise of the naturalization of primary accumulation strategies.

For this reason, love itself demands a critically savage and zoöphilic evaluation lest we be committed here to limiting a multitudinous exopedagogy to the education of irrational (and possibly fascist) antimodern mythologies of the primeval, or to reactionary combinations of either nature/culture or human/nonhuman that work curricularly throughout society to reinscribe the domination of nature proper. In other words, we do not imagine love as a form of monstrous copulation or hybridization that occurs through immoral consubstantial identifications with an essentialized nature by those who would claim the right to authoritarian violence as spokespersons on its behalf.[5] Likewise, we also cannot envision a working vivisection laboratory as a sensible example of an ethical space inhabited by a liberatory love, even though we acknowledge that it (as with any place) could possibly serve as a future uncanny home for zoömorphic and perhaps savage imaginings to suddenly reappear. Simply crossing borders is not necessarily evidence of a progressive form of love, nor is it transformatively educational. Such action may be a challenge to certain forms of Power from below, but it may also be a colonialist invasion from above. A critical exopedagogical reading of myriad interactionist (Tuana 2008), intra-actionist (Barad 2003), and trans-corporeal (Alaimo 2008) contexts is demanded by the desire to know more about how love is socially situated in any given instance.

In our view, the ancient philosopher Heraclitus was therefore correct: "Nature loves to hide" (Kahn 1981, 33). Knowledge of nature is always mantic—it neither declares nor conceals itself absolutely, but rather takes the form of an enigmatic sign that demands transversal deciphering by a monstrously zoömorphic imagination. Accordingly, exopedagogy looks to emergent exocultural valences and gothic/surrealist avant-garde representations to critically listen for novel generative themes that might be the germinative subjects of multitudinous dialogues—Haraway's "otherworldly conversations" (2008b, 174)—on behalf of a new science of life. But exopedagogy also reads global cultures against the grain after the manner of a critical public pedagogy in order to isolate the superstitious and anthropocentric vectors of the imagination stimulated by a host of spectacular wonders proffered by capitalism. What results, we imagine, is a cultural studies for "posthumanist posthumanism" (Wolfe 2010) that is libidinally invested in a revolutionary zoömorphic and savage love, the monstrous nature of which is articulated well by Jacques Derrida:

> the future is necessarily monstrous: the figure of the future, that is, that which can only be surprising, that for which we are not prepared, you see, is heralded by species of monsters. A future that would not be monstrous would not be a future; it would already be a predictable, calculable, and programmable tomorrow. All experience open to the future is prepared or prepares itself to welcome the monstrous arrivant, to welcome it, that is, to accord hospitality to that which is absolutely foreign or strange, but also, one must add, to try to domesticate it, that is, to make it part of the household and have it assume the habits, to make us assume new habits. This is the movement of culture. (In Weber 1995, 387)

PENGUINS, WOLVES, AND ALIENS: LOVELY ENTANGLEMENTS OF FLESH, FUR, FEATHERS

Love as a hinge between human and nonhuman animal worlds is often depicted in media culture as a mediation point between species. In this section we will map out three valences of love within the postmodern bestiary, arguing that each misses the potential of the zoöphilia that exists when human and nonhuman animal distinctions are suspended. Take for instance the smash hit *March of the Penguins* (2005). As the second most successful documentary in North American history, we must ask why the life cycle of the Emperor penguin ignited so much fanfare, let alone many spin-off products featuring adorable penguins. Part of the fascination lies with the way the film transforms the mating cycle of these flightless birds into a moralizing love story—making penguins the central protagonists in a new humanist bestiary. The film begins with the narrator, wise Morgan Freeman, making the claim "Like all love stories, it begins with an act of utter foolishness." What follows is the projection of seemingly middle-class, white family values onto the torturous trials for survival of a group of penguins at the very bottom of the world. According to

Andrew Sullivan's critical analysis of the film, Christian evangelicals have claimed the film as direct evidence of intelligent design as well as the sanctity of traditional values such as monogamy and self-sacrifice. Sullivan quotes the antigay marriage activist Maggie Gallagher, who reportedly said of the film "Beauty, goodness, love and devotion are all part of nature, built into the DNA of the universe. Even in the harshest place on the Earth (like 21st century America?), love will not only endure, it will triumph" (2005, *Sunday Times*). Others have found in the film a celebration of yuppie family life in a flexible economy where mom and dad both have to work and share the responsibility for raising children.

Sullivan rejects the narrative of the film, highlighting the many inaccuracies of this moralizing description of penguin behaviors. As evidence he cites the existence of serial monogamy, rape, homosexuality, and nest-robbing as endemic to penguin communities. In an ironic twist, perhaps we could argue that Sullivan's attempts to rebuke the love thesis, in the end merely reinforces it! Isn't Sullivan's "scientific" description of the sexual politics of penguin society much closer to love as it actually exists in postmodern human animal communities? If the narration of *March of the Penguin*'s is seductive, it is not simply because it is anthropocentric, but rather that it is a fantasy screen for living out the impossible utopian aspirations of a mythological love of the family.

This projection of an overly moralizing life lesson about the natural and thus universal truth of the white, middle-class nuclear family cannot help but recall the limitations of David Icke's similar conundrum outlined in chapter two of this book. Icke argued that love is a universal strong force, but this love is coded as distinctly human in nature. Or rather it is coded along the lines of an idealized, liberal notion of self-love that in turn colonizes the animal other in the very gesture meant to promote ecological understanding. In this sense, the very moment of celebrating the common denominator uniting human and nonhuman animals (love), erases the potential of zoöphilic contamination—the surplus that exists in the state of exception that ruptures the coordinates of identification and recognition.

The second example of love is more complex (and compelling) than *March of the Penguins*. Caught within the media circuits of capitalism as a commodified product and yet resistant to the knowledge of the anthropological machine, the rather unusual television series *Living with the Wolfman* offers a field of play opened up for study when a man decides to live with and among wolves. This series charts the trials and tribulations of Shaun Ellis, also known as the "The Wolfman," and his fiancée, Helen Jeffs, who live besides wolves at the Combe Martin Wildlife Park in North Devon, England. In the series, Ellis attempts to introduce his fiancée, Jeffs, to the resident wolf pack. What is revealed through this process is the absolute fragility of living in the zone of indistinction that suspends the human and nonhuman animal dichotomy. The struggle to disidentify with either group causes a desubjectification process that Jeffs and Ellis find difficult to accept, but for different reasons. Ellis, whose life has been spent learning from wolves, has increasingly become detached from the world of the human, making it difficult to understand and empathize with the needs of his fiancée who remains connected to the common sense of the human community. Thus resubjectivizing himself as a human being has become a serious obstacle in his romantic life, creating a series of misunderstandings and comical attempts to live within the human commonwealth. For Jeffs, the same problem exists, only in reverse: desubjectivizing herself leaves her frustrated and anxious over the loss of human identification. Becoming-wolf proves to be an arduous task for Jeffs, who must undergo a certain form of anthropocentric death, and for Ellis, who must navigate two worlds through a pedagogical strategy that shifts continually between two signifying systems: the human animal and the nonhuman animal. The show does not convincingly demonstrate a monstrous, feral existence fully beyond the anthropological machine so much as it documents the frustrations of shuttling back and forth between humanist and posthumanist paradigms.

The difficulty of teaching Jeffs the ways of the wolves decisively captures this frustration. Ellis must translate the sensations, nonhuman rationalities, and verbal/nonverbal communications of the wolves back into knowledge of the anthropological machine in order to, paradoxically, overcome the anthropological machine that defines human and nonhuman animal relations. Thus becoming-wolf is constantly being captured and seized upon through an exopedagogy that names precisely what has no name in order to overcome the limits of these names. The results are paradoxical at best, and at one point in the series, Jeffs's emotional conflict becomes too overwhelming, and she leaves the wolf pack. As Ellis (2009) summarizes in his memoir, "Her [Jeffs's] way of dealing with what had happened [their breakup] was to get back to normal life [human life]; mine was to go down to the wolves. We both resorted to the worlds we knew" (243). If he wants to remain intimate with Jeffs, Ellis is therefore left to make a choice concerning his love for human

CONCLUSION   135

animal versus nonhuman animal companions, ultimately privileging
the former over the latter. In other words, the zone of indistinction,
of pure potentiality between human and animal, is thrown out of
joint, forced to articulate itself into a division, a "speciesist" separation between two kinds of love. Although Ellis does not fully leave
the pack, priorities shift as well as his residential location away from
the park. The restructuring of Ellis' interpersonal relationships in
order to save his love life with Jeffs casts his intimate relationship
with the wolves as a problem to be solved through a counter-peda-
gogy of humanization—a task that Jeffs takes upon herself in order
to "tame" the wolfman (a sort of comical, spectacular version of
Itard's pedagogy detailed in chapter one). In an ironic twist this
splitting of the self (a cleaving of the monstrous into the animal and
the human) does not cure the wolfman of his condition but rather
produces precisely the melancholic stain that defines the condition
of the wolfman as such!

The tension points are further multiplied through the simple fact
that this experimental drama is a media commodity that plays with
play in order to transform the pure potentiality of the in-between into
an exchange value. Yet even with this commodification and commercial packaging of Ellis, his show remains unique in the pantheon of
experientially oriented naturalists. As opposed to *Man vs. Wild*, *Living
with the Wolfman* does not encourage a domineering, antagonistic
relationship with nonhuman animals and the environment. Rather
its message is one of learning, sharing, and loving that cuts through
divisions demarking species. If Bear Grylls is a quintessential colonialist, utilizing nature as a formidable existential backdrop against
which he asserts his will to power (captured in the media spectacle of
chewing the heads off of small creatures for shock value alone), then
Ellis's attempts to overcome this metanarrative of the anthropological machine through a commitment to living with wolves is laudable.
Thus *Living with the Wolfman*, read diagnostically, offers a complex
image of the deterritorialization of the anthropological machine
through a becoming-wolf and the simultaneous reterritorialization of
this emergent, monstrous-becoming through human romance. The
zoöphilic vector of love is once again trumped by an anthropocentric
axiom, and in the process, the savage vector of Ellis's imagination is
tamed into accepting the authority of a decisively humanist Power. In
other words, the feral zone between humans and animals as a space
for the exploration of the surplus common is tamped down in order
to reinstall a distinction between the social (human) and the ecological (animal) commons.

Our third example of zoöphilia concerns the UFOther as an imaginative "assistant" poised between human and animal—the Na'Vi of the wildly popular film *Avatar* (2009). The word "avatar" has Vedantic origins meaning something akin to the "descent" or "manifestation" of a divinity in bodily form. It is the embodiment of the Holy Spirit (or in a non-monotheistic culture, spirits). In light of the cyberpunk generation, an avatar can now also be one's own digital representation—whether a representative icon for one's tweets and other social networking posts or an entire virtual person one can live through in cyborg media environments such as Second Life or Rock Band. Of course, *Avatar* is also the blockbuster film released in late 2009, which has gone on to be far and away the largest grossing movie domestically and worldwide (as of the time of writing: $2,731,058,342). In its blending of ambivalent meanings connoted by the concept of avatar, the movie self-consciously attempts to pitch for a monstrous pedagogical engagement of each with each in order to mediate and ultimately sublate the tension between the organic and the machinic (or the Epimethean and the Promethean[6]) traditions. The film ultimately poses the question whether it is a case of art imitating art, art imitating life, or, in the case of audiences moved to want to embody some of its characters' seemingly zoöphilic virtues, life imitating art.

In many respects, *Avatar* is the preeminent megaspectacular representation of revolutionary love to date, as it offers a boldly savage and zoöphilic allegory of current threats to sustainability and peace now posed by the military industrial complex along with a hopeful ending that the love of *zoë* will always result in the preservation of renewal within a community of integrity. The film, whether seen in 3-D or not, displays a richly romantic vision of the alien nature of the Alpha Centauri moon Pandora, which is populated by an indigenous race (the Na'vi) that is very much its wise and sustainable guardian. It centers upon a particular clan living in a giant "Hometree"—a veritable tree of life. Two other trees serve as sacred *axis mundis* for the Na'vi, a Tree of Voices, in whose shelter they can listen to their departed ancestors, and the Tree of Souls, that amounts to something like the primary hub coordinating and concentrating the biology of the planetoid's supraconsciousness called "Eywa."[7]

The Na'vi themselves are a large humanoid race, though with distinctive feline features. If in *The Matrix* (1999) members of the Nebuchadnezzar could "jack in" to bring their consciousness to bear on the stream of digital data being arranged by the machines to constitute a virtual world designed to pacify human agency, in *Avatar* the Na'vi (like other native species on Pandora) possess a tendril-like, braided organ that connects to their brain. By connecting this up with those of other flora and fauna, they achieve something akin to what we have been describing as a romantic version of E.T. contact consciousness with their lifeworld partners and so ritualistically establish the ethics of sustained relationship that is constitutive of Pandoran life. Thus, life on Pandora is presented as rooted in an ontology of relationship and, epistemologically, the Na'vi understand life as an unending series of dialogue and common bonding of the past with the present or the self with another. It is unsurprising, then, that the movie draws directly from Buber's *I and Thou* (1970, 70) for the manner in which they greet one another—"I see you," they say and thereby convey that in the relationship they perceive the zoöphilic unity of one with all. Yet unlike Buber and Levinas, here nature has a "face" that can be recognized as an other rather than simply a raw material to be consumed.

Avatar's script turns on the problem, then, that when human colonists colonize Pandora—in the form of a technocapitalist transgalactic corporation named Resources Development Administration (RDA), which includes armed soldiers, bureaucratic administrators, scientists and anthropologists, and other personnel—the Na'vi and Eywa become caught in a contradiction. Should they refuse the colonists outright as wrongful invaders? Considering that RDA is shown as desiring to lay waste to Pandora, dominate the Na'vi, and subject the mind-matter of Eywa under the Tree of Souls to primary accumulation in order to profit from it as an energy commodity named "unobtainium," a total resistance strategy could be justified. However, to do so would violate the ontological basis of relationship that constitutes the meaning of life on Pandora and the Na'vi's own understanding of what it means to be a people. In other words, it would reproduce an ideology of Other-as-pathogen that is the immunizing hallmark of community and that comes close to RDA's own position as regards the moon's *zoë* in the film—in explaining the corporation's intentions to the Na'vi, the double agent protagonist of *Avatar*, Jake Sully, declares, "This is how it's done. When people are sitting on shit that you want, you make 'em your enemy. Then you justify taking it."

Yet, if the Na'vi were to simply accept RDA on its own terms then they would voluntarily make themselves into a kind of *homo sacer* and sacrifice their zoöphilia on behalf of a Stoic's act of suicide—a thanatopolitics in resistance to the underlying thanatopower of RDA. Thus, they undertake a political position of liberal tolerance, with the important exception that it is decided that Jake Sully's Na'vi avatar will be incorporated into the tribe and taught its ways. The character of Sully therefore becomes the location of a potential "engaged pedagogy" (hooks 2010) within the biopolitical drama, and by refusing the Manichean thanatopower and zero-sum game of RDA, the Na'vi attempt to retain their integrity and plant a seed to enlarge the *zoë* community on Pandoran terms.

As many commentators have noted, despite *Avatar*'s supreme fantasy, its emplotment of the narrative of colonization—especially of indigenous peoples—could easily have been ripped from the headlines. RDA is Columbus and the Na'vi are peaceable Caribs (until Columbus starts chopping their hands off in search of gold). The synthetic personage of Jake Sully, a Marine transformatively turned into a diplomatic representative who might ethically speak for the Na'vi over the course of the film, represents him as a kind of Bartholomew de Las Casas figure. Of course, de Las Casas never went Croatan, nor was he perceived as a fated Clan leader by the indigenous populations that he recognized were the terrible objects of imperialist domination. Thus, in resolving itself by having Jake Sully reborn under the grace of Eywa as his Na'vi avatar in order to be a true avatar for universal peace, the film makes a superstitiously imaginative caricature of Hardt and Negri's call for a new human race based in a science of love . *Avatar* ultimately devolves in this way into a conservative white dream of zoöphilia on its own privileged terms—yes, it is the dominant Empire that is wrong; but it is in the end the dominant Empire that will make it right. Moreover, it will be welcomed by *zoë*'s multitudes and even crowned for its pedagogical achievement. For sure, there is an exopedagogy of the oppressor just as there is one for the oppressed, but *Avatar* likely overemphasizes the necessity of transforming the consciousness of average white male capitalist in order to achieve a meaningful revolution for earth democracy and beyond. For the dominant society, such revolution happens (as we have argued) in the form of the UFOther—itself a kind of alien invasion phenomenon; what is beyond the margins of the permissible will erupt into the center. It is less a matter of those at the centers of power going to teach and learn equally at the margins.

Perhaps the worst failure of *Avatar* as an artifact of exo-public pedagogy, though, is that while viscerally transcoding increasingly global fears about modern society's tendencies toward genocide, ecocide, and zoöcide, as with *The Matrix* series and other similar movies, it suggests to paying audiences that a spiritual world of social justice and biodiversity can be theirs if they will only take the first step of purchasing a ticket (and whatever other necessary items from the concession stand), suspend their will to disbelieve, and so engage in the repressive desublimation of its enchanted fairy tale complete with Hollywood happy ending. As noted by the social theorist and cultural critic Slavoj Zizek (2010), the awful irony about this awe inspired by *Avatar* is that similar indigenous struggles go on today in places such as central India (and we might add: throughout Latin America, Africa, Europe, the Middle East, Asia, Australia, Oceania, and yes—North America too!), but hardly anyone seems to notice or care, much less get involved.

The movie appears enough for most. Instead of a monstrous relationship to society, viewers are therefore repacked as pacified consumers and sent home to the sounds of the syrupy ballad, *I See You*—a snapshot in words of *Avatar*'s pedagogical adventure. As with all aspects of the film, here the lyrics too are decidedly ambiguous, potentially as much about a pathological relationship of self-flagellating, humanist masochism and internalized colonization as liberation:

> Walking through a dream, I see you
> My light and darkness breathing hope of new life
> Now I live through you and you through me, enchanted
> I pray in my heart that this dream never ends.
> Now I give my hope to you, I surrender—
> I pray in my heart that this world never ends.
> I see me through your eyes
> Breathing new life, flying high
> Your love shines the way into paradise—
> So I offer my life—
> I offer my love for you.

As we have attempted to illuminate through this critique, *Avatar* is a fairy tale rather than a faery tale. In other words, it lacks the uncanny, disturbing dimension of exopedagogy where common sense is suddenly ruptured by the appearance of the other-within opening a zone of indistinction that problematizes easily recognizable narratives. The friendship that emerges from such zones is not the liberal notion of mutual recognition but rather of mutual desubjectification. Here contact consciousness touches the strange kernel that rests between the animal and the human, the material and the imaginary. Regrettably, *Avatar* acts to conceal the uncanny advent of such friendship becoming a replacement for rather than lighting rod toward a new instantiation of the coming community of the multitude. Only when the movie is transformed into the diagnostic material for an exopedagogical lesson can its joy be reclaimed in the form of an apophatic liberation theology in which moviegoers (as proxies for the larger project for all citizens) refuse to accept scripts as handed to them and so write themselves back into the work of art as necessary as a proper response to their being in the world—an educational twist on the standard genre of the monster movie.

BESTIALITY IN THE POSTHUMAN BESTIARY?

The monstrous body is pure paradox, embodying contradictory states of being, or impossibilities of nature. It is both a sight of wonder—as a divine portent—and loathing, as evidence of heinous sin. The monster is both awful and aweful; and insofar as the monster synthesizes taboo and desire, it further articulates its ambivalence for its creators.
—Elaine L. Graham

Perhaps the farthest edge of the question of human and nonhuman animal love is bestiality. Zoöphilia is now used as a common synonym for bestiality amongst the wider public. While some subcultures that identify as zoöphilic have in fact begun to branch off from a core interest in sexual intercourse with nonhuman animals in ways that suggest the materialization of degrees of specialization amongst the broad category of bestialists, undoubtedly any attempt to reconstruct a revolutionary love amplified by zoöphilia requires a cultural analysis of the erotism displayed for nonhuman animals by elements of the human population. Per Graham's epigram given earlier, we suppose that bestiality represents a kind of monstrous performative body—at once a taboo and desire that is a natural impossibility in terms of its biologically procreative possibilities. A highly ambivalent cultural phenomenon, it is manifest within mainstream currents but almost always with the suggestion that it is either a psychiatrically or morally suspect behavior. Contemporary popular television shows such as *Family Guy* and *South Park*, and recent movies such as *Borat* (2006), *Clerks II* (2006), and *Sleeping Dogs Lie* (2005) have all drawn upon satirical narratives of bestiality in order to suggest themes of cultural devolution. That such comedy is effective at some level is perhaps because bestiality is widely considered to be generally deplorable by the majority of viewing audiences. But the monster is not just that which is banefully uncivilized. An evaluation of the manner in which bestiality incorporates states of wonder or awe is required in order to understand the interplay of love and various vectors of savage or superstitious, zoöphilic or anthropocentric imaginings. A survey of the anthropology of bestiality actually finds it to be shockingly common (Beetz 2004; Beetz and Podberscek 2009). The practice of human sexual relations with nonhuman animals appears to have existed within most every culture throughout history, and is a theme represented in a wide variety of people's literature, art, and myths the world over. Indeed, sex between humans and nonhuman animals can be dated back tens of thousands of years and is depicted on a number of prehistoric artifacts and cave paintings (Dekkers 1994). According to Dekkers and Hani Miletski (2002), who each offer copious histories of the subject, many cultures from ancient times up until the present have themselves shown forms of tolerance to bestiality for religious, ritualistic, and even recreational reasons. Still, practices of bestiality have also been, and remain, extremely controversial on the whole for societies rooted in Abrahamic religious traditions, which maintain important prohibitions against the practice. This is especially true of the Judaeo-Christian West, where some people have always tolerated bestiality in certain places and at certain times but, overall, bestial relations are associated with social stigma and religious forces have successfully advanced the idea in the popular mind that bestiality is a great moral outrage that is never to be condoned.

It is interesting to note that, as secular culture became instantiated throughout much of Europe and North America during the nineteenth and twentieth centuries, legislative concern with and the penalties for bestiality largely lessened (Miletski 2002). While for the Ancient Egyptians, Hebrews, and Romans, as well as throughout pre-Enlightenment Christian Europe, the human and nonhuman parties charged with bestiality could expect a punishment of torture and death, modern European nations such as the Netherlands, Sweden, and Belgium maintain that human sexual relations with nonhuman animals are ostensibly legal. Still, bestiality does remain officially criminalized in many countries throughout the world. Illinois became the first U.S. state to decriminalize sexual relations with animals in 1962, but the practice has been outlawed at the federal level in America and is once again considered criminal throughout all fifty states in the form either of explicit statutes against it or implicitly through a combination of animal cruelty and welfare laws. On the other hand, whether the commitment exists on the part of U.S. authorities to actively enforce prohibitions against bestiality, and then to vigorously prosecute and penalize offenders once they have been caught, is questionable.[8] In the absence of such a commitment, the pressure of socio-religious mores against bestiality remains the primary force preventing its wider adoption as an acceptable American practice.

As noted, these mores are hardly insignificant in many Western nations, where they have also given rise to stereotypes that often suggest bestiality is behavior more typical of uncivilized, rural, or agrarian-based peoples. Possibly lending credence to these stereotypes, early sex studies such as those famously conducted by Dr. Alfred Kinsey concluded that bestiality was primarily a rural phenomenon (Kinsey, Pomeroy, and Martin 1948), and it has been found that bestial relations are considered a much more normal part of sexual maturation in nomadic herding societies, such as throughout Africa and the Middle East, than in primarily urban cultures (Beetz and Podberscek 2009). Yet, other research over the last fifty years has demonstrated that--if it is not always possible to know who engages in such relations, or how often they do so, due to bestialists' frequent desire for anonymity—a broad spectrum of people in modern society have a statistically significant interest in bestiality themselves (Miletski 2002).

Perhaps no recent case better confirms this than when the *Seattle Times* published an article in 2005 on a local man who died from a perforated colon after having sex with a horse. Soon thereafter, a columnist for the paper found that due to unprecedented downloads of the article via the Internet, it was perhaps the most read piece of journalism ever published during the paper's 109-year printing history (Westneat 2005). Indeed, the story became so popular that it was turned into the centerpiece of a popular independent art film, *Zoo*, that was released in 2007. Another independent film on the subject of the subculture in a European Union context, entitled *Coming Soon— The Bestiality-Rights Movie*, was released to wide critical acclaim in 2008. This latter film in particular follows in the tradition of a 1999 British television documentary *Hidden Love: Animal Passions*, which was watched by millions of viewers. Yet another example of the popular fascination with bestiality is the 2002 Tony Award winning play by Edward Albee, *The Goat, or Who is Sylvia?*, in which a well-to-do architect destroys his bourgeois family's fantasy of peaceable happiness when his therapist leads him to reveal to them his ongoing practice of sexual intercourse with a female goat named Sylvia.

To return to the domain of the Internet, though, current understandings of bestiality demand recognition especially of how new media has been utilized pivotally to exchange information, educate others about lifestyle orientations associated with human sexual relations with nonhuman animals, and to trade pornography depicting the same (Beetz 2004; Miletski 2002). Additionally, some argue that the Internet has begun to establish and grow communities dedicated to varieties of bestiality, though the degree to which these communities occur offline and are constituted by face-to-face interactions remains unclear (Williams and Weinberg 2003). The first digital community of major importance was the Usenet newsgroup alt.sex.bestiality, which arose in the early 1990s. Over the last decade, there has been a tremendous proliferation of bestiality websites, chatrooms, listservs, and peer-to-peer file sharing networks, and thus it has never been easier to view explicit pictures and videos of men and women of a wide range of races and ages engaging in sexual intercourse with dogs, horses, cattle, snakes, birds, fish, rodents, reptiles, cats, sheep, goats, and other species. To put the demand for such material in perspective, consider the popularity ranking of a top bestiality website, Zootube365.com, on the traffic rank search engine Alexa.com. At the time of writing (April 24, 2010), out of the over 20 billion indexed websites in existence, Zootube365.com ranks 4545th in the world. By contrast, major left or progressive information hubs such as AlterNet, Common Dreams, and Democracy Now have websites ranked 6,429th, 15,069th, and 17,308th, respectively. In fact, Zootube365.com outranks Barack Obama's official website (5,407th). Even within the sphere of pornography proper, it is still approximately fifteen times more popular than the website of arguably the most famous and powerful porn star of the last decade, Jenna Jameson, whose ClubJenna.com ranks 74,957th.

Websites such as Zootube365.com and movies such as *Zoo* highlight the interchangeable aspects of the monikers "zoöphile" and "bestialist" for many involved in communities associated with bestiality. Still, scholars such as Miletsky (2002), Beetz (2004), and Williams and Weinberg (2003) have begun to argue for distinctions to be drawn between the terms. For while so-called zoophiles may engage in acts of bestiality, many claim that their zoöphilia[9] involves positive emotional feelings for nonhuman animals that go beyond the merely sexual or erotic and that does not necessarily require intercourse or pornographic titillation. Such persons could be categorized as "zoösexuals"—participant members who deeply identify with their community based on their sexual orientation, akin to how others orient as hetero-, homo-, bi-, or pan-sexuals. Thus, by these terms one can be a zoophile without engaging, or even wishing to engage at all, in sexual relations with nonhuman animals, just as one can conduct such relations as a purveyor of bestiality without thereby being a zoo-phile. This being said, many zoophiles will have zoösexual relations with nonhuman animals, and yet still differentiate themselves from other bestialists through the additional claims of equality and empathy between them and their nonhuman counterparts and themselves. These zoophiles can be distinguished from "zoösadists," or those who derive pleasure from inflicting pain in sexual and nonsexual ways upon nonhuman animals.[10]

While it is likely that the majority of those involved today in animal advocacy politics aspire to or identify with zoöphilic associations, it may be surmised that such activists are much less welcoming to the permissibility of zoösexual proclivities. Yet, the philosopher Peter Singer, author of the bible of animal welfare *Animal Liberation* (1975), wrote a piece "Heavy Petting" in 2001 that attempted to legitimate zoösexual ethics. While hardly condoning zoösadist practices, he sought to challenge long held cultural stigmas against zoöphilic interspecies sex based on irrational taboos. By noting that nonhuman animals often copulate as humans do and that some, such as domesticated canines, appear commonly to make humans the targets of their own sexual advances and desires, Singer argued that zoöphilia should not necessarily be understood as a solely human persuasion. If so, then the sharp boundaries between human and nonhuman animals can themselves be seen to be held in place by a taboo that should no longer treated uncritically in a rational society. Thus, Singer delineates an ethics of erotic love based upon an appreciation of the sentience that many nonhuman animals share with humanity, which is achieved in turn through an increased awareness of human creatureliness as sexual beings. If critical animal studies has convincingly demonstrated the broad distribution of subjectivities and linguistic invention across species (Wolfe 2010) then Singer pushes us even further, suggesting a broad distribution of libidinal desires below these subjectivities. What we want to argue is that an ethical practice of erotic love with nonhuman animals must couple zoöphilia with a savage imagination, otherwise zoösexuality will simply reinscribe oppressive forms of domination and appropriation of animal bodies by more powerful human agents. A savage imagination not only critiques irrational taboos against erotic loves but also remains vigilant against the reinscription of new antimodern irrationalities within emerging practices between human and nonhuman animals. Intensified by zoöphilic and savage imaginings the space of trans-species erotics is open to reinvention that resists

Oedipalized desires on the one hand and sheer speciesist instinct on the other.

LOVE'S MULTITUDE REVISITED

In order to navigate the various valences of love that emerge from within the postmodern bestiary, we must risk theorizing love out of bounds in the exopedagogical moment of savage and zoöphilic possibilities. Without an understanding of the imaginative vectors that intensify and sustain a revolutionary ethical practice of a posthumanist love, we will misidentify love as either corrupt or authentic—a mistake that Hardt and Negri have repeatedly made. Moving beyond the sentimentality of love and its connection to patriotism, the family, or the community, Hardt and Negri (2009) argue that revolutionary love is the productive force of the multitude and thus the radical affective engine of the commonwealth. As a biopolitical event, "Love—in the production of affective networks, schemes of cooperation, and social subjectivities—is an economic power" (180) that challenges the destructive force of war and capitalism. Gathering inspiration from Spinoza, Hardt and Negri argue that love is "joy, that is, the increase of our power to act and think together with the recognition of an external cause" (181). Counter to this productive form of love, corrupt love abounds. "Corruption of love" takes several shapes, including identitarian love (race love or nation love) and romantic love (where the ideal is to merge into one, singular identity), both of which reproduce sameness and unity over and against the production of singularities within the common. Evil is in fact derived from these distortions of love, creating a politics of inclusion that necessarily sacrifices the stranger, foreigner, or subhuman. In our terminology, we would argue that "evil love" is not the corruption of love as Hardt and Negri argue but rather an ethical commitment stimulated and amplified by a mixture of anthropocentric and superstitious vectors of the imagination. Within this imaginative register, love as a universal strong force is constricted into a form of in-group loyalty predicated on species belonging or a form of fetishization of animality captured in bestial pornography. On the other hand, love as a joyous ethic of the multitude is surcharged through a zoöphilic and savage imagination. In this formulation, love becomes the opposite of interpellation. If, as argued in relation to Victor's humanist education, interpellation is a violent hailing into a specifically defined subject position allotted within the family, community, or nation-state, then a zoöphilic and savage love is the opposite: an event of de-subjectification that opens up to the power of the transversal commonwealth to produce new monstrous becomings that escape the control of Power. Here, the melancholy of the divided subject is transformed into the joy of the singularity within the common.

In other words, a zoöphilic and savage love is an attentive care for the beautifully sublime nature of monstrous life as a suspension of species identification—it is a kind of free play *a la* Schiller that lacks predetermined hierarchies of value between sensation and sense, reason and affect, human and animal. In other words, love is an affective involution that does not collapse the two into one but rather opens a space of mutual becoming-different, becoming-singular in the shared (dis)location of exceptionality. To remain in love thus means "to live in intimacy with a stranger, not in order to draw him closer, or to make him known, but rather to keep him strange" (Agamben 1995, 61) and thus explore the gap that separates and in that separation remains open to an infinite exposure of the self to the experience of the monstrous. Love of the beautiful sublime is the ethic of connecting consciousness discussed in chapter two—an ethic that binds us not to the other but rather to the gap that joins and separates in the state of exception. It is a revelation not of a particular content but of the open potentiality of the monstrous as such. *Savagely zoöphilic love is always out of bounds.*

Love is the ethic that makes friendship possible in the coming community. Agamben's definition (2009) of friendship as a "con-division" (36) is a relation without sharing birth or law or place or taste but rather the simple existential fact of *life* beyond the anthropological machine. Friendship (a meeting of two singularities) renders inoperative every division instituted by Power. For us, this means that the love of friends cuts across identities or communities based on recognition and belonging. It is the sensation of common use (whatever value) by whomever (the multitude of singularities that comprise the surplus common). In other words, love is not the affective connection with this or that form of life (a belonging to this or that community whose image we see reflected in our self-conception), but is rather a closeness to the specialness of life as such—to the open potentiality of life that emerges when the ban of the anthropological machine is left to idle. Zoöphilia at its most savage is love of this monstrous terrain of unruly flesh, of the zone of indistinction between humans and animals, and in this sense is the quintessential act of love within the multitude.

Exopedagogy as the training in love gains a new urgency, helping to organize the imaginative impulses that animate our awareness of different kinds of loving relationships. The ultimate flaw with the love outlined earlier between human and nonhuman animals is that this love does not participate in the common field that emerges when the anthropological machine is suspended, and reduces nonhuman animals to objects rather than to actors in mutually joyful touching or simply replaces real world struggles for altermodernity with escapist fantasies of capitalist design (fairy tales). Against domination or appropriation, zoöphilic love becomes an ethic of divine violence that separates itself from the sacrifice of life by a sovereign decision. And like divine violence, it is educational. It is apprenticeship in the biopoetics of wherever and whatever that defines the common use of our collective relations between human and nonhuman animals. Love is the ethical use of divine violence to forge a new kinship bestiary that is strange, and in that strangeness opens itself up to a new form of learning out of bounds.

In *Empire*, Hardt and Negri (2000) extol the representative figure of St. Francis of Assisi in a culminating section entitled "MILITANT," where he is offered as a revolutionary figure of monstrous love:

> To denounce the poverty of the multitude he adopted that common condition and discovered there the ontological power of a new society. The communist militant does the same, identifying in the common condition of the multitude its enormous wealth. Francis in opposition to nascent capitalism refused every instrumental discipline, and in opposition to the mortification of the flesh (in poverty and in the constituted order) he posed a joyous life, including all of being and nature, the animals, sister moon, brother sun, the birds of the field, the poor and exploited humans, together against the will of power and corruption. Once again in postmodernity we find ourselves in Francis's situation, posing against the misery of power the joy of being. (413)

A real person of flesh and blood, unlike the Na'vi, Francis too was an enthusiastic friend and lover to the universe; a savage zoöphile.[11] He desired and achieved communion with all things. He was, above all else, monstrously passionate about germinal life in all its organic and inorganic permutations and combinations.

Francis of Assisi's "passion"—his sainted joy of being—was not a superstitious joy of the willfully and blissfully ignorant, however. In order to encounter his kingdom of God, paradoxically, he had to resist the social mores and institutions that attempted to mediate his ecstatic relationship with *zoë*. Thus, his joy is a complex covenant between spiritual affirmation and political resignation. A story from his life as recounted in *The Legend of Perugia* (Habig 1973) makes this clear. It is told that Francis was one day in the company of friars and scholars who sought to expound the proper conduct of their religious community, doing so through didactic reference to the authority of St. Augustine, St. Benedict, and St. Bernard, respectively. In response, Francis remained unconvinced. So, they brought him to a local Cardinal (and future Pope) in order that the Church's own authority might imprint upon Francis the necessity of finding inspiration in such saints as proposed for a properly attuned moral life. Instead, Francis took the Cardinal by the hand and announced, "My brothers, God called me to walk in the way of humility and showed me the way of simplicity. I do not want to hear any mention of the rule of St. Augustine, of St. Bernard, or of St. Benedict. The Lord has told me that he wanted to make a new fool of me in the world, and God does not want to lead us by any other knowledge than that" (1088–1089). A profane proclamation for sure—one that resists the temptation to sacrifice life for the virtues of saintly existence.

Leonardo Boff (1997) explains the Great Refusal of Francis of Assisi in this way, "This is St. Francis's new path: beyond existing systems; beyond the emerging bourgeois system; beyond the declining feudal system; beyond the prevailing religious monastic system. He is a fool (*passus*) only to the systems that he is leaving behind" (207). The joyful nature of Francis is his foolish pleasure. This is in some respects the "gay science" of Nietzsche—falling through the cracks of the established social order into a state of ontological anarchy, Francis learns to dance on the edge of an abyss. As camel, the Vatican was his burden. As lion, he articulates a new heretical order of faith. Then, in alternating the terms by which the world makes sense—in discovering that every grain of sand is holy (i.e., in common with the whole)—he is reborn as a divine child who can perceive the reason to have high spirits about a life of bare necessities.[12] Anticipating the mantra of 1960s guru Timothy Leary (1999), St. Francis "turned on, tuned in, and dropped out," not in the form of a linear pedagogical method, but consubstantially as an ever unfolding exopedagogical expression of his becoming-monstrous—an exodus from the relationship between love and recognition, community and belonging, and imagination and Power.

The term he used for "fool," *passus*, is semiotically rich in ways that demand our attention for a theory of the multitude. At once, it is rooted in the idea of "passion" (*passio*) but also in enduring "suffering" or "disease" (i.e., dis-ease). Hence, the notion of the Christian passion play is suggested. Moreover, *passus* is used in *The Civil Wars* (1914) by Julius Caesar to describe the "outstretched hands" and

arms of the conquered masses, supplicating and pleading in trepi-
dation for his protective mercy. Of course, the outstretched hands
are also representative of Jesus hanging on the cross (in *Matthew* 27:
45–46, "My God, my God, why hast thou forsaken me?"), and they
are also a common symbol of the pauper who begs alms ("Brother,
can you spare a dime?"). Still, yet another connotation of hands and
arms wide open is that of the friend reaching out in order to initiate
a grand embrace with the stranger, the foreigner, the alien. Thus, the
new humanity of Francis represents the occurrence of radical empathy
with *zoë* out of bounds of the ontological purity of the community
and its anthropological immunization. Monstrous love is both sublime terror and beautiful wonder.

The "outstretching" of *passus* is also etymologically related to the
Latin root *pando*—which means "to spread out," to unfold, to throw
open, and so in this way, to make known. It is Pandora's box releasing
its gifts upon the world. *Sporaia*, to be a Franciscan fool is to scatter
one's seeds of wisdom and pollinate one's truth. It is diasporic and
germinal. However, as bell hooks reminds us in *Belonging* (2009), the
history of diaspora in a social context additionally points both to the
mobile luxury of imperial privilege and the pain of refugees who seek
to flee the authoritarian orders of Empire. Thus, *passus* also intimates
qualities of "movement" of insurgencies and of Power. It is literally a
pace—a measure of how far one has moved. Poetically, a *passus* can
be a "footstep," or a track in the soil—an embodied orientation, a
biogram of movements, passages, speeds, and transformations rather
than a cognitive map of rational coordinates. Fransciscan foolishness
must therefore be interpreted as the desire to make a mark with one's
life in this fashion, which then becomes a historical gesture to a future
age for reconceptualizing *bios* and *zoë*.

Boff (1997) writes, "He [Francis] follows his own route and that
makes him, as biographer Thomas of Celano put it, '*homo alterius
saeculi*,' a man of a new age, a new paradigm" (207). We might say
that his sainthood was in setting out on a pilgrimage for a love destined for another time of utopian proportions (eternity). In desiring
to embody the impossible and so make it a possibility, Francis of Assisi
altered his own age and thus our own as well for we share a common
history. Yet, the pedagogical mystery of his monstrous riddle remains:
to follow him, we cannot make an *Avatar* of his life in the attempt to
make ourselves the avatars of his zoöphilic and savage commitments
to a form-of-life without name. The simple truth that drew him near
will always be more than what we can understand or make out of him,
and in a real way we do violence to the Franciscan event by hoping

that it could serve as a model through which we might learn to live and love. Even as we turn to him for educational clues, therefore, we find his message to us is, over and over again, that we are clueless. Yet, he is the model militant of another-time—an outrageous personage through and through. An untimely friend, an unhelpful assistant.

This notion of the outrageous is a central concern for exopedagogy as we have attempted to outline in this book. To be outraged is, by definition, to pass beyond reasonable bounds. In this it can seem excessive and even violent, or as we have related herein—monsterously divine. But this is always from the perspective of the hegemonic order and the dominant norms in place. Following Hardt and Negri's vision of a revolutionary multitude for absolute democracy, our intervention has been to offer that such a movement possesses (or is possessed by) a decidedly educational dimension. What we term exopedagogy is thus both the means and end to which this savagely zoöphilic movement must aspire. This educational vocation of the multitude seems now to manifest a planetary and posthumanist rhythm ("movement in time"). Can we come to understand how to uncover the secret history of the future and so then produce our own expansive songs of liberated joy and sustained "Yes!" making? This is our exopedagogical challenge, our monster in the closet. To embrace it with all our being may be both the most difficult and simple thing that we can learn to do.

In the strange space located out of bounds, the feral child, the UFOther, and myriad strangers that contaminate inside and outside we find the creaturely excesses and untimely friendships that inscribe a new vision of love. A love that is always profane, never sacred! Always poor, never rich! Always contaminated, never pure! Always common, never private! Always outrageous, never laudable! Always savage, never tame! Love is not the love of this or that but rather of specialness, and it is here that exopedagogy finds its final location: on the edge of the forest, standing with St. Francis, arms open to the joy that is this monstrous life.

NOTES

INTRODUCTION

1. See Asma (2009) as well as Daston and Park (2001) for definitive catalogs of these various manifestations of the monstrous.

2. In an interesting critique of Deleuze and Guattari, Donna Haraway (2008) has argued that their analysis of becoming-animal—which is zoömorphically inclined—reinscribes "misogyny, fear of aging, incuriosity about animals, and horror at the ordinariness of flesh" (30). In other words, while cloaked within a savage critique of capitalism and Oedipalization of the subject, their rendition of becoming-animal is superstitious of women and the intimate foreignness of dogs and cats, and the aging. At the same time, as Zipporah Weisberg (2009) points out, Haraway herself overly privileges genetically altered life forms such as oncomice without critically analyzing the capitalist systems of production underlying such experimentation. In other words, zoömorphic imaginings without savage supplementation overly valorize becomings without understanding how border-crossing between the human and the animal is not inherently politically progressive and in fact is the cultural logic of postmodern capitalism.

3. As we will examine later, zoöphilia is the dynamic movement that enlivens the imaginative production of zoömorphisms. Thus body and force are ontologically one, and our distinction is merely perspectival.

4. Although Gary Genosko (2002) has argued that Deleuze and Guattari utilize the bestiary in *A Thousand Plateaus* to rethink territoriality as a form of artistic expression rather than aggression, Bartkowski is the first contemporary theorist to explicitly identify the form of the bestiary as a critical tool for navigating what we are referring to as the contemporary monstrous state of exception.

5. For a slightly different description of education as a monstrous, inquiry-based practice, see Wallin (2008). Also it is important to note Cris Mayo's (2007) return to Aristophanes' story of the androgynes in order to theorize the political role of desire in genderqueer movements in public schools. For both Wallin and Mayo, the monster as imaginary excess is central to rethinking the matrix of desire, identity, and theories of knowledge that inform schooling practices.

6. If Heidegger (2000) once argued that the proper dwelling for the human is an uncanny homelessness (a being-foreign-to-what-is-familiar), then we would add that this dwelling in the uncanny is not metaphysical but rather purely historical—the result of living-labor's capacity for producing the surplus common that exists beyond the boundaries of community and nation-state and that transforms all dwelling into an exodus (see the Intermezzo of this book for a further discussion of the surplus common).

INTERMEZZO

1. In a radically different context, Asma (2009) argues that there are "uncanny" correspondences between Heidegger's existentialist analysis of angst and the cosmic fear induced by gothic horror auteur H.P. Lovecraft. For both Honig and Asma, the gothic is a defining imaginative matrix for social, existential, and political philosophy in the twentieth century.
2. Interestingly, Althusser (2001) argues that there is a strict separation between art and science. Art "makes us *see,* and therefore gives to us in the form of '*seeing,*' '*perceiving,*' and '*feeling*' (which is not the form of knowing)" (152). Thus art can only produce conclusions and not the premises. Yet if we read Marx carefully, his monstrous science is precisely located in a terrain between the aesthetic and the scientific—we cannot know *without* also feeling, we cannot *see* without also cognizing our perceptions. The educational role of the imagination as a feeling of thought's becoming is therefore lost in Althusser's formulation.
3. Our understanding of gothic narrative as a pedagogical technology is radically different from the romanticism espoused by educational philosopher Kieran Egan (1994). Egan emphasizes the connection between imagination and romantic identification with transcendental, heroic figures or virtues. Although both are concerned with the extremes of culture and society, the gothic narrative is more interested in uncanny (dis) identifications or strangely monstrous close encounters that throw into doubt the possibility of transcendental association with timeless ideals. In other words, one world is populated with swashbuckling heroes/rebels while the other with uncertain monsters.
4. Certainly Marx also gestures toward an allegory of the cyborg and of the automaton as monsters of capitalist industrialization. In his description of machinery in capitalist production, Marx (1990) writes, "Machinery is misused in order to transform the worker, from his very childhood, into a part of a specialized machine" (547). Because our book focuses on natureculture ecologies within a biomorphic imaginative diagram, we have chosen to focus our text elsewhere, and thus leave this work for future bestiaries that have yet to be written.
5. In this sense, Marx's bestiary stands in sharp contrast to the de-historicized and highly romantic bestiary of contemporary artist Gregory Colbert, whose

NOTES 153

"nomadic museum" contained exoticized photographs of indigenous animals and people living in harmony. Colbert referred to his migratory exhibit as a "universal bestiary" and a "family of animals" that celebrates biodiversity. As Nichole Shukin (2010) argues, Colbert's work is not simply harmless new-age romanticism, but is a dangerous form of animal fetishism where that animal other (interchangeable with "primitive" indigenous humans) is rendered through an orientalist framework. In typical colonialist fashion, Colbert—as a white, male explorer—produces exotic images of a lost wholism between nature and culture lacking in western industrialized countries. Shukin summarizes: "On the one hand, [Colbert] anthropomorphizes animals by attributing to them a subjectivity and an agency that are ostensibly readily transparent...enabling Colbert to play up their willing participation in the drama of interspecies intimacy he has staged...On the other hand, Colbert demotes the human subjects appearing in his photos to a dumb animality by excluding them from the rhetoric of collaboration and the possession of subjectivity that it connotes" (197). As opposed to the reinscription of colonialist hierarchies and anthropocentric wish-fulfillment, the critical bestiary that we propose challenges such hierarchies and abuses of power by focusing on the *exotic stranger within*: capitalism itself as a monstrous, historically specific set of social and economic relations. In this sense, we are calling for a bestiary that recognizes its own historical and political embeddedness against anthropocentric and superstitious imaginings in order to join in the fight for human-animal-becomings that escape domination and exploitation in the suspended state of the monstrous.

6. It is also interesting to note another connection between the vampire and contemporary models of bioproduction. Bram Stoker's novel *Dracula* famously begins with the English solicitor Jonathan Harker traveling to the Carpathian Mountains to meet with Count Dracula. Harker's mission is to provide legal consultation to the count for a major real estate transaction overseen by Harker's employer. Thus the story is set in motion by a movement from a remote feudal estate to the imperial hub, London, with its "teeming millions." The question of premodern forms of rent at the center of *Dracula* foreshadows the growing importance of ground-rent within the bioproduction of the metropolis over and above wage labor (Hardt and Negri 2009, 141). While rent was often thought to be a premodern anachronism, in post-Fordist production, rent has returned with new importance as a source of profit. Hence a new justification for Fredric Jameson's (2009) urgent call for a new spatialized logic of capitalist dialectics.

7. See Wolfenstein (1993) for a further analysis of how the commodity form becomes internalized as a model for subjectivity.

8. See, for instance, Hardt and Negri's (1994; 2000; 2009) ongoing critique of the state form as a territorializing force.

9. Here we might turn to Jacques Rancière (2010) who argues that the politically democratic nature of the aesthetic regime is found in its insistence

on the immediate identity of logos and pathos without hierarchy. This "identity of contraries" (23) is precisely the "end of an ordered state of relations between what can be seen and what can be said, knowledge and action, activity and passivity" (21). In this book, we will repeatedly emphasize how this democratic state of exception is an aesthetic moment of deformation between human and nonhuman animals, between the sublime nature of the monstrous and the beauty of the community of equals.

10. At the outset we must be clear, the multitude does not abandon Marx's theory of class struggle. According to Negri (2008), the multitude "is also a concept of working class—and it is certainly a concept of exploited labour power, but it is more extensive than the concept of working class, because, inasmuch as the whole of society is today dominated—and exploited—by capital, the multitude corresponds to this social dimension of exploitation. The multitude is not the same as the working class because the temporal and spatial dimensions of exploitation have been utterly transformed. The form of labour power which is today hegemonic over the fabric of production is immaterial, intellectual, relational and linguistic labour—and a labour power which is flexible both in space and in time...the multitude is mobile and migrant" (46). Multitude is "an internally different, multiple social subject whose constitution and action is based not on identity or unity (or, much less, indifference) but on what it has in common...The multitude is the only social subject capable of realizing democracy, that is, the rule of everyone by everyone" (Hardt and Negri 2004, 100). In sum, the multitude is composed of singularities working collectively to produce the common or social life through networks of immaterial production. If the working class produced material goods through factory labor, the multitude is an expanded notion of production that includes the linguistic, affective, and intellectual dimensions of life itself—production that includes biopolitics (the conduct of our collective lives) and what we would call biopoetics (specific ways of living and imagining social relations). In other words, immaterial labor is the biopolitical transubstantiation of class labor into a multitudinous uprising. Where the question of revolution once concerned the dialectical overcoming of wage labor, within the monstrous state of exception, revolution now directly revolves around the continual production of the surplus common in all its dimensions. The critical political question thus becomes: Can the multitude manage the surplus common or will this surplus be transformed back into the dialectic of private versus public property?

11. Our reading of Hardt and Negri should be seen as an attempt to highlight the most progressive elements of their theory. For a more complex reading of residual anthropocentrisms in Hardt and Negri's work, see Lewis (in press), Shukin (2010), and LaCapra (2009).

12. Our appropriation of Haraway in this instance is intentionally *selective*. As Weisberg (2009) has convincingly argued, Haraway's more recent

work on companion species is not so much a furtherance of her previous socialist-feminist inspired critical posthumanism as it is a betrayal.
While emphasizing the inter-relational nature of becomings, her theory of companion species unfortunately reinscribes a sado-humanist
dominance over the nonhuman animal that she otherwise decries. In
this sense, we want to amplify the politically progressive valences of her
imagination while also recognizing superstitious limitations.

13. As a small footnote, in his chapter on primitive accumulation in
Capital: Volume One (1990), Marx writes, "In the history of primitive
accumulation, all revolutions are epoch-making that act as levers for
the capitalist class in the course of its formation; but this is true above
all for those moments when great masses of men are suddenly and forc-
ible torn from their means of subsistence, and hurled onto the labor-
market as free, unprotected and rightless proletarians" (876). What we
want to emphasize in this passage is a slippage in translation that has
potentially important ramifications for understanding Marx's nascent,
zoömorphic imagination. The phrase "free and unprotected" is a translation of the German word *vogelfrei*, which could also be rendered as
"free as a bird." Here Marx's fleeting utopian imagination is captured
by the movement of birds, and the nonhuman animal becomes the
inspiration for a new freedom beyond capitalism and beyond the law of
the human.

CHAPTER 1

1. If, as Nicole Shukin (2010) reminds us, we must "develop the material
unconscious of capitalist modernity as the denied, disavowed historicity
of animals and of animal rendering [both literal and figurative]" (92) so
too is there a material unconscious linking humanist pedagogy to animal taming.

2. Summarizing Friedrich Schiller's vision of free play, Jacques Rancière
argues that in play there is a true moment of indistinction between the
intellect and the sensible, between activity and inactivity, and we might
add between the human animal and the nonhuman animal. Quoting
Rancière (2009), "If aesthetic 'play' and 'appearance' found a new community, then this is because they stand for the refutation, within the
sensible, of this opposition between intelligent form and sensible matter
which, properly speaking, is a difference between two humanities [or in
our case two species]" (31).

3. Espositio not only turns to Nietzsche for his affirmative reconstruction
of biopolitics but also to Hannah Arendt and her concept of natality.
While we agree that a shift from death to birth and thus an opening up
of community to the arrival of the new is an important political and educational move, we would also like to suggest that the concept of natality
must be positioned in relation not only to biopolitics but also posthumanist theory. For Arendt (1998), natality is a central feature of the

human condition that enables individuals to engage in political action. It is this anthropocentrism that must be questioned. If natality is only for the human actor, and never for the inhuman, posthuman, or nonhuman, then natality is part and parcel of an anthropocentric imagination that constrains our understanding of political resistance and transformation. In other words, let us really introduce something new into the world precisely by rupturing the necessary and exclusive link between natality and the human condition! Let natality be monstrous!

CHAPTER 2

1. Nuwaubians are a group that mixes the politics of afrocentric black nationalism with ideas about the alien origin of humanity and an eschatological return of alien civilization. Posadists are followers of the once leading Latin American Trotskyite Juan Posadas, who equate post-revolutionary society with a Socialism brought to earth from what they believe is an alien future. Raëlians recently grabbed headlines by claiming to be the first to successfully clone human beings (in fact their organization Clonaid claimed two!), but while the movement believes in the humane and progressive use of science and technology to live in accordance with the alien powers that are its true origins, Raëlians additionally believe in sensualism and other doctrines that give this group a unique agenda with wide popular appeal. We use "New Age" loosely here as a signifier that points to a general class of post-1960s literature and the spiritually minded people who have made a culture around it.
2. Although Daston and Park dismiss tabloid interest in UFOs, aliens, and the paranormal as no longer capable of subversion or sublime education (banal media culture merely demonstrates a yearning for lost wonderment), we would argue that there is still the possibility of encountering the strange, rare, and wondrous within certain forms of media culture that (perhaps fleetingly) ignite and intensify our savage and zoömorphic imaginations.
3. The prefix "exo-" denotes a state of being beyond not simply the earth but of common sense as such. Thus, theorizing about alien practices is the study of an exoculture, and our work here is in part exocultural studies.
4. Some utopias may in fact be fictive narratives about "no place" or projects that lay out plans and laws for a perfect world, but we do not take that up here and it would be a mistake to associate either David Icke or our own work with these traditions.
5. For a much more detailed description, refer to David Icke's *The Biggest Secret* and *Children of the Matrix*.
6. This theory is an example of how Icke combines various narrative strains under one signification, theorizing that the Anunnaki come from the

Draco star system, with connotations, therefore, of dragon, draconian law, and Count Dracula.

7. Before becoming a full-time alien conspiracy expert, Icke had served as a UK Green party spokesperson.

8. For instance, Icke's own name tends to outsize and dominate even his own book titles and conference fliers, sending the message that it is the star-status of his personality that is ultimately being sold more than the infotainment he provides—which is wholly in line with the logic of Hollywood spectacle and is a marketing technique often used by the movie-trailer industry to generate audience share.

9. In his work, Icke also makes much use of the analysis of the negative imagery of the owl, which he describes as a Freemasonic emblem signifying a relationship to Babylonian Aryan/reptoid cults. In conclusion, along with UFO groups that posit that alien dolphinoids have arrived on earth in order to save humanity, Icke commonly uses the representation of the dolphin as signifying cosmic peace and justice.

10. It should be pointed out that in his most recent work Icke critiques the Christian and far-right, thereby distancing himself from that association.

CHAPTER 3

1. The Cottingley fairies were a spectacular hoax perpetrated by two young cousins, Frances Griffiths and Elsie Wright, who lived in Cottingley, England. In 1917, they produced the first of a series of photographs that appeared to display them cavorting with fairies and gnomes in their country garden. Sir Arthur Conan Doyle published the photos and wrote a book, *The Coming of the Fairies* (1921), that defended their authenticity. In 1978, however, it was definitively revealed that the girls had produced their fairies by cutting them out of Arthur Shepperson's *Princess Mary's Gift Book* (1915) and in 1981, the cousins finally confessed their fakery. Frances Griffiths insisted until the end of her life, though, that they really *had* fairy experiences that had served to generate the idea for their photographs. Two 1997 films, *Photographing Fairies* and *Fairy Tale: A True Story*, dealt directly with the subject of the Cottingley fairies.

2. According to the top website dedicated to tracking movies' box office sales, http://www.boxofficemojo.com, the recent film trilogy of J. R. R. Tolkien's *Lord of the Rings* has generated sales totaling $2,916,919,070 worldwide (as of May 2008). Of course, Peter Jackson's films and Tolkien's work itself contain allegorical elements that support a critical faery narrative, such as we argue for here, and so must be considered a contested terrain of meanings. For one compelling interpretation of *Lord of the Rings*, see http://www.youtube.com/watch?v=vkmczhkrKYA&NR.

3. Similar work has been done analyzing Disney's animated strips and movies; see Dorfman and Mattelart (1984) and Giroux (2001).

4. Etymologically, "faery" is simply the older variant of "fairy" and the words can be used interchangeably. Trubshaw (1998) writes, "The English word 'fairy' comes to us, via the Old French *faerie*, from the Latin *fata*, meaning 'fate.' This means the roots are with the classical Greek Fates, who were believed to control the fate and destiny of the human race." He also links it to the Greek concept of *phasma*, which served to identify a range of liminal beings. Indeed, the recent urban invention of fairies as tiny winged people occludes the more common folk belief that figures them as a myriad of ghostly beings occurring in all shapes and sizes (Evans-Wentz 2002; Spence 1997; Stewart 1995). Spence (1997, 114–115) provides the most careful etymology of the term and additionally notes its connection to the latin word *fatare*, meaning "to enchant." Harte (2004) traces how the terms of "elf" and "fairy," as well as "puck" and "dwarf," became synonymous out of the developing historical literature of various European traditions since the Middle Ages.
5. The terms share a common origin in the Greek concept of *psyche*.
6. A "fairy" is also slang for male homosexuals. While derogatory today, it appears to have had a positive valence when it arose in late nineteenth-century New York to characterize the transvestite men who populated secret mixed-race clubs that existed on the fringes of city life in Red Light districts such as the Bowery. Middle class gentlemen would frequent these environs after hours to cavort with "the fairies." While not technically faery in our usage of the term, these fairies function similarly in their ability to disrupt patriarchal and heterosexual hegemonic norms while remaining invisible to society and existing beyond the bounds of authority. Of importance for our work here, contemporary neopagan faery subcultures have been noted for their uncharacteristic tolerance of homosexual, lesbian, and transgendered identities (Pike 2001). At least some of these neopagan communities are considered "Radical Faerie" communities, an eclectic spiritual offshoot of the Gay Liberation movement. The Radical Faerie movement is generally considered to have begun in 1979, when the founder of the modern gay movement, Harry Hay, helped to issue a call for a "Spiritual Conference of Radical Faeries." A leading Radical Faerie website is: http://www.radfae.org. A recent treatment of the subculture can be found in Rodgers in Hume and McPhillips (2006) as well as in Povinelli (2006).
7. See their website at http://www.fairycongress.com. In photos archived there, humans in fairy costumes are shown parading in the moonlight in front of a "fairy tree," surrounded by an atmosphere of "orbs" (i.e., lights considered to be spiritual faery beings).
8. On the New Age movement, see Melton (2001).
9. By "land" we do not intend a landscape devoid of cultural communities, but rather seek to delineate a natureculture spatial terrain in which people attempt to produce multiple forms of sustainable agrarian place-based literacies (Donehower et al. 2007).

10. Of course today's thanatopolitics is zoöcidal, though not in the sense that it destroys *zöe* (which cannot be destroyed by definition). Rather, in instituting a transnational network of murder over life, capitalist life is zoöcidal in that it seeks to colonize any and all spaces in which cultures based on exopedagogical relations of teaching and learning with animal others can thrive.

11. Indeed, virtual Paganism is aptly named because much of its growth as a movement is due to the Internet (Davy 2007), which is used to organize the subculture and advertise its activities in ways typical of other online subcultures. This is an ambiguous development for Neopaganism, however, as the religion is by definition about emplaced relationships to the land and nature, whereas the Internet is a manifestation of the global industrial order and can represent threats to place-based land ethics even as it is utilized to serve them.

12. Hereon, by "Neopagan" we intend "virtual Pagan" in contrast to "Eco-Pagan."

13. The Starwood Festival and Tripsy the fairy are chronicled in Pike (2001).

14. The spectacular nature of global media culture, however, works against faery and for fairy. Hence, critical readings of *Pan's Labyrinth* that extol its exopedagogical virtues must also speak to its role as a major film industry commodity that has grossed over eighty-three million dollars (as of May 2008). This monetary success has led to its director, Guillermo del Toro, being chosen to direct *The Hobbit*, the fourth in the global blockbuster *Lord of the Rings* movie series (see note 2). He also was chosen as the director of *Hellboy II: The Golden Army*, a 2008 film based on a popular comic book series in which Hellboy, a Nazi-bred demon cum maverick superhero who fights thanklessly for justice, must save the world from an underworld faery rebellion that seeks to destroy humanity and establish rule over the Earth. The original film, *Hellboy*, has grossed nearly one hundred million dollars (as of May 2008). Interestingly, a major part of the marketing campaign for *Hellboy II* has been to create a fictitious activist organization called HETFET, or Humans for the Ethical Treatment of Fairies, Elves and Trolls. The "organization" has its own real website updating its progress of protecting magical forest denizens since the 1960s (see http://hetfet.org) and a real press release was also sent to various media outlets claiming that a mass protest occurred during February 2008 at New York City's Jacob Javits Center in which HETFET activists protested with Save the Trolls picket signs until being arrested and dispersed by police (see http://blog.wired.com/underwire/2008/04/hellboy-ii-hetf.html#previouspost). Such tongue-in-cheek marketing reveals the contradictory nature of the context in which we consider del Toro as a potential faery auteur.

15. On the wild hunt, see http://en.wikipedia.org/wiki/Wild_Hunt.

Conclusion

1. Relatedly, in discussing the figure of the monster, Jacques Derrida imagined it as a new "species"—to quote: "A monster is a species for which we do not yet have a name, which does not mean that the species is abnormal, namely, the composition or hybridisation of already known species. Simply, it shows itself [*elle se montre*]—that is what the word monster means—it shows itself in something that is not yet shown and that therefore looks like a hallucination, it strikes the eye, it frightens precisely because no anticipation had prepared one to identify this figure" (in Weber 1995, 385–386). It is, to use our language, the UFOther. Whether the monstrous figure of a new humanity is best analyzed in terms of reconstructions of race, class, gender, species, or other social analytics is a quintessential exopedagogical problem posed by the present moment. Without dismissing single-issue approaches *in toto*, the dialogical and dialectical nature of a multitudinous exopedagogy seeks to create emancipatory relationships between single-issue groups or theorists. It thereby craves a utopian politics of friendship that aims for "total liberation" (Best 2006b; Kahn and Humes 2009) from predetermined subject positions.

2. Ché's reflections on the interconnection between love, revolution, and what Ivan Illich would describe as "deschooling" society stand in stark contrast to Theodor Adorno's warning that overcoming fascist psychology through love is a dangerous illusion. In the essay "Education After Auschwitz" (1998) Adorno offers a picture of hard, cold, and manipulative character traits that must be overcome through an education that promotes "critical self-reflection" (193). Progressive educational imperatives to love children are not a cure for this condition but rather act as part of the ideology of coldness itself. Adorno writes, "The exhortation to love—even in its imperative form, that one *should* do it—is itself part of the ideology coldness perpetuates. It bears the compulsive, oppressive quality that counteracts the ability to love" (202). Bearing in mind this dialectical paradox (that the educational mandate to love, or the revolutionary clarion call to "love the people," can turn into an instrumentalized command that negates the immediacy and spontaneity of love), our project hopes to create the preconditions for a new savage and zoöphilic love that ruptures imaginary identifications with Power from a location out of bounds of humanist pedagogical interventions where love is conveniently Oedipalized, nationalized, or instrumentalized.

3. While our claim is that zoöphilia acts as an educative force, our social focus on the pedagogy of love moves us beyond teacher-student or school-focused discussions offered by theorists such as Cho (2005); Garrison (1997); Darder (2002); and hooks (2010; 2004). While our conception has not been consciously developed out of their positions, our approach to educational love shares sympathies with the larger cultural and political treatment given by Burch (2000) and hooks (2009), as well

as Freire (1998) but with a new inflection. Often theorists such as Freire and hooks have spoken about radical love in education as the affective possibility for producing a political/historical common body. Yet the talk of love tends to get read romantically and idealistically. As an alternative, we want to emphasize that zoöphilia is *always* a zoömorphics in which a body-in-(love)relation is in exodus from itself, simultaneously pushing the boundaries of our sensual apparatus as well as our imaginative diagrams. Thus, theoretically, to the degree we can posit novel zoömorphic imaginings, we open space for new forms of zoöphilia as sociopolitical happening; likewise, to the degree that we involve ourselves in modes of radical zoöphilia, our imagination becomes open to new morphologies of revolutionary *zoë* beyond the controls of biopower and its internal relationship to death.

4. We anticipate that the reader may wonder if it is altogether fair, much less scholarly sound, to associate the form of love denoted by the concept "*philia*" (e.g., zoöphilia) with mythic figures such as Aphrodite or Ishtar. Suffice it here to say that while the Greek "*philos*" is often translated to mean the love inherent in friendship, this disguises the polysemic range of emotional meanings actually identified by the term. In truth it characterized everything from a mode of formal address to fellow citizens to the love of one's family and that which one held most dear, as well as the amorous feelings for a mistress or life mate (in current parlance, one's "significant other" is definitely a *philos*). It is also the distant root of the concept of "affiliation," and we therefore seek to use the idea of zoöphilia inclusively as a space in which the multitude of qualities common to the act of love can be affiliated with one another through theoretical reflection—if you will, *zœffiliation*—as a way of reconceptualizing a new notion of friendship out of bounds in the state of monstrous exception.

5. The work of Slavoj Zizek (2008) on "divine violence" deserves consideration in this regard. While we leave in-depth discussion of this point for the future, here we would note that Zizek's point about figures such as Robespierre and Guevara (202) is exactly that they do not claim a foundational relationship to an essential ground (i.e., nature) for their revolutionary acts. Rather, it is their radically subjective courage to act in the face of their knowledge that such a ground is necessarily lacking that distinguishes them in his mind as potential bearers of truth-as-Event. Considering charges of eco-fascism made against groups such as Earth First! by the social ecologist Murray Bookchin in the 1990s, it remains to be clarified as to whether today's eco-radicalist groups or individuals are closer in kind to the early twentieth century *volkische* movement that inspired German fascism or to the anti-foundationalist revolutionary ethics favored by Zizek.

6. The name Pandora references the Greek myth of Epimetheus and Prometheus. Notably, this myth is the concluding centerpiece of Ivan Illich's famous work *Deschooling Society* (1970), in which he called for the return in a new age of Epimethean individuals whose values would

align with what we now imagine as sustainability. For Illich, we needed a turn away from the dangers and toil wrought by Promethean culture (akin to Marcuse), but Epimetheans distinguish themselves all the same by practicing collaboration with their Promethean counterparts even in their stark differences. While Pandora is often considered one who looses great sin and plague on the earth by foolishly opening her box containing them, Illich celebrates that from an Epimethean standpoint her name means "All Giver," and that her box was really a womb or sanctuary conserved to contain only "hope." On these terms, the meaning of the myth is to teach Promethean culture the true nature of hope, which is not in Illich's opinion the production of unquenchable needs, but the dignified joy found in a philosophical state of necessity (see Kahn 2009).

7. *Avatar* endows the Na'vi with an idealized form of, what in indigenous educational circles is called, "Traditional Ecological Knowledge" or TEK (see Berkes 1993). Indeed, a study of the cultural understandings and practices of the Na'vi in light of the book *Power and Place: Indian Education in America* (2001) by Vine Deloria and Daniel Wildcat would prove fruitful. Deloria and Wildcat suggest therein that indigenous cultural systems almost universally predicate themselves on a cosmological understanding of what they call "power"—an all-pervasive force that in this book we identify as "*zoë.*" For Deloria and Wildcat, such power is always in relation to a place, and when emplaced it takes the form of a particular "personality"—a *bios*, or biography. Such personalities exist collectively over time in the lived form of what they further term the "habitude" of a people. Yet, make no mistake, we are not arguing here that *Avatar* is an appropriate representation of TEK. As we suggest, the film clearly activates a social critique based on the Rousseauian "noble savage" and so is more akin to a white liberal colonial fantasy of TEK's zoöphilia in many respects than an accurate biography of indigenous eco-spiritual knowledge systems. In this it links up with a variety of New Age appropriations of indigenous education and culture that can be called "plastic shamanism" (on TEK in contemporary context; see Kahn 2010).

8. As noted by Beetz (2004), there is a paradox at work in that the rise of animal welfare concerns in secular nations has, with important exceptions such as documented by the Home Office (2000) in Britain, perhaps led to an increase in the desire to criminalize bestiality-related acts in recent years. On the other hand, secular views of liberal tolerance have moved to identify such behavior as individually criminal and not a humiliation to human species-being as in times past. Moreover, the move to create criminal statues for bestiality itself serves as a kind of proof of its continued practice amongst a significant percentage of the population.

9. We should note that "zoöphilia" was first scientifically defined in the nineteenth century by the psychiatrist Richard von Kraft Ebing, who

used it to denote that a person had an erotic attraction to animals' fur or excitement upon viewing the copulation of animals. He did not believe zoöphilia involved the desire for intercourse with nonhuman animals and this was not included in his definition. In the twentieth century, conversely, zoöphilia was identified by the American Psychiatric Association (APA) as a form of paraphilia, or clinical form of perverse sexual and psychological dysfunction in individuals due to their attraction to and desire for intercourse with nonhuman animals. The most recent version of the APA's professional handbook (DSMIV) continues to think of zoöphilia as a human sexual and psychological affinity for nonhuman animals, but no longer considers it as a form of disorder unless an individual's attraction to nonhuman animals causes personal distress.

10. Green criminologist Piers Beirne (2009) has arguably been the leading advocate challenging this differentiation from a strong animal rights perspective. Beirne believes that zoophiles incorrectly assume that their nonhuman animal partners can signal forms of consent, which would thereby transform acts of zoösadistic bestiality into zoöphilic relationships based in reciprocity and mutual affection. According to Beirne, nonhuman animals can never consent in this way and, additionally, human sexual relations with them almost always involve some degree of coercion. Further, he believes that zoöphilic and bestial relations with nonhuman animals often result in the latter suffering injury and even death. Therefore, he concludes that with a robust legal commitment to animal welfare, human sexual relations of any kind with nonhuman animals would be considered "interspecies sexual assault" and that this then is the rightful basis for unflinching social intolerance to them. While we are equally outraged by anything resembling interspecies sexual assault and in no way seek to defend or provide openings for it, we believe that encounters between humans and nonhumans involve communication and agency on both sides, thereby allowing for potential consent from nonhuman parties. Further, we follow research by those such as Beetz and Williams and Weinberg that document that zoösexuals are often extremely careful in their actions so as not to coerce or harm their partners. Our main point is that zoösexuality in its most radical form is not simply Oedipalized sexual desire but is a new, de-Oedipalized notion of erotic touch that disperses desire in particularly feral ways across multiple erogenous zones of fur and feather. In this sense, zoösexuality is out of bounds, dwelling in a no-man's-land between species.

11. In this sense we disagree with the critique of Hardt and Negri's endorsement of St. Francis offered by Dominick LaCapra (2009), which we find too strong.

12. The reference to camel, lion, and child refers to a famous section, "On the Three Metamorphoses of the Sprit," in *Thus Spake Zarathustra* (Nietzsche 1976, 137–140).

BIBLIOGRAPHY

Adorno, T. 1998. *Critical Models: Interventions and Catchwords.* New York: Columbia University Press.

Agamben, G. 1993a. *Stanzas: Word and Phantasm in Western Culture.* Minneapolis: University of Minnesota Press.

———. 1993b. *The Coming Community.* Minneapolis: University of Minnesota Press.

———. 1995. *The Idea of Prose.* New York: State University of New York Press.

———. 1998. *Homo Sacer: Sovereign Power and Bare Life.* Stanford: Stanford University Press.

———. 1999a. *Potentialities: Collected Essays in Philosophy.* Stanford: Stanford University Press.

———. 1999b. *The Man without Content.* Stanford: Stanford University Press.

———. 2000. *Means without End: Notes on Politics.* Minneapolis: University of Minnesota Press.

———. 2004. *The Open: Man and Animal.* Stanford: Stanford University Press.

———. 2005. *The Idea of Prose.* Albany: State University of New York Press.

———. 2007. *Profanations.* London: Zone Books.

———. 2009. *What is an Apparatus?* Stanford: Stanford University Press.

Alaimo, S. 2008. Trans-corporeal Feminisms and the Ethical Space of Nature. In S. Alaimo and S. Hekman (eds.), *Material Feminisms.* Bloomington, IN: University of Indiana Press, 237–264.

Aldred, L. 2000. Plastic Shamans and Astroturf Sun Dances: New Age Commercialization of Native American Spirituality. *American Indian Quarterly* 243: 329–352.

Althusser, L. 2001. *Lenin and Philosophy and Other Essays.* New York: Monthly Review Press.

Althusser, L. and E. Balibar. 1979. *Reading Capital.* London: Verso.

Anderson, H. M. 2007. Learning and Leaving the Comforts of Home: A Radical Pedagogy of Homeplace. In N. Burbules (ed.), *Philosophy of Education Society Yearbook, 2007.* Urbana-Champaign: University of Urbana-Champaign, 103–111.

Ansell-Pearson, K. 1999. *Germinal Life: The Difference and Repetition of Deleuze*. New York: Routledge.

Arendt, H. 1998. *The Human Condition*. Chicago: University of Chicago Press.

Asma, S. T. 2009. *On Monsters: An Unnatural History of Our Worst Fears*. Oxford: Oxford University Press.

Ayers, W. 1997/98. The Criminalization of Youth. *Rethinking Schools Online* 12, no. 2: n.p.

Badmington, N. 2003. Theorizing Posthumanism. *Cultural Critique* 53: 10–27.

———. 2004. *Alien Chic: Posthumanism and the Other Within*. New York: Routledge.

Bahktin, M. 1993. *Rabelais and His World*. Bloomington, IN: Indiana University Press.

Balibar, E. 2009. Reflections on *Gewalt*. *Historical Materialism* 171: 99–125.

Barad, K. 2003. Posthumanist Performativity: Toward an Understanding of How Matter Comes to Matter. *Signs* 28.3: 801–831.

Barnard, M. 1986. *Sappho: A New Translation*. Berkeley: University of California Press.

Barrie, J. 1995. *Peter Pan; or the Boy who would not Grow Up*. Oxford: Oxford University Press.

Bartkowski, F. 2008. *Kissing Cousins: A New Kinship Bestiary*. London: Verso.

Battaglia, B. 2006. *E.T. Culture: Anthropology in Outerspace*. Durham: Duke University Press.

Bean, R. 1906. The Negro brain. *Century Magazine*. September, 778–784.

Beetz, A. 2004. Bestiality/Zoophilia: A Scarcely Investigated Phenomenon between Crime, Paraphilia, and Love. *Journal of Forensic Psychology Practice* 4.2: 1–36.

Beetz, A. and A. L. Podberscek. 2009. *Bestiality and Zoophilia: Sexual Relations with Animals*. West Lafayette, IN: Purdue University Press.

Beirne, P. 2009. *Confronting Animal Abuse: Law, Criminology, and Human-Animal Relationships*. Lanham, MD: Rowman & Littlefield.

Benjamin, W. 1968. *Illuminations*. New York: Shocken Books.

———. 1978. *Reflections*. New York: Shocken Books.

———. 1985. *The Origin of German Tragic Drama*. London: Verso.

Berkes, F. 1993. Traditional Ecological Knowledge in Perspective. In J. T. Inglis (ed.), *Traditional Ecological Knowledge: Concepts and Cases*. Ottawa: International Development Research Centre: 1–10.

Berman, M. 1982. *All That is Solid Melts into Air: The Experience of Modernity*. London: Verso.

Best, S. 2006a. Senator James Inhofe: Top Terrorist Threat to Planet Earth. *Impact Press Winter*. Online at: http://www.impactpress.com/articles/winter06/bestwinter06.html.

————. 2006b. Rethinking Revolution: Animal Liberation, Human Liberation, and the Obsolescence of Left Humanism. *The International Journal of Inclusive Democracy* 2.3. http://www.inclusivedemocracy.org/journal/vol2/vol2_no3_Best_rethinking_revolution.htm.

Best, S. and D. Kellner. 2001. *The Postmodern Adventure: Science, Technology and Cultural Studies at the Third Millennium.* New York: Guilford Press.

Blake, W. 1994. *The Marriage of Heaven and Hell. Mineola.* NY: Dover Publications.

Bleakley, A. 2000. *The Animalizing Imagination: Totemism, Textuality and Ecocriticism.* New York: St. Martin's Press.

Bloch, E. 1996. *The Principle of Hope.* Vol. 1. Trans. Neville Plaice, Stephen Plaice, and Paul Knight. Cambridge, MA: MIT Press.

Bloom, W. 1998. *Working with Angels, Fairies and Nature Spirits.* London: Judy Piatkus Limited.

Boff, L. 1997. *Cry of the Earth, Cry of the Poor.* Maryknoll, NY: Orbis Books.

Braidotti, R. 1996. Signs of Wonder and Traces of Doubt: On Teratology and Embodied Differences. In N. Lykke and R. Braidotti (eds.), *Between Monsters, Goddesses, and Cyborgs: Feminist Confrontations with Science, Medicine, and Cyberspace.* London: Zed Books, 135–152.

Berman, M. 1988. *All That is Solid Melts into Air.* London: Penguin.

Breton, A. 1969. *Manifesto of Surrealism* commonly referred to as the "first manifesto of surrealism," in Manifestoes of Surrealism. Ann Arbor, MI: University of Michigan Press.

Brown, N. O. 1966. *Love's Body.* Berkeley, CA: University of California Press.

Buber, M. 1970. *I and Thou.* New York: Scribner and Sons.

Bullard, T. E. 2000. UFOs: Lost in the Myths. In David M. Jacobs (ed.), *UFOs and Abductions: Challenging the Borders of Knowledge.* Lawrence: University of Kansas Press, 141–191.

Burch, K. 2000. *Eros as the Educative Principle of Democracy.* New York: Peter Lang.

Burkert, W. 1991. *Greek Religion: Archaic and Classical.* London: Wiley-Blackwell.

Butler, J. 1997. *The Psychic Life of Power.* Stanford: Stanford University Press.

Caesar, J. 1914. *The Civil Wars, with an English Translation by A. G. Peskett.* New York: Macmillian Co: 335.

Cajete, G. 2000. *Native Science: Natural Laws of Interdependence.* Santa Fe, NM: Clear Light Publishers.

Carlson, L. 2003. Rethinking Normalcy, Normalization, and Cognitive Disability. In R. Figueroa and S. Harding (eds.), *Science and Other Cultures.* New York: Routledge, 154–169.

Casarino, C. and A. Negri. 2008. *In Praise of the Common: A Conversation on Philosophy and Politics.* Minneapolis: University of Minnesota Press.

Cho, D. 2005. Lessons of Love: Psychoanalysis and Teacher-Student Love. *Educational Theory* 55.1: 79–96.

Clark, J. 2000. The Extraterrestrial Hypothesis in the Early UFO Age. In David M. Jacobs (ed.), *UFOs and Abductions: Challenging the Borders of Knowledge*. Lawrence: University of Kansas Press, 122–140.

Cohen, J. J. 1999. *Of Giants: Sex, Monsters, and the Middle Ages*. Minneapolis: University of Minnesota Press.

Cohen, J. J. Ed. 1996. *Monster Theory: Reading Culture*. Minneapolis: University of Minnesota Press.

Cook, Y. 2003. It's A Way with the Fairies: A Lesson in New Age Beliefs is as Valid As Any Other Academic Discipline. *The Independent*, September 2. Online at: http://www.independent.co.uk/news/education/higher/its-a-way-with-the-fairies-578699.html.

Cowley, J. 2000. The Icke Files. *The Independent*, October 1: 6–7, 9.

Crumey, A. 2001. David Icke and Other Weird Creatures. *Scotland on Sunday*, April 15: 12.

Dali, S. 1966. *Diary of a Genius*. Trans. Richard Howard. London: Hutchinson Press.

Darder, A. 2002. *Reinventing Paulo Freire: A Pedagogy of Love*. Boulder, CO: Westview Press.

Daston, L. and K. Park. 2001. *Wonders and the Order of Nature*. London: Zone Books.

Davy, B. J. 2007. *Introduction to Pagan Studies*. Lanham, MD: Rowman & Littlefield.

Dean, J. 1998. *Aliens in America: Conspiracy Cultures from Outerspace to Cyberspace*. Ithaca, NY: Cornell University Press.

Dekkers, M. 1994. *Dearest Pet: On Bestiality*. Trans. P. Vincent. New York: Verso.

Deleuze, G. 2003. *Francis Bacon: The Logic of Sensation*. Minneapolis: University of Minnesota Press.

Deleuze, G. and F. Guattari. 1983. *Anti-Oedipus: Capitalism and Schizophrenia*. Trans. Robert Hurley, Mark Seem, and Helen R. Lane. Minneapolis: University of Minnesota Press.

———. 1987. *A Thousand Plateaus: Capitalism and Schizophrenia*. Trans. Brian Massumi. Minneapolis: University of Minnesota Press.

Deloria, V. and D. Wildcat. 2001. *Power and Place: Indian Education in America*. Goldon, CO: Fulcrum Resources.

Derrida, J. 2002. The Animal that Therefore I am More to Follow. *Critical Inquiry*, 28 Winter.

———. 2006. *The Specters of Marx: The State of Debt, the Work of Morning and the New International*. London: Routledge.

———. 2009. *The Beast and the Sovereign: Volume One*. Chicago: University of Chicago Press.

Dewdney, C. 1998. *Last Flesh: Life in the Transhumant Era*. Toronto: Harper-Collins.

Dewey, J. 1980. *The School and Society.* Carbondale: Southern Illinois University Press.

Dolar, M. 1993. Beyond Interpellation. *Qui Parle* 62: 75–96.

Donehower, K., Hogg, C., and Schell, E. 2007. *Rural Literacies.* Carbondale: Southern Illinois University Press.

Dorfman, A. and Matterlart. 1984. *How to Read Donald Duck: Imperialist Ideology in the Disney Comic.* Amsterdam: International General.

Douthwaite, J. 1997. *Homo Ferus:* Between Monster and Model. *Eighteenth-Century Life* 212: 176–202.

Doyle, A. C. 1999 [1921]. *The Coming of the Fairies.* London: Pavilion Books.

Doyle, R. 2003. *Wetwares: Experiments in Postvital Living.* Minneapolis: University of Minnesota Press.

DuBois, W. E. B. 1968. *The Autobiography of W.E.B. Du Bois.* New York: International Publishers.

Dunnewind, S. 2006. Pixie Power; Marketers Try to Capture Little Girls' Hearts Anew with Fairy Books and Toys. *The Seattle Times,* March 11, C1.

Egan, K. 1994. Teaching the Romantic Mind. *The English Journal,* 83.4: 16–25.

Encyclopaedia Britannica. tat tvam asi. Encyclopædia Britannica Premium Service. Online. February 2005. http://www.britannica.com/eb/article?tocId=9071370 (accessed February 20, 2005).

Ellis, S. 2009. *The Man Who Lives with Wolves.* New York: Harmony Books.

Esposito, R. 2008. *Bios.* Minneapolis: University of Minnesota Press.

———. 2010. *Communitas: The Origin and Destiny of Community.* Stanford: Stanford University Press.

Evans-Wentz, W. Y. 2002 [1911]. *The Fairy-Faith in Celtic Countries.* Mineola, NY: Dover Publications.

Ferguson, P. 1987. The Social Construction of Mental Retardation. *Social Policy* Summer: 51–56.

Foucault, M. 1980. *Herculine Barbin: The Recently Discovered Memoirs of a Ninetheenth-Century French Hermaphrodite.* New York: Pantheon.

———. 1990. *History of Sexuality Volume One: An Introduction.* New York: Vintage Books.

———. 2003a. *Society Must Be Defended: Lectures at the College de France, 1975–76* New York: Picador Press.

———. 2003b. *Abnormal.* New York: Picador.

Freire, P. 1998. *Pedagogy of the Heart.* New York: Continuum.

———. 2000. *Pedagogy of the Oppressed.* New York: Continuum.

Freud, S. 2003. *The Uncanny.* London: Penguin Classics.

Garland, D. 2006. To Cast a Giant Shadow: Revolutionary Ecology and its Practical Implementation through the Earth Liberation Front. In S. Best and A. J. Nocella, II (eds.), *Igniting a Revolution: Voices in Defense of the Earth.* Oakland, CA: AK Press: 59–70.

Garrison, J. 1997. *Dewey and Eros.* New York: Teachers College Press.

Genosko, G. 2002. A Bestiary of Territoriality and Expression: Poster Fish, Bower Birds, and Spiny Lobsters. In B. Massumi (ed.), *A Shock to Thought: Expression after Deleuze and Guattari*. New York: Routledge, 47–59.

Geoghegan, V. 1987. *Utopianism and Marxism*. London: Methuen.

Giroux, H. A. 1994. *Disturbing Pleasures: Learning Popular Culture* New York: Routledge.

———. 2000. Public Pedagogy as Cultural Politics: Stuart Hall and the "Crisis" of Culture. *Cultural Studies* 14.2: 341–360.

———. 2001. *The Mouse that Roared: Disney and the End of Innocence*. Lanham, MD: Rowman & Littlefield.

———. 2010. Zombie Politics and other Late Monstrosities in the Age of Disposability. *Policy Futures in Education* 8.1: n.a.

Goldman, E. 1934. *Living my Life*. New York: Knopf Publishers.

Graeber, D. 2002. The New Anarchists. *New Left Review* 13. http://www.newleftreview.org/A2368.

Graham, E. 2002. *Representations of the Post/Human: Monsters, Aliens, and Others in Popular Culture*. New Brunswick: Rutgers University Press.

Grebowicz, M. 2010. When Species Meat: Confronting Bestiality Pornography. *Humanimalia: A Journal of Human/Animal Interface Studies* 1.2. http://www.depauw.edu/humanimalia/issue02/grebowicz.html.

Greene, M. 2000. *Releasing the Imagination: Essays on Education, the Arts, and Social Change*. New York: Teachers College Press.

Grice, E. 2006. Cry of an Enfant Sauvage. *Telegraph*. http://www.telegraph.co.uk/culture/tvandradio/3653890/Cry-of-an-enfant-sauvage.html.

Grof, S. 1985. *Beyond the Brain: Birth, Death and Transcendence in Psychotherapy*. Albany, NY: State University of New York Press.

Guattari, F. 2000. *The Three Ecologies*. Trans. Ian Pindar and Paul Sutton. London: The Athlone Press.

Guevara, C. 1965. Socialism and Man in Cuba. http://www.marxists.org/archive/guevara/1965/03/man-socialism.htm.

Haase, Donald. 2003. Children, War, and the Imaginative Space of Fairy Tales. *The Lion and the Unicorn* 24: 360–377.

Habermas, J. 1982. The Entwinement of Myth and Enlightenment: Re-reading. Dialectic of Enlightenment. *New German Critique* 26. Spring–Summer: 13–30.

Habig, M. A. Ed. 1973. *St. Francis of Assisi—Writings and Early Biographies: English Omnibus of the Sources for the Life of St. Francis*. Chicago, IL: Fransciscan Herald Press.

Halpin, D. 2009. Pedagogy and Romantic Love. *Pedagogy, Culture, & Society* 121: 89–102.

Hanssen, B. 2000. *Walter Benjamin's Other History: Of Stones, Animals, Human-Beings, and Angels*. Berkley: University of California Press.

Haraway, D. 1991. The Promises of Monsters: A Regenerative Politics for Inappropriate/d Others. In L. Grossberg, C. Nelson, and P. Treichler (eds.), *Cultural Studies*. New York: Routledge.

———. 1997. *Modest_Witness@Second_Millennium.FemaleMan©_Meets_ OncoMouse™: Feminism and Technoscience*. New York: Routledge.

———. 2003. *The Companion Species Manifesto: Dogs, People, and Significant Otherness*. Chicago, IL: Prickly Paradigm Press.

———. 2008a. *When Species Meet*. Minneapolis, MN: University of Minnesota Press.

———. 2008b. Otherworldly Conversations, Terran Topics, Local Terms. In S. Alaimo and S. Hekman (eds.), *Material Feminisms*. Bloomington, IN: University of Indiana Press, 157–187.

Harding, J. 2001. Inside the Black Bloc. *Financial Times*, October 15.

Hardt, M. 2007. *Michael Hardt Presents Thomas Jefferson*. London: Verso.

Hardt, M. and A. Negri. 1994. *Labor of Dionysus: A Critique of the State Form*. Minneapolis: University of Minnesota Press.

———. 2000. *Empire*. Cambridge: Harvard University Press.

———. 2004. *Multitude: War and Democracy in the Age of Empire*. New York: The Penguin Press.

———. 2009. *Commonwealth*. Cambridge: The Belknap Press of Harvard University Press.

Harris, A. 1996. Sacred Ecology. In C. Hardman and, G. Harvey (eds.), *Paganism Today*. London: Thorsons [HarperCollins].

Harte, J. 2004. *Explore Fairy Traditions*. Loughborough, UK: Heart of Albion Press.

Hassig, D. 1995. *Medieval Bestiaries: Text, Image, Ideology*. Cambridge: Cambridge University Press.

Hayles, N. K. 1999. *How We Became Posthuman: Virtual Bodies in Cybernetics, Literature, and Informatics*. Chicago: University of Chicago.

Heidegger, M. 1995. *The Fundamental Concepts of Metaphysics*. Bloomington: Indiana University Press.

———. 2000. *Introduction to Metaphysics*. New Haven: Yale University Press.

Heller-Roazen, D. 2007. *The Inner Touch: Archaeology of a Sensation*. London: Zone Books.

Helliwell, T. 1997. *Summer with the Leprechauns*. Nevada City, CA: Blue Dolphin Publishing.

Hewitt, A. 2005. *Social Choreography: Ideology as Performance in Dance and Everyday Movement*. Durham: Duke University Press.

Higgins, C. 2009. Modest Beginnings of a Radical Revision of the Concept of Imagination. In S. Blenkinsop (ed.), *The Imagination in Education*. New Castle: Cambridge Scholars Publishing.

Hodson, G. 1982. *Fairies at Work and Play*. Wheaten, IL: Theosophical Publishing House.

Home Office. 2000. *Setting the Boundaries: Reforming the Law on Sex Offenses*. London: Home Office Communications Directorate.

Honig, B. 2001. *Democracy and the Foreigner.* Princeton: Princeton University Press.

Honig, B. 2009. *Emergency Politics: Paradox, Law, Democracy.* Princeton: Princeton University Press.

hooks, B. 2004. *Teaching Community: A Pedagogy of Hope.* New York: Routledge.

———. 2009. *Belonging: A Culture of Place.* New York: Routledge.

———. 2010. *Teaching Critical Thinking.* New York: Routledge.

Horkheimer, M. and T. W. Adorno. 2002. *Dialectic of Enlightenment Philosophical Fragments.* Stanford, Calif: Stanford University Press.

Hume, L. and K. McPhillips. 2006. *Popular Spiritualities: The Politics of Contemporary Enchantment.* Aldershot, UK: Ashgate Publishing.

Icke, D. 1999. *The Biggest Secret.* Wildwood, MO: Bridge of Light.

———. 2001. *Children of the Matrix.* Wildwood, MO: Bridge of Light.

———. 2002. *Alice in Wonderland and the World Trade Center Disaster.* Wildwood, MO: Bridge of Light.

Illich, I. 1970. *Deschooling Society.* London: Marion Boyers.

Itard, J. 1972. *The Wild Boy of Aveyron.* New York: Monthly Review Press.

Jameson, F. 1992. *The Geopolitical Aesthetic: Cinema and Space in the World System.* Bloomington: Indiana University Press.

———. 1994. *Seeds of Time.* New York: Columbia University Press.

———. 1995. *Postmodernism or the Cultural Logic of Late Capitalism.* Durham: Duke University Press.

———. 2009. *Valences of the Dialectic.* London: Verso.

Jefferson, T. 1999. *Political Writings.* New York: Cambridge University Press.

Jung, C. G. 1959. *Flying Saucers: A Modern Myth of Things Seen in the Sky.* Trans. R.F.C. Hull. New York: Signet.

———. 1990. *The Undiscovered Self.* Trans. R. F. C. Hull. Boston: Little Brown.

Khanna, R. 2003. *Dark Continents: Psychoanalysis and Colonialism.* Durham: Duke University Press.

Kahn, C. H. 1981. *The Art and Thought of Heraclitus: An Edition of the Fragments with Translation and Commentary.* Cambridge, UK: University of Cambridge Press.

Kahn, R. 2005. Reconsidering *zoë* and *bios*: A Brief Comment on Nathan Snaza's "Impossible Witness" and Kathy Guillermo's "Response." *Journal of Animal Liberation Philosophy and Policy* 3.1. http://www.criticalanimalstudies.org/cas-publications/journal-for-critical-animal-studies/JCAS/Journal_Articles_download/Issue_4/Reconsidering_Zoe_and_Bios.pdf.

———. 2006. The Educative Potential of Ecological Militancy In An Age of Big Oil: Towards a Marcusean Ecopedagogy. *Policy Futures in Education* 41: 31–44.

———. 2009. Critical Pedagogy Taking the Illich Turn. *The International Journal of Illich Studies* 1.1: 37–49.

———. 2010. *Critical Pedagogy, Ecoliteracy, and Planetary Crisis: The Ecopedagogy Movement.* New York: Peter Lang.

Kahn, R. and B. Humes. 2009. Marching Out From Ultima Thule: Critical Counterstories of Emancipatory Educators Working at the Intersection of Human Rights, Animal Rights, and Planetary Sustainability. *The Canadian Journal of Environmental Education* 14.1: 179–195.

Kapil, B. 2006. *Incubation: A Space for Monsters.* New York: Leon Works.

Kearney, R. 2003. *Strangers, Gods, and Monsters.* New York: Routledge.

Keel, J. 1970. *UFOs: Operation Trojan Horse.* New York: Putnam.

Kellner, D. 1995. *Media Culture: Cultural Studies, Identity and Politics between the Modern and the Postmodern.* London: Routledge.

———. 2003a. *From 9/11 to Terror War: The Dangers of the Bush Legacy.* Lanham, MD: Rowman & Littlefield.

———. 2003b. *Media Spectacle.* London: Routledge.

Kinsey, A. C., W. B. Pomeroy, and C. E. Martin. 1948. *Sexual Behavior in the Human Male.* Philadelphia, PA: W. B. Saunders Company.

Knight, P. 2002. *Conspiracy Theory: The Politics of Paranoia in Postwar America.* New York: New York University Press.

Kristeva, J. 1991. *Strangers to Ourselves.* New York: Columbia University Press.

Kumar, K. 1991. *Utopianism.* Buckingham, Eng.: Oxford University Press.

LaCapra, D. 2009. *History and Its Limits: Human, Animal, Violence.* Ithaca: Cornell University Press.

Lavin, T. 2010. The Listener. *The Atlantic* 305.1: 68–76.

Leary, T. 1999. *Turn On, Tune In, Drop Out.* Berkeley, CA: Ronin Publishing.

Lemm, V. 2009. *Nietzsche's Animal Philosophy: Culture, Politics, and the Animality of the Human Being.* New York: Fordham University Press.

Lepselter, S. 2005. Why Rachel Isn't Buried at Her Grave: Ghosts, UFOs, and a Place Called the West. In D. Rosenberg and S. Harding (eds.), *Histories of the Future.* Durham: Duke University Press, 256–279.

Letcher, A. 2000. Virtual Paganism or Direct Action? The Implications of Road Protesting for Modern Paganism. *Diskus* 6. http://web.uni-marburg.de/religionswissenschaft/journal/diskus/letcher.html.

———. 2001. The Scouring of the Shires: Fairies,Trolls and Pixies in Eco-Protest Culture. *Folklore* 112: 147–161.

———. 2004. Raising the Dragon: Folklore and the Development of Contemporary British Eco-Paganism. *The Pomegranate* 62: 175–198.

Lewis, T. 2007. Biopolitical Utopianism in Educational Theory. *Educational Philosophy and Theory* 39.3: 1–20.

———. In press. Swarm Intelligence: Rethinking the Multitude from within the Transversal Commons. *Culture, Theory, and Critique.*

Lewis, T. and D. Cho. 2006. Home is Where the Neurosis Is: A Topography of the Spatial Unconscious. *Cultural Critique* 64.Fall: 69–91.

Linebaugh, P. and Rediker, M. 2000. *The Many-Headed Hydra: Sailors, Slaves, Commoners, and the Hidden History of the Revolutionary Atlantic.* Boston: Beacon Press.

Lukacs, G. 1971. *History and Class Consciousness.* Cambridge: MIT Press.

Mack, C. and D. Mack. 1998. *A Field Guide to Demons, Fairies, Fallen Angels and Other Subversive Spirits.* New York: Owl Publishers.

Mack, J. E. 2002. Deeper Causes: Exploring the Role of Consciousness in Terrorism. *IONS Noetic Sciences Review* June–August: 11–17.

Maclean, D. 1990. *To Hear the Angels Sing: An Odyssey of Co-creation with the Devic Kingdom.* Hudson, NY: Lindisfarne Press.

Mannoni, O. 1972. Itard and His Savage. *New Left Review* 74.July–August: 37–49.

Martin, J. R. 2007. *Educational Metamorphoses.* Lanham: Rowman and Littlefield.

Marx, K. 1978. *The Marx-Engels Reader: Second Edition.* New York: W. W. Norton.

———. 1990. *Capital Volume One.* London: Penguin Press.

Mason, F. 2002. A Poor Person's Cognitive Mapping. In P. Knight (ed.), *Conspiracy Theory: The Politics of Paranoia in Postwar America.* New York: New York University Press, 40–56.

Massumi, B. 2002a. *Parables for the Virtual: Movement, Affect, Sensation.* Durham: Duke University Press.

———. 2002b. That Thinking Feeling. In B. Massumi (ed.), *A Shock to Thought: Expression after Deleuze and Guattari.* New York: Routledge, xiii–xxxix.

Mayo, C. 2007. Disruption of Desire: From Androgynes to Genderqueer. In N. Burbules (ed.), *Philosophy of Education Yearbook, 2007.* Urbana, IL: University of Illinois at Urbana-Champaign, 49–58.

McAlpine, K. 2005. Don't Move That Rock…You'll Kill the Fairies. *The Sun* November 22.

McGuigan, J. 1992. *Cultural Populism.* New York: Routledge.

McIntosh, A. 2005. Fairy Faith in Scotland. In J. Kaplan and B. Taylor (eds.), *The Encyclopaedia of Religion and Nature,* 2 volumes. London & NY: Continuum International Publishing.

McLaren, P. 1999. *Schooling as a Ritual Performance: Toward a Political Economoy of Educational Symbols and Gestures.* Lanham, MD: Rowman and Littlefield.

———. 2000. *Che Guevara, Paulo Freire, and the Pedagogy of Revolution.* Lanham: Rowman and Littlefield.

Melton, J. 2001. New Age Transformed. University of Virginia. Institute for the Study of American Religion. Online at: http://web.archive.org/web/20060828130904/religiousmovements.lib.virginia.edu/nrms/newage.html.

Miletski, H. 2002. *Understanding Bestiality and Zoophilia.* Bethesda, MD: East West Publishing.

Milojevic, I. 2006. Hegemonic and Marginalized Educational Utopias in the Contemporary Western World. In M. Peters and J. Freeman-Moir (eds.), *Edutopias: New Utopian Thinking in Education*. Rotterdam: Sense, 21–44.

Mishlove, J. 1993. *The Roots of Consciousness: Psychic Exploration through History, Science and Experience*. New York: Marlowe.

More, M. 1998. The Extropian Principles, v. 3.0. http://www.maxmore. com/extprn3.htm.

Morgan, C. 2009. *The Way of the Fairies: A Workbook for Healing the Earth and Ourselves*. Denver: Guiding Light Publisher.

Narváez, P. 1997. *The Good People: New Fairylore Essays*. Lexington, KY: University of Kentucky Press.

Negri, A. 1991. *The Savage Anomaly*. Minneapolis: University of Minnesota Press.

———. 1992. *Insurgencies: Constituent Power and the Modern State*. Minneapolis: University of Minnesota Press.

———. 2003a. *Time for Revolution*. New York: Continuum.

———. 2003b. N for Negri: Antonio Negri in Conversation with Charles Guerra. *Grey Room* 11: 86–109.

———. 2007. Art and Culture in the Age of Empire and the Time of the Multitude. *SubStance* 36.1: 48–55.

———. 2008. *Empire and Beyond*. Malden, MA: Polity Press.

Newitz, A. 2006. *Pretend We're Dead: Capitalist Monsters in American Pop Culture*. Durham: Duke University Press.

Newton, M. 2002. *Savage Girls and Wild Boys*. London: Faber and Faber.

Nietzsche, F. 1976. *The Portable Nietzsche*. Ed. and trans. Walter Kaufmann. New York: Penguin Books.

———. 1990. *Twilight of the Idols/The Anti-Christ*. London: Penguin Press.

———. 2002. *Beyond Good and Evil: Prelude to a Philosophy of the Future*. Cambridge, UK: Cambridge University Press.

———. 2004. *Ecce Homo*. Mineola, NY: Dover Publications.

Noel, D. C. 1997. *The Soul of Shamanism: Western Fantasies, Imaginal Realities*. New York: Continuum.

Norris, M. 1985. *Beasts of Modern Imagination: Darwin, Nietzsche, Kafka, Ernst, and Lawrence*. Baltimore: John Hopkins Press.

Noske, B. 1997. *Beyond Boundaries: Humans and Animals*. Montreal, Can.: Black Rose Books.

Otten, C. F. 1986. *A Lycanthropy Reader: Werewolves in Western Culture*. New York: Syracuse University Press.

Panagia, D. 2009. *The Political Life of Sensation*. Durham: Duke University Press.

Peebles, C. 1994. *Watch the Skies! A Chronicle of the Flying Saucer Myth*. Washington, DC: Smithsonian.

Pickering, A. 1995. *The Mangle of Practice: Time, Agency, and Science*. Chicago, IL: University of Chicago Press.

Pickering, L. J. Ed. 2003. *The Earth Liberation Front: 1997–2002.* South Wales, NY: Arissa Publications.

Pike, S. 2001. *Earthly Bodies, Magical Selves: Contemporary Pagans and the Search for Community.* Berkeley and Los Angeles, CA: University of California Press.

Povinelli, E. 2006. *The Empire of Love: Toward a Theory of Intimacy, Genealogy, and Carnality.* Durham: Duke University Press.

Pritchard, A., D. E. Pritchard, J. E. Mack, P. Kasey, and C. Yapp, Eds. 1994. *Alien Discussions: Proceedings of the Abduction Study Conference Held at MIT.* Cambridge, MA: North Cambridge Press.

Protevi, J. 2009. *Political Affect: Connecting the Social and the Somatic.* Minneapolis: University of Minnesota Press.

Radley, A. 1995. The Elusory Body and Social Constructionist Theory. *Body & Society* 12. London: Sage.

Rancière, J. 2006. *The Politics of Aesthetics.* London: Continuum.

———. 2007. *On the Shores of Politics.* London: Verso.

———. 2009. *Aesthetics and Its Discontents.* New York: Polity Press.

———. 2010. *The Aesthetic Unconscious.* Malden, MA: Polity Press.

Reuters News Service. 2003. Amazon Destruction Accelerates. *MSNBC* June 27, 2003. http://stacks.msnbc.com:80/news/932187.asp (accessed August 2003).

Roth, C. 2005. Ufology as Anthropology: Race, Extraterrestrials, and the Occult. In D. Battaglia (ed.), *E.T. Culture: Anthropology in Outerspace.* Durham: Duke University Press, 38–93.

Rousseau, J. 1979. *Emile or On Education.* New York: Basic Books.

Rutsky, R. L. 2007. Mutation, History, and Fantasy in the Posthuman. *Subject Matters: A Journal of Communication and Self* 3.2; 4.1: 99–112.

Sandlin, J. A., B. D. Schultz, and J. Burdick. 2009. *Handbook of Public Pedagogy: Education and Learning Beyond Schooling.* New York: Routledge.

Sands, P. 2003. Octavia Butler's Chiastic Cannibalistics. *Utopian Studies* 14.1: 1–14.

Sargisson, L. 1996. *Contemporary Feminist Utopianism.* New York: Routledge.

Shakespeare, W. 1998. *As You Like It.* New York: Signet Classic.

Shattuck, R. 1980. *The Forbidden Experiment: The Story of the Wild Boy of Aveyron.* New York: Kodansha International.

Shaviro, S. 2002. Capitalist Monsters. *Historical Materialism* 104: 281–290.

Shukin, N. 2010. *Animal Capital: Rendering Life in Biopolitical Times.* Minneapolis: University of Minnesota Press.

Singer, P. 1975. *Animal Liberation: A New Ethics for Our Treatment of Animals.* New York: Random House.

———. 2001. Heavy Petting. *Nerve.* March/April. http://www.nerve.com/ Opinions/Singer/heavypetting.

Sitchin, Z. 1995. *Genesis Revisited.* New York: Avon.

Skal, D. J. 1998. *Screams of Reason: Mad Science and Modern Culture.* New York: W.W. Norton.

Spence, L. 1997. *The Fairy Tradition in Britain.* Whitefish, MT: Kessinger Publishing Company.

Spence, M. D. 1999. *Dispossessing the Wilderness: Indian Removal and the Making of the National Parks.* New York: Oxford University Press.

Starhawk. 2003. Toward an Activist Spirituality. *Reclaiming Quarterly,* Fall. http://www.starhawk.org/pagan/activist_spirituality.html.

Steiner, R. 1992. *Spiritual Beings in the Heavenly Bodies and in the Kingdoms of Nature.* Great Barrington, MA: Anthroposophic Press.

Stewart, R. J. 1992. *Earth Light.* Great Britain: Element Books Limited.

———. 1995. *The Living World of Faery.* Glastonbury: Gothic Image Publications.

Stillman, P. G. 2003. Dystopian Critiques, Utopian Possibilities, and Human Purposes in Octavia Butler's Parables. *Utopian Studies* 14.1: 15–35.

Summers, M. 2003. *The Werewolf in Lore and Legend.* Mineola: Dover Publications.

Suvin, D. 1980. SF and the Novum. In Teresa de Lauretis, Andreas Huyssen, and Kathleen Woodward (eds.), *The Technological Imagination: Theories and Fictions.* Madison, WI: Coda Press, 141–158.

Taylor, B. 2005. Earth First! and the Earth Liberation Front. In B. Taylor (ed.), *The Encyclopedia of Religion and Nature.* London: Continuum International, 518–524.

Taylor, S. 1997. So I was in this bar with the son of God.... *The Observer,* April 20.

Thacker, E. 2003. Data Made Flesh: Biotechnology & the Discourse of the Posthuman. *Cultural Critique* 53.Winter: 72–98.

Tolkien, J. R. R. 2001. *Tree and Leaf.* London: HarperCollins Publishers.

Trubshaw, B. 1998. Fairies and Their Kin. *At the Edge* 10: n.p.

Tuana, N. 2008. Viscous Porosity: Witnessing Katrina. In S. Alaimo and S. Hekman (eds.), *Material Feminisms.* Bloomington, IN: University of Indiana Press, 188–213.

Turner, V. 1995. *The Ritual Process: Structure and Anti-Structure.* Chicago, IL: Aldine Publishing.

Tucker, R. 1967. *Philosophy and Myth in Karl Marx.* London: Cambridge University Press.

Tyack, D. 1970. *The One Best System: A History of American Urban Education.* Cambridge, MA: Harvard University Press.

Vallee, J. 1993. *Passport to Magonia: On UFOs, Folklore, and Parallel Worlds.* Columbus, OH: McGraw-Hill.

Virno, P. 2004. *A Grammar of the Multitude.* Los Angeles: Semiotexte.

Virno, P. and Hardt, M. 2006. *Radical Thought in Italy: A Potential Politics.* Minneapolis: University Of Minnesota Press.

Wall, D. 2000. Snowballs, Elves, and Skimmingtons. In B. Seel, M. Paterson, and B. Doherty (eds.), *Direct Action in British Environmentalism.* London: Routledge, 79–92.

Wallin, J. 2008. Living with Monsters: An Inquiry Parable. *Teaching Education* 19.4: 311–323.

Weber, E. Ed. 1995. *Points—Interviews 1974–1994*. Stanford, CA: University of Stanford Press.

Weber, M. 1958. *The Protestant Ethic and the Spirit of Capitalism*. New York: Charles Scribner's Sons.

Weisberg, Z. 2009. The Broken Promise of Monsters: Haraway, Animals, and the Humanist Legacy. *Journal of Critical Animal Studies* 3.2: 21–61.

Westneat, D. 2005. Horse Sex Story was Online Hit. *The Seattle Times*, December 30.

Williams, C. and M. Weinberg. 2003. Zoophilia in Men: A Study of Sexual Interest in Animals. *Archives of Sexual Behavior* 32.6: 523–535.

Wolfe, C. 1998. *Critical Environments: Postmodern Theory and the Pragmatics of the Outside*. Minneapolis: University of Minnesota Press.

———. 2003a. *Animal Rites: American Culture, the Discourse of Species, and Posthumanist Theory*. Chicago: University of Chicago Press.

———. Ed. 2003b. *Zoontologies: The Question of the Animal*. Minneapolis: University of Minnesota Press.

———. 2010. *What is Posthumanism?* Minneapolis: University of Minnesota Press.

Wolfenstein, E.V. 1993. *Psychoanalytic Marxism: Groundwork*. New York: Free Association Press.

Wordsworth, W. 2004. *Poems in Two Volumes, Vol. 2*. Whitefish, MT: Kessinger Publishing.

Yeats, W. B. 1996. The Stolen Child. In R. J. Finneran (ed.), *The Collected Poems of W.B. Yeats*. New York: Scribner, 18.

Young, B. 1991. Three Creation Myths: An Historical Overview of the Whereabouts of Gnomes and Elves, Fauns and Faeries, Goblins, Ogres, Trolls and Bogies, Nymphs, Sprites, and Dryads, Past and Present. *Firehart* 6: 8–10.

Zipes, J. 1997. *Happily Ever After: Fairy Tales, Children, and the Culture Industry*. New York: Routledge.

———. 2002. *Breaking the Magic Spell: Radical Theories of Folk and Fairy Tales*. Lexington, KY: University of Kentucky Press.

Zizek, S. 2008. *Violence: Six Sideways Reflections*. New York: Macmillan.

———. 2010. Return of the Natives. *New Statesman*, March 4: http://www. newstatesman.com/film/2010/03/avatar-reality-love-couple-sex.

INDEX